ACCOUNTABLE TEACHER EVALUATION!

Toward Highly Qualified and *Competent* Teachers

By HANS A. ANDREWS

NEW FORUMS PRESS INC.

Stillwater, Okla., U.S.A.

NEW FORUMS PRESS INC.

Published in the United States of America
by New Forums Press, Inc.1018 S. Lewis St.
Stillwater, OK 74074
www.newforums.com

Library of Congress Cataloging-in-Publication Data Pending

This book may be ordered in bulk quantities at discount from New
Forums Press, Inc., P.O. Box 876, Stillwater, OK 74076 [Federal I.D.
No. 73 1123239]. Printed in the United States of America.

International Standard Book Number: 1-58107-087-X

Cover design by Katherine Dollar.

Praise for *Accountable Teacher Evaluation!*

This practical handbook on teacher evaluation is a thorough guide through the intricate issues surrounding teacher evaluation. The information, tools, and strategies contained in this guide enhance the opportunity to move teacher evaluation from the task of fulfilling regulatory guidelines to improving teacher performance and increasing student achievement.

RICHARD A. FLANARY, *Director, Center for Principal Development; National Association of Secondary School Principals*

This book is a call to action for K-12 and community college instructional administrators. Its message is compelling: supervisory evaluation of teaching is generally lacking and this needs to be corrected-fast! Based on extensive research and experience, Hans Andrews presents a convincing case for why reform of faculty evaluation practices, improvement strategies and reward processes is needed. Simply stated, students deserve it and the public demands it. Using case studies and examples from the field, the author provides theory and practice that can be adapted at the local level to ensure that teachers perform effectively in the classroom over their entire career.

CHRISTINE M. LICATA, *Associate Vice President for Academic Affairs at NTID/Rochester Institute of Technology and Senior Scholar, American Associate for Higher Education*

Evaluation inflation" must be stopped. Dr. Andrews' latest treatise offers many practical and proven suggestions for improving the evaluation of teachers at the community college and K-12 levels. He includes an overview of research on a variety of significant components, comments from various union officials. Administrators who are developing or revising their teacher evaluation procedures and criteria will find much to ponder in this handbook.

ROBERT SMITH, *Attorney, Seyfarth, Shaw, Fairweather & Geraldson, Chicago*

Contents

Acknowledgments

Special thanks to the many good people I've had the opportunity to work with over 35 years in the field of improving teaching and student learning. Dr. John Allen, Louis Borio, Carol Haas, Dr. John Erwin, Dr. William Marzano, William Uebel, Harold Barnes, Dr. Linda Knight, Ed Anderson, Dr. Samuel Rogel, and Lewis Cushing were all part of the evaluation team at Illinois Valley Community College.

Mr. Terry Bruce, Dr. Jackie Davis, Dr. Judy Johnson, and Donna Henry, all worked toward quality in teacher evaluation within the Illinois Eastern Community Colleges and Olney Central College in particular.

Thanks also go to Fran Stencel, Charlotte Bruce, Evelyn Moyle, Carol Bird and Jan Vogelgesang for research support over the years. Carla Gardner, Tammy Harmon, and Judy Day also deserve recognition as administrative support persons in ordering and preparing segments of materials used in this book. Special thanks goes to my wife Carolyn for her support and encouragement.

Over the years Dr. Alfred Wisgoski and Dr. Richard Whitmore supported these efforts to improve instruction in their roles as college presidents at Illinois Valley Community College and Kellogg Community College respectively. Attorneys Bruce Mackey, Robert Smith, and Cynthia Mooney added exceptional practical support to problem areas of evaluation over the years. My research partners, Chris Licata and BeverlyJo Harris, have encouraged and helped publish national research on the topic of evaluation in the community college system. I also need to note the high level of encouragement from Blouke Carus to get this message out to educators everywhere. Ralph C. Bedell, deceased, continues to have an influence on my work of combining research with practical applications.

Accountable Teacher Evaluation

Prologue

> If your research doesn't result in practice your re-
> search is no good, and if your practice is not based on
> research, your practice is no good.
>
> *Ralph C. Bedell*
> *Bourne (1988)*

Many school reforms have been mandated by state and national legislation over a thirty-year period. The national alert regarding the lack of quality teaching taking place in many American schools was sounded when *A Nation at Risk: The Imperative for Educational Reform* was published in 1983. The *No Child Left Behind* legislation in the early 2000's, promoted by President George W. Bush and his administration, called for highly qualified teachers in all classrooms.

Preparing and identifying highly qualified teachers as required in the No Child Left Behind law is not in itself enough! This definition only relates to having teachers properly credentialed with a major, minor, or specifically outlined course work in the subject areas and levels of subjects to be taught. It does not identify the competence of these teachers. Competence is manifested in classroom teaching and delivery to students and in student outcomes. Evaluation of faculty by competent administrators is necessary to document either competency or lack of competency in classroom teaching. *Accountable Teacher Evaluation* provides the blueprint necessary to assure that highly qualified and competent teachers will be present in every classroom.

Many experiences of this author as a student in K-12 classrooms and as a college student, business teacher at the secondary school level, counselor at two high schools and a community college led me years ago to believe that the teachers need stronger support. In part, our teachers' status was suffering due to administrators and boards allowing some very

---

good teachers to be neglected and to leave the field. In addition, they allowed some very poor teachers to continue teaching year-after-year.

In all levels of my own education I experienced some exceptional teachers, many other acceptable teachers and a few who, for one reason or another, were not teaching anywhere near an acceptable level. My curiosity peeked during my college years when it was more difficult to understand why some poor teachers were allowed to work in higher education.

The student movement in the 1960's had as part of its agenda the ranking of teachers on a number of college campuses. These rankings were developed to provide a "warning system" to unsuspecting future student enrollees about who the exceptional teachers were as well as identifying the poor ones. The ranking systems grew out of the frustration of students finding that complaining about poor faculty members led to no action on the part of the college administrators.

As a counselor at both the secondary school and community college levels, it became a moral dilemma for me and the other counselors when it came time to place students in classes with those faculty well known to be incompetent or lazy. When the classes of the "best" faculty members became filled first, we counselors found ourselves having to place many of the weakest and the late-enrolling students in classes of the least competent teachers.

It was also a major surprise to learn that outstanding teachers went unrecognized in most educational institutions. The most common type of recognition given appears to have been in the area of longevity of service, i.e., five-, ten-, and twenty-years of service in a K-12 school or college. These ceremonies, while important, had nothing to do with recognizing high quality teaching and strong student outcomes.

Where were the instructional administrators who would ensure students quality teaching in every classroom? Why didn't administrators or governing boards respond when it became known that poor teaching existed in their schools and colleges? Why did schools allow their quality teachers to leave instead of creating an environment of support in order to keep them?

In several roles I assumed during my career as an instructional administrator I decided to explore these questions with a passion and determine what could be done. I found much of the educational research and literature lacking in substance when it came to dealing with these important and necessary questions.

My doctoral advisor, Dr. Ralph C. Bedell, University of Missouri, supported the need for research and practice going hand-in-hand. He was quoted by Bourne (1988) in an interview late in his life saying, "If your research doesn't result in practice, your research is no good, and if your practice is not based on research, your practice is no good" (p. 138).

The above scenario continued to haunt me as I learned the importance of evaluating both part-time and full-time teachers at the community college level. It struck me early on that very little of the colleges' resources were being used to assist faculty members in their needs to be upgraded, to attend meetings with fellow teachers at the state and national levels, or to assist them in improving classroom teaching techniques.

At Illinois Valley Community College I had the opportunity to train and assist division chairs and deans in evaluating faculty members throughout the college. It became the number one quality check for improving instruction at the college. The college president and board of trustees were supportive of a recognition system to reward those teachers that the instructional administrators had identified through the evaluation process as doing outstanding work in their teaching and other job responsibilities.

These were years when we were able to "put our money

where our mouths were" in terms of our philosophy of supporting faculty development and improvement needs. We started sending faculty to teacher workshops designed to improve their teaching. In addition we also brought in outstanding resource people to talk with our faculty about effective teaching strategies, sponsored faculty at state and national meetings in their teaching fields, and utilized our own most competent faculty to conduct in-house workshops on teaching techniques that they had found successful. Faculty who had already received special recognition were subsequently sent to master teacher workshops around the country to strengthen their skills and to make presentations on their special teaching techniques.

There was another smaller, but very significant, group that was evaluated as not providing quality teaching for their students. Each of these teachers was given clear and specific objectives to work on to improve their teaching and eliminate their defects and deficiencies in their work. Some succeeded in improving but a number did not and were eventually dismissed after a remediation process proved unsuccessful. A number of the newer faculty were not awarded tenure if they were receiving poor evaluations and found not to be improving sufficiently during their first, second or third year with the college. These were tough and excruciating decisions and actions for the administration, board of trustees and faculty. They were, however, the right decisions necessary to guarantee students quality teachers in every classroom.

As a teacher, administrator and researcher I have continued to research and practice those techniques and teaching strategies that work most effectively. This had led me to be invited for numerous speaking engagements in the United States and Canada on the topics of teacher evaluation and recognition programs. It has also offered the stimuli for writing and publishing over forty articles and chapters, and with this book, four books on the topics of teacher evaluation, recognition and improved learning outcomes for students.

Why the focus on K-12 and Community Colleges?

The American elementary, middle schools, and high schools (K-12) and community colleges all share the same need to have quality teachers in every classroom. While universities and other four-year college institutions value good instruction, their faculty members are, in fact, not always hired for teaching expertise. They most often have to present a record of quality research and publication success and, as the third most important criteria, teaching ability.

Some years ago after making a presentation to some of my former faculty members at the University of Missouri in Columbia, Missouri, a most interesting discussion evolved. Three of the faculty and administrators present were questioning a fourth one about his recent hiring process for a new faculty member for his department. He was asked, "Why did you put so much emphasis on whether or not the candidates could teach? You make them think this is a priority in our university when they are asked to present a lesson in front of the selection committee."

This was one further confirmation for me that teaching was not nearly as highly valued as was research and publishing at the senior college and university levels. In fact, the professor, while defending his position on the teaching emphasis, appeared to be looked down upon by his colleagues that day.

In the K-12 and community colleges systems we 'live or die' by the quality of teaching from the faculty members we hire for our students. It is with this similarity of purpose for quality teaching in mind that this book is focused on the K-12 and community college teachers. Quality evaluation systems to assess classroom teaching should be paramount in these schools and colleges.

Teaching can be improved through teacher evaluation if

it is taken seriously, accomplished by competent administrators, and supported by serious governing boards intent on improving instruction in their schools and colleges. There must be teamwork and support from the faculty, evaluators, administration and governing boards. If any one of these groups "breaks down" in the delivery of the process, effective evaluation will cease. The important processes that will lead to successful and legally supportable teacher evaluation processes are presented throughout this book.

Board members, teachers at all levels, administrators, legislators, parents, school administrators and teacher and administrator preparation programs in the universities should all gain valuable insights into the need to focus on quality and meaningful evaluation of teachers to improve the quality of American education. We cannot afford to continue to neglect programs that recognize our finest teachers. We must try to improve all others who are willing to improve, and discontinue the services of those unable or unwilling to make the quality improvements necessary. Serious students of school improvement will find the book most helpful.

The Author

HANS A. ANDREWS has been a leader in the field of faculty evaluation as both a practitioner and a researcher in community colleges and secondary schools for over 35 years. He has had three previous books published on the topic of faculty evaluation. His experiences include being dean of a community college evening program, vice president for community and student services, dean of instruction and a community college president. He has evaluated over 600 faculty members and conducted over 1,500 classroom visitations including written reports and oral evaluation sessions with each individual faculty member.

Dr. Andrews' previous books on the subject of faculty evaluation are *Evaluating for Excellence* (1985), *Merit in Education* (1987) and *Teachers Can Be Fired: The Quest for Quality* (1995). Andrews has had over 35 journal articles published on this subject and over 40 other professional articles on related higher education topics. In addition, he published the first book on the dual-credit movement across America entitled *The Dual-Credit Phenomenon: Challenging Secondary School Students Across 50 States* (2001). His articles have appeared in the *American School Board Journal, New Directions for Community Colleges* series, *The Journal of Applied Research in the Community College, Trustee Quarterly, NASSP Journal, The School Administrator, Journal of Personnel Evaluation in Education, Community College Review, American Community College Journal, The Community College Enterprise, Journal of Faculty Development, Community/Junior College Quarterly, The Journal of Staff, Program & Organization Development* and several other journals. His work on teacher evaluation and recognition programs also appeared in *Psychology Science Collection* in the People's Republic of China.

Andrews has served on four editorial boards: *The Journal of Staff, Program & Organization Development; The Community Services Catalyst; Community Education Journal;* and, *Administrator: Practical Ideas and Key Issues in Higher Education.*

Andrews is often a speaker at national community college and trustee conferences on the topics of evaluation, teacher recognition programs, and the development of dual-credit programs. In addition, he consults with individual colleges and secondary schools on these topics.

Andrews has conducted research projects on evaluation and merit programs with grants from the American Association of Community Colleges (AACC), American Association for Higher Education (AAHE), and North Central Community Junior College Association (NCCJCA). He has been a faculty member for the North Central Dean's Academy and the National Division Chairs' Academy for Community Colleges as well as a management consultant for the American Association of Community Colleges (AACC). In addition, he has consulted with a number of state superintendent and principal organizations, education associations, and numerous community and technical college faculty and administrative groups in both the United States and Canada. Andrews also had the opportunity to present his concepts of effective evaluation at Northeastern University in Shenyang, People's Republic of China.

In addition to his 35 years in community colleges, Andrews' experiences include several years of secondary school experience as a teacher and a director of guidance and counseling. He has also taught as a part-time professor at Illinois State University. Andrews is now the Distinguished Fellow in Comunity College Leadership at Olney Central College in Olney, Illinois.

The rewards that come from improved instruction for students, resulting from faculty development, is the driving force in Andrews' administrative, teaching, and publishing efforts.

Section I
JUSTIFICATION FOR *ACCOUNTABLE EVALUATION SYSTEMS*

Accountable Teacher Evaluation

CHAPTER 1

ACCOUNTABLE TEACHER EVALUATION FOR IMPROVEMENT OF INSTRUCTION

evaluation..... *the system of determining the merit, value, and worth of someone (the evaluee, such as a teacher, student, or employee)*
Teacher Evaluation Kit Glossary *(2003), p. 12*

If ever there was a time to make teacher evaluation programs meaningful and accountable to students, parents, taxpayers, and local, state, and federal funding sources, it is now! The *No Child Left Behind* legislation (2003) calls for a highly qualified teacher in every K-12 classroom. In addition, a national study of community college faculty leaders and instructional administrators by Andrews, Licata, and Harris (2002c) documented that both groups want quality teacher evaluation processes with meaningful outcomes.

Community colleges, while not under the *No Child Left Behind* legislation, are still mandated by their regional accrediting agencies and state coordinating bodies to maintain teachers who have specific qualifications. At a minimum, and in most areas, these credentialed teachers must possess a baccalaureate degree. In the associate degrees designed for transfer to university course areas a Master's Degree is normally required. Some exceptions in technical and vocational training are made if the teacher has had adequate years of experience in the field of the subject matter.

Olson (1999) summarized the movement toward student "results" in American education as "accountability" (p. 1). She pointed out that accountability is here to stay and forty-eight states had mandated student testing while thirty-six had published report cards on individual schools.

A Saint Louis Post-Dispatch (1999, November 21) editorial, *Accountability is Coming,* pointed out that two-thirds of the nation's universities were involved with or considering post-tenure evaluation reviews for their faculties. It also noted that these universities should reward teaching excellence as one of the outcomes.

Lashway (1999) states that the new accountability systems are emphasizing "results." He cited the Southern Regional Education Board (1998) as having five essential elements: (1) rigorous content standards; (2) testing of student progress; (3) professional development aligned with standards and test results; (4) results that are publicly reported; and (5) results that lead to rewards, sanctions, and targeted assistance (p. 1).

In this opening chapter I will support the need for teacher evaluation. This will demonstrate why evaluation of teachers is possibly the most important process in the improvement of instruction in our K-12 schools and our community and technical colleges.

Evaluation of teachers is a very important and serious business. It can be one of the most rewarding jobs of administrators and boards as they work to provide the best education possible for their students. *It is an important enough job to make it the number one quality control available to schools and colleges!* Rice (2003) reported that the National Center for Education Statistics 2000 had recorded close to 2.9 million teachers educating over 46 million public elementary and secondary school students (p. 2).

Arreola (1995) emphasized that *values* are a major guide in faculty evaluation system development. Andrews (2000a) pointed out, in his guide to governing boards on personnel policies, "The product of the community college is instruction. The quality of that instruction is one of the major concerns that administrators, faculty, and boards of trustees must keep as a priority focus"(p. 26). The expected *outcome* from quality instruction is *improved student learning*. Andrews offered the following as values to be considered by governing boards:

Value 1: Quality in every classroom
Value 2: Meeting individual development needs of teachers
Value 3: A recognition plan for outstanding faculty
Value 4: A strong stand on placing poor teachers into a remediation process and, if necessary, movement toward termination.

MAJOR NATIONAL K-12 LEGISLATION

The *No Child Left Behind Act* in the revised version of the Elementary and Secondary Education Act of 2001 has become the key legislation for school improvements. The *Act* focuses on increasing *accountability* for student performance and on having *highly qualified teachers in every classroom* (*Education Week* on the Web, 2003, August 6).

The research of Sanders and Rivers (1996) presented a high degree of correlation between quality of teachers and student academic achievement. This type of research has led the federal government to provide a mandate on each State Education Agency (SEA) to develop plans for assuring "highly qualified" teachers in every classroom by the end of the 2005-2006 school year. These "highly qualified" teachers are identified in the *Act* as having full certification, a bachelor's degree, and having demonstrated competence in subject knowledge and teaching skills (U. S. Department of Education. MyED.gov, 2003a, p. 1).

In addition, the Act requires principals to attest to compliance with the "highly qualified" teacher requirements. This information is to be made available to the public if so requested. Yearly progress reports on this item are required.

Dr. William Sanders, a University of Tennessee statistician, researched the impact of teachers in the Tennessee educational system since 1992. He reviewed the records of student progress with some 30,000 teachers and concluded that, "a bad one [teacher] can thwart a child's progress for at least four years" (Marks, 2000). He went on to note, *Teachers are clearly the most important factor affecting students*" (p. 1). When asked about test scores that he analyzed as being only part of the equation that also includes poverty and parent involvement he emphatically stated, "We've been able to demonstrate that you can separate out the influence of a teacher, over and over again" (p. 2).

Mathis (2003), in referring to the *No Child Left Behind* legislation, warned that, "alas, the promises are far greater than the reality" (p. 679). While the legislation promises that by 2014 it is expected that 95% of all student groups will be passing their state test standards, Mathis is concerned whether the federal government and state legislators will properly fund this movement in order to make it successful.

Levin and Quinn (2003) reported that large city school systems had set up a new teacher recruitment system that had been self-defeating. They found many "highly qualified" teachers applying for the jobs in the large school systems but they were being contacted *too late* in the summer to still be available for hire. Levin and Quinn cited information to show that the more aggressive schools could, indeed, attract large numbers of applicants. One district had received over 4,000 applications for their 200 positions.

The schools waiting until late in the summer to hire saw from 31 to 60 percent of the original applicants no longer available or having withdrawn their applications. Levin and Quinn found many of the applicants for the urban schools were "serious" about wanting to work in *high-need* positions. Late decision-making and interviewing were found to cause most of this problem and, therefore, prevent the high-need schools from obtaining many of the brightest and most qualified candidates.

A NATIONAL COMMUNITY COLLEGE STUDY

Contrary to an opposite widespread preconception, there is solid research evidence that teachers will support effective supervisory evaluation, provided that it meets certain standards of fairness and objectivity. In a national research study on community college evaluation systems, there was strong support among faculty leaders and chief academic administrators for faculty evaluation. This support centered on evaluation with the goals of *improving instruction* and offering *development for improving teachers* in their instructional roles (Andrews, et al., 2002c). There was also support from both groups that the small minority of incompetent teachers should be given remediation, and should it fail, be "weeded out" of the institution.

Faculty leaders and administrators in the study often found evaluation carried out ineptly in their community colleges. There was widespread agreement that present evaluation methods in many of their colleges provided ineffectual outcomes and little to no follow-up.

SOME NATIONAL PERSPECTIVES: NEED FOR *QUALITY* IN EVALUATION

Walberg (2002), with 35 plus years of experience as an educational psychologist suggested, "educators should choose those methods that positively, consistently, and powerfully affect how much children learn" (p. 56). He referred to the hundreds of studies that have been made available through the years showing which teaching methodologies and practices work best.

At a national evaluation institute Shinkfield (1995) spoke to the need for major changes in teacher evaluation systems.

> To be effective schools must make decisions based on considerably better evaluations than presently are the case. It is now accepted that schools must be accountable for achievement levels and expenditure. This accountability is inextricably linked to good evaluations (p. 21).

He had found that schools normally do not choose one best model of evaluation but are more likely to choose an eclectic approach. This is done after reviewing and selecting models or making adaptations to meet their values and goals in the process.

Shinkfield further suggested that since the teaching cohort is virtually fixed in the United States, it could only improve if these teachers improve in their skills. This is done, in his research, in large part through effective teacher evaluation practices (p. 3).

William Bennett (2002), former Secretary of Education, has highlighted the differences a good teacher can make over a poor teacher in regards to impact on students:

The difference between a good teacher and a bad teacher is so great that fifth-grade students who have poor teachers in grades three through five score roughly 50 percentile points below similar groups of students who are fortunate enough to have effective teachers (p. ix).

Rosenthal (2003) identified teaching as consisting of "having a broad knowledge; curriculum and standards; enthusiasm, a caring attitude and a love of learning; knowledge of discipline and classroom management techniques; and a desire to make a difference in the lives of young people" (p. 1). She identified the *characteristics* that make for "*great teachers*:"

1. High expectations for all students
2. Clear, written-out objectives
3. Preparation and organization
4. Engaging students and getting them to look at issues in a variety of ways
5. Forming of strong relationships with students and showing that they care about them as people
6. Masters of their subject matter
7. Frequent communication with parents (p. 2).

The identifiers of *a poor teacher* outlined by Rosenthal were:

1. Your child complains that his teacher singles him out repeatedly with negative remarks.
2. The teacher is the last one to arrive in the morning and the first to leave in the afternoon. He doesn't return phone calls or respond to written communication.
3. Your child rarely brings work home from school.
4. Homework assignments are not returned.
5. The teacher does not send home frequent reports or communications to parents.

6. The teacher exhibits limited knowledge of the subject he is teaching.
7. Lessons lack organization and planning.
8. The teacher refuses to accept any input from parents (pp. 2-3).

A significant amount of the book is dedicated to highlighting quality teaching methodologies and teacher traits. It is important for anyone involved in teacher evaluation to see how these methods and traits become the basis of any evaluation system. If, for example, it is important for a teacher to be knowledgeable, always on time for classes, and enthusiastic in ones' teaching, these then should be included on the evaluation form utilized. This book will also document that tenure, contrary to a popular *myth*, does not guarantee that poor teachers cannot be dismissed for poor performance. Numerous cases are presented showing that courts have upheld dismissal of poor or ineffectual tenured faculty. The firing of poor teachers is presented as a last resort in the evaluation process. This process includes proper identification of weaknesses, a remediation process and a chance to resign prior to being terminated through a formal process by the governing board.

Albert Shanker, long-time president of the American Federation of Teachers, responded to a *U. S. News and World Report* (1996b, February 26) article entitled, "Why Teachers Don't Teach," which was very critical of the teacher unions and their role in keeping poor teachers in the educational system (*U.S. News and World Report*, 1996, March 18):

> We don't run colleges, teacher-education programs or licensing systems, though we've aggressively pursued much higher standards in all of them. And we're not the ones who routinely game the modest teacher-licensing standards by issuing emergency credentials to people who don't pass muster. Nor do unions hire, evaluate, promote or grant tenure; school boards and princi-

pals do that. You don't like the results, yet want to give them an absolute, incontestable right to fire the teachers they evaluated favorable for years and tenured. What makes you think their judgment will be any better than when they had unchecked power over teachers jobs, as they do before a teacher gets tenure and some due process rights? Tenure is a right to due process, not a job guarantee. Like democracy, it is hardly perfect, but it's better than the alternatives (p.10).

Mr. Shanker's words were clearly and honestly stated and have much to offer to boards, administrators, and state and national educational leaders in terms of reflecting what has been poor decision making over a long period of time. His response should cause these leaders to reflect on how the system of evaluation and tenure has been, and has continued to be, poorly conducted by many administrators and governing boards across the country.

Cashin (1996) identified that helping faculty improve their performance was an almost universally accepted primary goal of faculty evaluation within the higher education arena (p. 1). I will present much evidence to support the fact that good faculty evaluation systems can improve instruction. The evidence will also support the need for recognition programs for outstanding teachers. The recognition systems presented are the kind of recognition programs that have proven to meet the needs of the teachers as well as having support from both teachers and their unions. Unlike merit pay, recognition programs have shown significant success in reinforcing quality work by teachers.

Faculty evaluation is both a very difficult and a rewarding job. It requires much time, expertise and seriousness of intent. Honest and descriptive documentation is important at each stage in an evaluation system whether it be for a first-year or a long-term or tenured teacher. Faculty input during the developmental stages of the system and subsequent support during the implementation of the evaluation processes are vital to its success, and I will explore ways this can be accomplished.

THE NEED FOR EVALUATION

Andrews, Licata and Harris (2002b), in their national survey of instructional administrators and faculty leaders in community and technical colleges, documented strong support from both groups for evaluation of teachers:

- Both instructional administrators and faculty leaders strongly believed that tenured or long-term faculty should be evaluated.
- Most administrators and faculty felt that the emphasis of evaluation should shift from providing a basis for assessment of performance and decisions on retention, remediation and dismissal to providing a basis for individual faculty development and improvement.
- Significant percentages of both administrators and faculty questioned the effectiveness of current evaluation practices.
- Another important goal of evaluation was identified as the 'weeding out' of incompetent faculty, but neither group felt that this goal was being met (p. 1).

This national survey received a 71 percent (664) return from instructional administrators and a 57 percent (530) return from faculty leaders. A total of 565 administrators and 442 faculty also felt that faculty development programs were *necessary* as a part of tenured and long-term faculty evaluation practices.

Ackerman (1996) stressed the need for a quality faculty appraisal program as a means of maintaining high standards

---

for an institution. The appraisal is to be used for assessing individual teachers in their job performance. Ackerman felt that teachers meeting or exceeding performance criteria that has been agreed upon should be rewarded.

RECENT UNIVERSITY MOVEMENT INTO POST-TENURE REVIEW

It is not one of the purposes of this book to focus on the university system. The following information will show, however, that post-tenure review is also becoming an accountability program at the university level in recent years. I will identify some elements of evaluation that appear in the university system that are similar to those in K-12 and community college evaluation systems.

In a national study of post-tenure review of American colleges and universities, Aper and Fry (2003) surveyed those institutions with graduate programs at the master's, doctoral, and research level. Their data was summarized and concluded with, "these data suggest that up to this point, post-tenure review has been more ritual than substantive and more driven by politics and appearances than by deeply rooted intentions to change the status of the faculty within the academy" (p. 260).

Licata (1998) stated that post-tenure review at the college and university level almost always emphasizes faculty development as a goal of the process (p. 4). More than half of the public graduate institutions surveyed reported having post-tenure review in place. An additional 30 percent of the institutions reported they were in the process of developing such a policy. This is a recent development for many universities. Fifty-two percent of the universities reporting put post-tenure review policies in place between the years of 1994 and

1999. The Association of American Universities (2001) reported that the majority of their members had these policies put in place since 1995.

Aper and Fry referred to Leatherman's (2002) survey of faculty members, which had been conducted in 1999 by the National Opinion Research Center. The survey found only 6 percent of the faculty responding agreeing with the statement that "post-tenure review has impacted faculty performance" (p. A19). This is a very *low level* of impact considering the time involved in developing and implementing post-tenure evaluation processes within universities.

THE *IDEAL* AND *DISLIKED* EVALUATOR

The quality and competence of the administrators and/or supervisors conducting evaluations is a concern mentioned in surveys of faculty leaders. The following is an "ideal evaluator" profile as presented by Turner (1986):

> The evaluator is genuinely interested and concerned. He's a common sight in the classroom making many formal and informal visits throughout the year. He spends plenty of time observing, knows the classroom and students well, and is on hand to point out the teacher's strengths and weaknesses. He talks with the teacher before and after each evaluation, gives specific suggestions, and welcomes the teacher's input. The situation is relaxed and comfortable; the evaluation, nonthreatening and fair. The principal's purpose is to help the teacher improve her teaching, period" (p. 58).

This composite was put together from over 1,000 teachers responding to a poll on teacher evaluation and positive and negative evaluator traits.

The following profile of "the most disliked evaluator,"

also compiled by Turner, was drawn up from responses of these same teachers. They described the most disliked evaluator as one who alienates teachers from the evaluation process and is likely to conform to the following stereotype. These evaluators:

1. Spend 15 minutes in the classroom once a year;
2. Are more concerned with how the bulletin board looks than how a teacher interacts with her students;
3. Offer no feedback, no suggestions for improvement, and no interest in what the teacher has to say.

It means very little for a teacher to receive high marks from an evaluator like the one just described. Over 52 percent of the teachers responding to the survey conducted by *Learning 86* magazine felt that their evaluators and their subsequent follow-up reports had either a negative effect or no effect at all on their teaching.

A LEGALLY DEFENSIBLE SYSTEM

Legally defensible – *an action, conclusion, or statement that can be upheld under current legislation, governmental mandates, and court decisions.*
Teacher Evaluation Kit Glossary (2003a, p. 18)

As a dean of instruction, a college president, and a national researcher and speaker on the topic of evaluation, I have had many discussions with faculty and administrators on the importance of having a "legally defensible" faculty evaluation system. These discussions have confirmed my view that support does exist among teachers for fair and meaningful evaluation of teaching. I have also learned that there is a need for both faculty and administrators to have a clearer understanding of what can be accomplished through effective classroom evaluation. It is also important to learn how evaluation can be made less threatening for faculty involved.

Faculty evaluation systems must include elements necessary to meet state or local board mandates, legislation, and board policies and procedures. These elements must also be able to stand the scrutiny of a third-party evaluator such as an arbitrator as well as prove to be defensible in the courts.

In a research study by Johnson et al. (1985) a total of 935 elementary teachers in 15 schools were surveyed on school climate as related to evaluation. Teachers' attitudes were much more positive about evaluation in those schools that had high morale. Getting along well together within the school, having a principal whose behavior was personal and direct, and having a school staff committed to quality teaching and learning were some of the other key factors that were correlated to positive attitudes of teachers.

A HISTORICAL PERSPECTIVE

A report from 1911 dealing with the quality of teaching, listed the "causes of failure among elementary school teachers" (Littler, 1914). The researcher had surveyed 50 county, 50 city, and 50 town and village superintendents and another 50 ward principals in Illinois. An additional group of superintendents in Iowa, Indiana, Wisconsin, and Missouri were also included in the study. Out of a total of 400 questionnaires sent out to these schools, a follow-up response of 281 replies was received for an outstanding 70 percent response. The response from the school administrators reported that 676 elementary teachers had been dismissed (see Table I below).

Littler also reported the following "merit" qualities of the *best elementary teachers*. They were ranked as follows:

1. Discipline
2. Teaching Skill

3. Initiative
4. Personality
5. Studiousness
6. Follow Suggestions
7. Health

This 1911 study presented a number of concerns and positive teacher traits that still exist at the beginning of the twenty-first century.

SOME TEACHERS' PERSPECTIVES

Several years ago, during a discussion with the middle school faculty in Spring Valley, Illinois, I was bombarded with the teachers' expectations of an improved evaluation system that we had been discussing. The following is a summary of their expectations from that meeting:

1. Improved instruction;
2. Better communication between administration and

TABLE 1: Causes of Failure among Elementary School Teachers (1911)

Reason for Failure	Number	Percent of Total
1. Lack of discipline	105	15.53%
2. Lack of proper personality	100	14.79%
3. Lack of interest in work or too much interest in outside work	71	10.50%
4. Lack of scholarship	53	7.83%
5. Lazy—made no daily preparation	48	7.10%
6. Lack of preparation	29	4.29%
7. Lack of instructional skill	29	4.29%
8. Lack of pedagogical training	26	3.86%
9. Failure to cooperate	25	3.69%

teachers;

3. Elimination of poor teachers who do not follow remediation procedures;
4. A chance to see weaknesses and the opportunity to improve on them in a constructive way;
5. An opportunity for administrators to see the realistic situations that teachers encounter;
6. Improved public relations when incompetent teachers are removed;
7. Upgraded community opinion of the teaching profession.

It was evident that these teachers wanted some significant improvements and outcomes. It was also important to them that they remain anonymous relative to the individual responses written by them. This was not an unusual response as teachers are often anxious that their honesty might cause them problems with their administrators.

A national survey conducted by Filan (1992) identified topics that instructional leaders felt to be of the greatest concern to be addressed at the First National Conference for Community College Chairs. The number one choice of 298 of the respondents was *faculty evaluation*. Division chairpersons and chief academic administrators were those surveyed. The following is a list of the three items checked most often as needed to improve performance in their present jobs. Individuals could check more than one item (pp. 1-2):

1. Faculty evaluation   298
2. College and division/department
    strategic planning   284
3. Curriculum design   268

As the presenter at this conference on faculty evaluation, I found that community college chairpersons through-

---

out the U.S. and Canada wanted quality faculty evaluation, but most of them had received very little training to prepare them in this most important area of their jobs.

At a workshop I conducted on *improving faculty evaluation practices* with 45 faculty and division chairpersons at Aims Community College in Colorado, the first day feedback, from the largest number of respondents, was the need to focus much more directly on the evaluation practices at their college and on how they might work to change them. Small groups discussed "what can be salvaged from your present system" and "what needs to be done to strengthen evaluation at your college." The participants most frequently voiced the following responses:

What can be salvaged from our present system?
1. Nothing!
2. Student evaluation, but in a revised form
3. Re-evaluate supervisor form

What needs to be done?
1. Include 'teaching' in annual evaluation.
2. Don't visit and evaluate only when problems exist.
3. Eliminate the 'fear' factor of being observed.
4. Revise the faculty evaluation form to focus on teaching.
5. Develop a consistent approach (throughout the system.)
6. Define expectations and define quality teaching.
7. Have a board/president policy approved.
8. Keep in mind the system must be fair.
9. Determine the primary purposes of what the evaluation system should accomplish: *Improvement of instruction.*

There was a nearly unanimous wish to move away from what were considered inept attempts at faculty evaluation.

The small groups came to a consensus on what they felt was needed to improve instruction – - an evaluation process that has consistency and defines quality teaching and then goes about measuring it.

The question, "what motivates you to want to improve your evaluation practices," solicited the following responses:

- We are tired of teacher-bashing and we need professionalism to gain the status teachers deserve. We need to police ourselves.
- Get the deadwood out and regain our pride.
- Consensus is that the current system doesn't work. It is not fair and consistent.
- We really do believe that a revamped system could improve instruction.

In dealing with in-class observations the faculty stressed the need to reduce fear, ensure consistency and fairness, and have well-trained evaluators. They also felt that they "must be comfortable that the evaluator is well trained and competent so as to create trust."

Faculty leaders' perspectives

The research of Andrews and Licata (1990a) and Andrews et al. (2002b) reinforce the above comments. In both studies they found faculty leaders supportive of quality evaluation proposals to improve instruction. In neither study did faculty leaders, as a group, feel that their present evaluation systems were nearly as effective as they should be.

The survey of faculty leaders (Andrews and Licata, 1990a) in the 19-state North Central Association (now called Higher Learning Authority) brought 158 responses for a 51 percent rate. The number one stated reason for post-tenure evaluation by 59 percent of the respondents was *individual faculty development*. Only 27 percent rated their system as "very effective" or "effective." This contrasted with administrative leaders, which as a group had 56 percent rating evaluation as "very effective" or "effective."

Seventy-three percent of faculty leaders, who gave responses of "uncertain" or "ineffective," were asked to describe in more detail why they felt so negative about the effectiveness of their systems (pp. 18-19).

The following major reasons were checked:

1. Pays only "lip service" to faculty development;
2. Has no mechanism to measure competence/incompetence;
3. Does not have adequately trained evaluators (p. 19).

Faculty leaders and administrators both agreed that, "there should be post-tenure evaluation for tenured faculty." This question showed 96 percent of the faculty and 100 percent of the administrators "agreeing" or "agreeing strongly" with the statement (p. 20).

Feedback, as a part of the evaluation system, does not occur for the majority of the teachers according to Peterson (1995). He found feedback for improving practice for teachers was only happening for a small minority of the teachers.

Miller et al. (2000) found evaluation *systems* to be rare. They defined a system as having components such as student ratings, classroom observation, self-evaluation (portfolio), and colleague evaluation linked together. They also found two-year colleges reluctant to admit that faculty evaluation is often taken lightly or used as a façade to cover the public demand for accountability (p. 14).

CONCERN ABOUT POOR INSTRUCTORS

Both the faculty leaders and administrative respondents in the Andrews and Licata (2002b) study were asked if evaluation in their colleges "*should* lead to the weeding out of incompetent faculty." Both groups *strongly agreed* that it should. The responses were 354 (72 percent) for faculty leaders and 434 (68 percent) for administrators. The next statement, "post-tenure evaluation *does* lead to the weeding out of incompetent faculty," provided very *strong disagreement* with the statement. The faculty leaders had 376 responses (77 percent) selecting "disagree or strongly disagree" compared to 543 responses (82 percent) from administrators selecting the same responses (p. 8).

McDaniel and McDaniel (1980) saw principals with some conflicting roles in their positions. They saw them serving their faculty in both roles of consultant and evaluator. Principals having trouble reconciling or balancing these roles, they found, will usually lean toward "the positive role of consultant rather than the negative role of evaluator" (p. 35).

Painter (2001) studied principals in elementary and middle schools relative to the barriers that kept them from doing an effective job of evaluating poor teachers. They identified teacher-tenure laws, procedures, problems with the teacher's union, the collective-bargaining agreement, and time constraints as reasons they were unable to properly evaluate teachers in their schools.

Gaynes (1990) says the first year of employment of a teacher is key for making "continuation" or "dismissal decisions." The principal needs to actively monitor and evaluate all probationary teachers. Only the best teachers should be kept in the classroom beyond the first year according to Gaynes (p. 30-32).

Van Sciver (1990b) expressed concern that administrators may not give top priority to understanding the evaluation instruments and finding time to evaluate teachers. He said, "it is ironic, for schools exist first and foremost to educate our children." He continued, "allowing other concerns to intrude on the effectiveness of that mission seems counterproductive" (pp. 318-319).

Incompetent teachers were found to be relatively few by Bridges (1985). The number of students being taught by these teachers, however, was substantial. Parental complaints play a major role in signaling that something may be radically wrong in the classrooms of certain teachers. Too often Bridges found the administrator leaving these teachers alone. When a meeting is called to discuss problems, there are two distinct purposes that need to be considered. One is when the administrator is trying to "salvage the teacher." Bridges found few such teachers actually being salvaged and suggested that the "incompetent veteran teacher is nearly impossible to make into a good teacher." The second situation, where the administrator tries to get rid of the incompetent teacher, is not easy, especially when dealing with a tenured teacher. Non-tenured dismissals do not offer nearly as much of a challenge. Bridges found in California that poor tenured teachers were being "eased out" about 20 times as often as they were dismissed.

Bridges concluded that granting of tenure may well be the most important single decision facing administrators and governing boards everywhere. He found incompetent teachers being allowed to continue indefinitely, and unless the public and student pressures become almost intolerable, little or no action was taken to dismiss such poor instructors.

Bridges pointed to the fact that most states have passed laws that make it possible to move toward termination of those faculty found incompetent. Such termination, however, requires a well-defined evaluation system and adequate support of the administration and governing board. He concluded that "coaching out" incompetent faculty is more successful when a school has an evaluation system that commits the administration to evaluating a teacher over a period of time and has allowed the person ample time to improve (p. 24).

TENURE

A definition of tenure was provided by the Teacher Evaluation Kit Glossary (2003):

TENURE: An employment status conferred upon a teacher by state law or institutional regulation after successful completion of a probationary period. Tenure provides substantial but not complete protection against arbitrary or capricious dismissal and entitles the teacher to due process procedures and other protections that may not be available to the non-tenured teacher (p. 26).

Nisbet (1973) concluded that tenure did indeed mean a guarantee of a lifetime job for most teachers. He found very few faculty had been dismissed from tenure positions. Nisbet suggested that there are many institutions where a tenured faculty member has *never been dismissed.* He stated: "To argue that tenure is not a refuge for the lazy, incompetent and delinquent, that 'with cause shown' such individuals may be dismissed, hardly carries conviction when, as the record makes plain, tenure *is* such a refuge" (p. 47).

He also described the frustration that a new university president, along with board members and a substantial number of faculty members face when they wish to make significant improvements: "What must be the emotions running through the mind of such a president as he looks at the layer on layer of mediocrity, sloth, incompetence and disdain for effort, the heritage of years, and at the budgetary and appointment problems made inevitable by inability to reduce these

---

layers, protected as they are by an iron doctrine of tenure?" (p. 53).

QUESTIONABLE SYSTEMS AND RESULTS

Seldin (1982) described the failure of evaluation systems on several points: (1) failing to distinguish between poor, adequate, and good teaching; (2) failing to motivate teachers to improve their performance (p. 93).

Another concern Seldin presented was that the evaluation program may start out flawed by being so vague that no one may know how it works. He said it can also become "so comprehensive and detailed, down to assigned weights to publications, classes, professional and community activities, that it will not work" (p. 94). Cohen and Brawer (1982) also found evaluation procedures being developed into "labyrinthine complexity" (p. 75). Seldin concluded that, "how the evaluation program is developed and administered can be almost as important to program success as program content" (p. 94).

WORKING TOWARD A MORE EFFECTIVE SYSTEM

Hunter (1988a) suggested a slogan for teacher evaluation as "good, better, best. Never let it rest until good becomes better and better becomes best (p. 32)!" Her view of an ideal system on which sophisticated supervisors and evaluators should base their teacher evaluations follows:

1. Teaching is seen as a learned profession, not a genetic endowment.
2. Many principles governing effective teaching are described, taught, observed, and documented in practice.

3. All teachers (and all administrators) continue to grow in professional effectiveness and artistry, and this is required as a condition of continued employment.

4. Increasing the quality of educational practice is encouraged, stimulated, and demanded by formative and summative evaluation.

5. Career opportunities and psychological incentives for continuing growth are available to excellent teachers. Stimulation and incentives for growth are provided for "average" teachers. Compassionate but rigorous and effective remediation is required for teachers who need it. Removal with dignity takes place for those very few teachers for whom remediation is not effective.

6. Daily teaching is seen as the most critical professional duty of a teacher.

7. The summative evaluation is fair and has the following three qualities: First, it is based on many performance samples (not on one observation or on hearsay); second, only an adequately trained evaluator conducts it; last, it is based on stipulated criteria with meanings common to teacher and evaluator.

8. The evaluators are competent and demonstrate expertise in two key areas: They possess knowledge of the research-based, cause-effect relationships between teaching and learning, and they demonstrate competence in observation and conferencing skills (pp.34-35).

SOME QUALITY EVALUATION SYSTEMS

Wise et al. (1984) found four districts—Salt Lake City, Utah; Lake Washington, Washington; Toledo, Ohio; and Greenwich, Connecticut—that were best able to identify incompetent teachers and to improve teacher performance. These districts spent more administrative time, money, and care in the implementation of faculty evaluation. These "exemplary" systems made sure their evaluators were competent, sought cooperation from both teachers and administrators, and tailored a system of evaluation to fit their particular district's educational and political characteristics (p. 63).

Over a nine-year period the Salt Lake City district removed 37 teachers who were found to be incompetent. The Lake Washington upper-middle-class suburban district used a highly structured system, with both pre- and post-observation conferences and personal development plans. Over a five-year period 56 faculty were "counseled out" of their system (p.100).

A BILL OF RIGHTS: *THE INSTITUTION*

A "bill of rights for faculty evaluation" was proposed by Strike (1990). It defines the powers of the institution as related to evaluation:

1. Educational institutions have the right to exercise supervision and to make personnel decisions intended to improve the quality of the education they provide.
2. Educational institutions have the right to collect information relevant to their supervisory and evaluative roles.

3. Educational institutions have the right to act on such information in the best interest of the students whom they seek to educate.

4. Educational institutions have the right to the cooperation of the teaching staff in implementing and executing a fair and effective system of evaluation (p. 358).

A BILL OF RIGHTS: *THE FACULTY*

Andrews (1986c) developed the following as a "faculty evaluation bill of rights" as a result of his many evaluation experiences and workshops with faculty from elementary schools through the community college level:

1. Competent evaluators should be expected and used.
2. The evaluators and faculty members should have a clear understanding of the evaluation system and instruments to be used.
3. Consistency should be expected.
4. Fairness is a "must" element of the system.
5. Both verbal and written evaluations should be part of the feedback to teachers.
6. Teachers should be allowed to express disagreement, both verbally and in writing.
7. Feedback from the evaluator should be expected to occur in a reasonably short time.
8. Recognition for excellence in one's work should be given.
9. A reasonable amount of time should be given for those areas of teaching that may need some form of remediation due to a weakness.
10. Privacy of results should be expected—except when an open meetings act in a state may call for board action in open session of the board on a "notice to

remedy," or on a personnel dismissal being recommended.

These "bills of rights" can be used as guidelines in providing for the professionalism necessary to assure trust, support, and positive expectations by faculty.

UNION LEADERS: *SUPPORT FOR QUALITY EVALUATION*

When he was newly elected president of the National Education Association, Robert F. Chase stated a major concern: "The imperative now facing public education could not be more stark. We must revitalize our public schools from within or they will be dismantled from without" (Gergen, 1997, p. 100).

Futrell (1986), while president of the National Education Association (NEA), explained that teachers were supportive of having their supervisors evaluate them providing that such evaluation is professionally carried out. The faculty bill of rights above includes several of the ingredients Futrell suggested faculty should expect.

Former American Federation of Teachers (AFT) president, Albert Shanker, (Shanker, 1985) pointed to poor administrators being responsible for poor instructors being kept in place rather than being dismissed:

> The machinery for dealing with incompetent teachers is in place in every community and has not been compromised by any negotiated settlement. One cannot deny that this is often an unwieldy, time-consuming, thankless process. And the truth is that most teachers are as troubled by the situation as are supervisors. Incompetent teachers reflect badly on the profession and their fecklessness usually ends on the back of their colleagues (pp. 224-225).

Chait and Ford (1982) did not find the American Association of University Professors (AAUP) having an official position relative to post-tenure evaluation. They believed, however, that the AAUP would denounce the process if it were employed to terminate tenured faculty without cause. The chance for remediation and due process would have to be key elements if post-tenure evaluation was to be sanctioned.

THE GOAL: *COMMITMENT AND COMPETENCE*

In their recommendation on improving teacher effectiveness and decreasing the variability that presently exists among teacher performances, Rivers and Sanders (2002) see two factors as *key* in the process: (1) identification through measurement and (2) professional development (p. 21). The improvement of teacher quality was seen as the way of assuring that more students will be able to reach their potential. This student improvement came, according to Rivers and Sanders, "because they benefited from effective teachers *every year*" (p. 23).

The primary goal of tenure review according to Brand (1999) is for renewal of professionalism. If this renewal does not occur through the review process for a teacher "it may be appropriate to fire him or her" (p. A-64). Brand made a distinction between the process of termination and post-tenure review.

In a report by the National Commission of Higher Education Issues (1982) several conclusions were drawn relative to post-tenure evaluation:

1. It should assure that the tenured faculty member has maintained the appropriate level of competence and is performing at a satisfactory level.
2. The responsibility lies with faculty and administra-

---

tion to see that unsatisfactory performance is remedied.

3. Ultimately, incompetent faculty members must not be protected at the expense of the students or the maintenance of quality (p. 10).

Bridges (1990) states that if a teacher is assisted with good faith efforts, but cannot be considered for future employment due to a lack of improvement, "the administration must be able to justify its dismissal decision to an impartial third party" (p. 154). These third parties are court judges, hearing officers, or a commission on professional competence. Credible evidence for the decision must be presented as the administration is under pressure to justify its decision. Written records that document a pattern of poor performance are necessary. The evidence must be focused on the pattern of behavior rather than on isolated incidents that might be considered remediable. When the administration is unable to document a pattern of deficiency and defects in the teaching or other job responsibilities, those who must sit in judgment of the evidence will not allow dismissal.

SUMMARY

This chapter has laid the foundation for the need for effective faculty evaluation. It has provided evidence that various levels of faculty understand the need for effective evaluation. It has also presented research and testimonials to show that there are many problems with evaluation systems, and often a lack of qualified and quality evaluators. Further there is a fear by some faculty of speaking out about such problems unless their anonimity can be protected.

Support is dependent upon *skilled* and *trusted* administrative evaluators. In addition to trust, this support is also dependent upon faculty input into the system, and administration of the process in a manner that is consistent and fair.

Recognition for quality teachers and support for improvement are key elements in successful evaluation programs. There is a strong need for recognition plans for those faculty who are working hard and providing high quality teaching with the results being increases in student achievement. Faculty members are looking for a system that recognizes good performance as well as identifying shortcomings and providing appropriate opportunities for development.

Differences do exist between decisions regarding nontenured and tenured faculty and with how governing boards, arbitrators and the court system deal with non-tenure and tenured dismissals. Non-tenured dismissals, when challenged in the appeals processes, have been upheld in most cases. A solidly conceived and administered evaluation system strengthens the legal position of administrators and governing boards. Tenured faculty dismissals, however, are much more difficult to accomplish.

It is a difficult and time-consuming job to document teacher incompetence. Some administrators tend to leave incompetent faculty in a school district or community college. This may well be due to a lack of motivation to conduct effective evaluation practices that (1) leads to improvement of instruction or (2) to a decision to remove poor instructors who refuse to or cannot improve.

The *No Child Left Behind Act* does not leave this type of discretion up to K-12 principals and superintendents. This act, guaranteeing quality teachers in every classroom, makes removal of incompetent teachers imperative. Community colleges, while not operating under this legislation, have similar concerns about removal of incompetent faculty. The Andrews, Licata, and Harris national study (2002c), reported faculty leaders expect *meaningful outcomes* from evaluation to include remediation and dismissal for those colleagues who do not improve.

Laws in most states support sound evaluation systems. Faculty union leaders have pointed out that the mechanisms for dealing with poor and incompetent teaching are in place. It is the responsibility of competent administrators to use such mechanisms when needed.

The two bills of rights offered in this chapter consist of the elements of (1) consistency, (2) fairness, (3) competency in evaluators, (4) recognition, (5) mutual respect, and (6) privacy of results. These elements must permeate all quality evaluation systems.

SUGGESTED EXERCISES

1. Define what can be done to make supervisory evaluation a successful process in a school or college. What are the important elements that should be included in a supervisory system that will gain faculty support?

2. Identify those personal characteristics a supervisor needs to generate trust and confidence from the faculty.

Accountable Teacher Evaluation

CHAPTER 2

DEVELOPING FACULTY AND UNION SUPPORT FOR ADMINISTRATIVE EVALUATION

> A teacher affects eternity; he can never tell where his influence stops.
>
> *Henry Brooks Adams*

> A bad one [teacher] can thwart a child's progress for at least four years, says a University of Tennessee statistician, who has quantified just how much teachers matter.
>
> *Marks,* The Teacher Factor, *2000, p. 1*

After working in faculty evaluation for some 35 years the question most often presented to me in workshops has been, "How do faculty respond to a system of administrative evaluation?" It continues to surprise some faculty, governing boards and administrators to learn that there are many faculty members and some faculty union leaders openly supporting an evaluation system that includes in-class observations of faculty by members of the administrative staff.

Faculty union leaders in America over the years have felt it is most important for their teaching membership to do a good job in their classrooms and other job responsibilities. These same leaders have also pointed out that many school governing boards lack proper policies and procedures to carry

---

out an effective faculty-supported evaluation system. In return, they see these administrators and boards hiding in the shadows of faculty unions and tenure to justify why they are not able to conduct evaluations leading to meaningful outcomes.

Albert Shanker expressed innovative ideas near the end of his long-term career as the leader of the American Federation of Teachers. His new vision of the union and teaching was considered radical at the time (U. S. News and World Report, 1996b). He advocated changes that he felt were necessary to keep the unions in a survival mode. These changes included viewing quality teaching as part of the union's responsibility. He warned, "Unless we restore the public's faith in what we do, public education is going to collapse. Convincing people to change has been a damn difficult thing to do" (p. 71).

Nolin (1994) reported on a survey relating to formal evaluations based on nearly 1,000 elementary teachers in K-6 grades.

1. Most teachers (89 percent) believe their last performance evaluation provided an accurate assessment of their teaching performance.
2. A total of 94 percent knew the evaluation criteria prior to assessment.
3. A total of 92 percent reported classroom observation was used.
4. A total of 99 percent said subject matter knowledge should be a consideration in these performance evaluations.
5. Most perceived their evaluators to be competent to judge performance in most areas of their teaching (p. 1).

These results support quality evaluation carried out with known criteria and by competent evaluators.

Marks (2000) reported that in 1992, Dr. William Sanders, a University of Tennessee statistician, conducted a major research project to define the impact that teachers have on students. In his work he analyzed six million student records. He also evaluated performance records of more than 30,000 elementary school teachers. The outcome of his quantified research was that, "a bad one [teacher] can thwart a child's progress for at least four years" (p. 1).

Cashin (1996) recommended that faculty leaders be significantly involved in developing their system of evaluation in higher education institutions. In this way the evaluation system will become equally accepted and co-owned by both administration and faculty (p. 2).

Wise et al. (1984) suggested that, "a well-designed, properly functioning teacher evaluation process provides a major communication link between the school system and teachers. On the one hand, it imparts concepts of teaching to teachers and frames the conditions of their work. On the other hand, it helps the school system structure, manage, and reward the work of teachers" (p. 61).

NECESSARY COMPONENTS FOR OBTAINING FACULTY AND UNION SUPPORT

The following are four fundamental components that this author has identified over the years as necessary in any school system developing an *effective* administrative evaluation system. Such a system must gain support within the faculty and its union organization:

1. *Trust.* It is difficult to imagine a faculty evaluation system having any chance of success without trust between the board, administrators and faculty. Faculty want to trust those persons selected to supervise them in their classroom

and other job responsibilities. This trust can only be earned through experience working with faculty. McLaughlin (1990) says, "teacher evaluation will be no more effective than the extent to which teachers support it; and an effective evaluation system insists on trust between teachers and administrators" (p. 404). Trust was defined by the Teacher Evaluation Kit Glossary (2003) as: "a common understanding of the purpose and potential of teacher evaluation, and a cooperative spirit between the teacher and the evaluator for maximizing the benefits of doing the evaluation. Trust is related to such factors as confidentiality of communication, careful consideration of the accuracy of evidence from such sources as hearsay or complaints, honesty, openness, sharing, and sincerity on the part of both the teacher and the evaluator" (p. 27).

2. *Input.* The best faculty members understand what it takes to be effective in the classroom. It, therefore, behooves the administration and board to seek the input of faculty in the development of the evaluative instrument. This will create feelings of joint-ownership that are very important in encouraging acceptance of the evaluation system.

3. *Feedback.* Faculty want both oral and written feedback on the supervisor's observations. This feedback needs to be given as soon as it is practical following classroom observations. At this time teachers have an excellent opportunity to respond to the observations. They want to have the options of learning how to improve in their teaching and to be able to disagree and have their viewpoints heard and respected.

4. *Remediation.* It is most important for a supervisor to tell a teacher what teaching areas or methods need to be improved or changed. It is also important that a specified period of time is set for these remediation areas to be accomplished. Wheeler, et al., describe remediation as "those techniques or strategies designed to improve a teacher's performance with respect to general deficiencies or specific areas of weakness"

(p. 22).

Licata's (1986) recommendations for institutions interested in developing or modifying a plan to evaluate their tenured faculty members include the following:

1. The purpose for the evaluation should drive all other aspects of the evaluation plan. Will the evaluation be formative or summative in nature?
2. Faculty must be involved in the design of the plan.
3. Faculty and administrators should agree upon the specifics of the plan.
4. A post-tenure evaluation plan should be flexible and individualized.
5. Faculty development programs should be linked to a post-tenure evaluation system.
6. Innovative approaches to post-tenure evaluation and institutional planning are needed (pp. 67-68).

Licata pointed out the importance of item five (5) if "institutional commitment to faculty development and provision for faculty rewards *cannot* be delivered, then institutions should seriously question the usefulness and effectiveness of such evaluation" (p. 68).

In a report entitled *Action for Excellence*, the Task Force on Education for Economic Growth, Education Commission of the States (ECS), (1983), presented several recommendations, one of which was for faculty input in the development of evaluation systems:

> We recommend that boards of education and higher education in each state—in cooperation with teachers and school administrators—put in place, as soon as possible, systems for fairly and objectively *measuring the effectiveness of teachers and rewarding outstanding performance.*
>
> We strongly recommend that the states examine and tighten their procedures for selecting not only those

who come into teaching, but also those who ultimately stay . . . Ineffective teachers—those who fall short repeatedly in fair and objective evaluations—should, in due course and with due process, be dismissed (p. 39).

THE CASE FOR FACULTY INVOLVEMENT

Wise, et al. (1984) presented a study of four school districts with well recognized evaluation systems that found all four allowed the teachers' organizations to play a major role in designing and implementing the evaluation process. They recommended that school districts "should involve teacher organizations in the design and oversight of teacher evaluation to ensure its legitimacy, fairness, and effectiveness" (p. 111).

Van Sciver (1990) suggested working with both the teacher union leadership and school board members. The emphasis, he indicated, must be on how important quality instruction is to the school operation for students. One of the outcomes he feels will result from such cooperation is board support for removing poor teachers when properly documented information is brought to them at the proper time (p. 41).

Seldin (1982) called for both faculty and administrators to lend their support to the development of faculty evaluation systems. He pointed out that such systems need to recognize that the goal is to make "improvement" and "not perfection" (p. 98).

In 1987 the faculty senate at Miami-Dade Community College in Miami, Florida, invited me to present the tenants of an effective faculty evaluation process. Two teachers who were former faculty union presidents at community college District 513 in Illinois were interviewed on videotape in preparation for the Miami Dade presentation. They were questioned about the administrative evaluation system at their college: How well was it accepted by the teachers? How about faculty input in developing the instrument? How do you feel about evaluations leading to dismissal of some of your fellow teachers? Mary Sue Myers, a physical fitness instructor, and Robert Mueller, a teacher of English and literature, were the respondents who consented to the interview with William Danley, Director of Public Information, for the college. Following are the interview questions and responses:

Faculty Involved in Evaluation as Union Leaders: An Interview

Interviewer: This college is somewhat unusual in that faculty are evaluated in the classroom by a department chairperson, associate dean and dean. Bob, would you start by commenting about how being evaluated in the classroom makes you feel. Does being evaluated in the classroom make you feel ill at ease? Some instructors have expressed such a feeling.

Robert: Yes, I think evaluation is something that we are going to have to live with. It has always been with us. As faculty members we have had input into the instrument that we are going to be evaluated on, and on the procedures involved. As a union president we have negotiated fringe benefits but have never really talked about teacher evaluation. It has been a non-negotiable item.

As far as a feeling about faculty evaluation is concerned, no matter how long you are in teaching, when you are being evaluated there is a little tenseness and *perhaps that's good.* Perhaps that gives you that edge and you go from there. Our visits are unannounced by the division chair people, also by the dean of instruction. I think it's something that at least we have been involved in developing some of the key elements that have made up the evaluation form. In that way the faculty feel that they are a little more at ease than if the evaluators were coming in with a different instrument being forced upon us.

Mary Sue: I guess my personal feeling is that it is helpful to know what is expected. When the evaluators are in evaluating I kind of know the expectations, and when I go into the classroom I *am prepared.* I feel on any day they could come in and I would feel comfortable with an evaluation. I know what the expectations are and I don't have a problem with it.

Interviewer: You would have occasion to know most of our faculty on a personal basis. Are the feelings you expressed generally the feelings of the faculty at large?

Robert: I think so. In talking, and that's what faculty do best, we do talk around coffee and I think that everyone is in agreement that, number one, the evaluation is part of our job; and number two, that the instrument is fair in that it does evaluate those areas that are important in teaching, like the course syllabus— are you following it? I think it is one of our requirements as a teacher and that it becomes our bible of instruction. I think that the written evaluation is far superior to any kind of checklist mainly because it allows for some kind of specificity; it allows for those areas that were observed. Following a classroom visitation there is a discussion with the teacher and the person who has done the evaluating. The faculty member will sign the form, but only after you have reviewed each item that is on the evaluation form.

That feedback is a strong point of the instrument because if I'm being evaluated and I'm having something written that I feel deserves an explanation, then I'm allowed that opportunity to say what you observed is atypical or whatever. There is room for discussion, and what I'm hearing from the faculty is that they are in agreement with that. Sue can maybe comment on that.

Mary Sue: I think they see the instrument as, number one, a way of improving instruction, and I think the faculty does take pride in the reputation of our students doing well. And I think this is just part of the pride that we have that we all want to do well, and we see this [evaluation] as one of the ways that will help us to do a better job. Again, it was important that, in developing the instrument, we had input. I was involved when it was being set up and I can remember some very tough discussions we had with the administration. I was representing the union at that time, but I think that we came up with some things we can all live with here.

Robert: The instrument does allow in the written format a means of remediation and I think that that is an important part of evaluation. Is the evaluator coming into the classroom to evaluate objectively as much as she/he can, or is the evaluator coming in to solidify a pre-conceived idea? In other words, if my reputation is that I'm not doing a very good job, does that slant the evaluation? I don't think that would be reflected in an instrument relying on numbers. The written form helps, especially when I have the chance to go one-on-one with the person who has evaluated me. I can say, 'well, I can do this or I can do that or I can see where this area needs improvement or that one may not.' I can see where the feedback is the essential part of the instrument.

Evaluation and improved instruction

Interviewer: Do you have a feel for whether the system of evaluation has a system wide tendency to improve instruction?

Robert: I believe that in our conversations the faculty is in agreement that evaluation here is to improve instruction. I know there is a tendency once in awhile to say that, 'if they want to get me, they can get me,' which is true under any situation. The instrument isn't at fault there. If they want to, they can build a case if you are in that situation. We have had some in that situation who have been evaluated several times, given remediation dates; those had not been met, and they have been discharged from the faculty. As a union president that is a very difficult situation to be in because you are caught right in the middle. But I think that the instrument does allow, as I say, the feedback, which is important. And also if I'm doing something wrong, tell me, give me a chance to remediate, and than come on back and evaluate. In that way I think its improving instruction. Its not a vendetta, its not a solidification of a preconceived idea; it's an evaluation.

Mary Sue: I think some things that I find in my own teaching, even now, I'm improving upon. I have been recently evaluated so I'm kind of thinking they won't be back in for a while. On the other hand, I find myself stating objectives each day that I go in. Do the students know what is expected? In summing things up, these are the kinds of things they are looking for in the evaluation and I find that I am just more careful that I do these things, and I think these are educationally sound kinds of things that we should all be doing. Some people, I think, are sometimes a little careless. So again, I think evaluating us helps the students, with us being better teachers. These are just some of the kind of feelings you get as a result of being evaluated and having these things pointed out, that these are important things, and that you really should be doing them in each class.

Robert: I really think that if you're not evaluated it doesn't help you a great deal, because you really don't know and you get into you own way of doing things and you think its working, and so on. At least this is how I look at it: I'm happy to have someone come in and then give me that interaction to help me to become a better teacher. Here we're our own best public relations because the faculty here has traditionally been strong on the transfer successes of our people, so something good is going on in that classroom. I think the evaluation allows discussion of those methods of what's being done, what's good, what works, what doesn't work. What Sue mentioned, and it's true, the form has comments about the course syllabus: Are the students given direction? Do they know what you're covering today? What's going to be coming up the next meeting, or the next? And as Sue mentioned, I think it is very true that those are sound educational principles.

Mary Sue: I guess I really don't have anything else to add here other than, I just get back to the point that educationally this is a very sound approach to things and I just think it very definitely can make better teachers out of all of us.

Removing poor faculty

Interviewer: Some of our faculty, of course, did not survive the evaluation system and you folks were involved, in that these were colleagues, and also you were in union leadership positions. Candidly, would you tell how you felt about that sort of thing? Obviously, it couldn't have been easy.

Mary Sue: I think I was the one who was involved when all of this was going on. I was president of the local association for two years, and it was during these two years that there was some hard evaluating going on here. And, truly, it was personally a very hard time for me because I was involved with some of these individuals. Some of them were my close friends. I think in looking at it; I think it was helpful, both for the administration and for the faculty involved, to have me, not just me as a person, but sort of this [union leader] position. I think that I could see things happening oftentimes when we would have meetings trying to see where problems were. Oftentimes, I found that the faculty person who was involved would sit in the meeting but wouldn't really hear what was being said. Basically, I was there as an observer and also to maybe add some helpful comments.

I guess that I would say the meetings I was involved in were always in the tone of trying to help the person. But I could see that we would come out of a meeting and the person would say, 'thus and so,' and I would say, no, that isn't what they were really saying. I was sometimes a go-between and really felt nobody was my friend. But I could see that the administration was making, you know, great efforts to try to help these people and sometimes they just weren't hearing what was trying to be said to them.

I feel that the administration probably did the best job that they could to try to get them to hear. I know that I did, and other people that were involved in the other union offices would sit down with these people and look at the evaluations and try to help them to see where changes needed to be made. And as I say, sometimes they were just not willing to admit that there was a problem. We couldn't change their interpretation of what the situation was. Being the one in the middle, it was one of the worse things that I had ever been through, but I think it made it a little easier for both sides.

Robert: If I could pick up on that, I think that coming out of the dismissals of several of our instructors came, very clearly, some guidelines for people who are in the classroom. I'm going to be very specific now: number one, some people get in trouble for not following the course syllabus. As a union president, as a faculty member, I have very little sympathy for a person who doesn't follow the course syllabus. I think that that's our job, that's our responsibility. We also have the responsibility to be up-to-date in what's happening in our field. How we do that is by going back to conferences or by going back to school or by doing something other than the normal teaching. The college has been supportive of travel. I know we appropriate monies and then we distribute them among our faculty. On the other side again—and what Sue said is very true— there is this chance for remediation if you don't meet the standard. Dates to submit updated course outlines, or syllabus, or whatever; those are dates that you should follow, because that's in the remediation process. If they are not adhered to you are held responsible for that, and I don't know that a union can protect you in that way for not meeting your responsibilities.

Mary Sue: Yes, I think that was a thing that I could see that the administration made it very clear what was expected of the people in the remediation. They had their options to make the needed changes or not. As I said, some of the people were quite defensive and maybe didn't perceive the problems or whatever. But they, in cases I was aware of, knew clearly what was expected of them in remediation.

[End of interview]

This interview proved to be very helpful in the Miami Dade workshop with the Faculty Senate membership of around 170 persons. Key points made in the interview were: (1) faculty were involved in the development of the process and instrument; (2) it was a fair system, and the administrators always tried to assist those teachers who were having problems; (3) knowing what was expected of the teachers was important; and (4) in the tough decisions that had to be made in terminating some instructors, the administration gave clear guidelines on what to improve and the teachers had the option of choosing to do those things or to ignore those things. Some did not take action necessary to keep their jobs.

SUMMARY

The material presented in this chapter reinforces the importance of having the support of teachers and their unions. Teachers do support an administrative evaluation system if it has certain key elements, and they see that the process is administered fairly. There are four elements that are essential in getting faculty to support an administrative evaluation system: (1) trust between faculty and administrators; (2) faculty involvement in development of the evaluation system; (3) both oral and written feedback from supervisors and a chance to respond; and (4) due process procedures and adequate time to allow one to remediate defects and deficiencies.

Wise, et al. (1984), recognized evaluator competence as possibly being the most difficult part of the process in evaluation. Their concern centered on the fact that, no matter how well developed an evaluation process may be, a lack in background, knowledge, and expertise of the evaluator can render such a process ineffective (p. 86).

The participation of faculty in the process is a sound management practice. The two teachers who had been union presidents presented strong evidence from their own experiences about the importance of the shared ownership that evolved in their community college. This faculty input does much to foster the trust that is necessary to ensure the success and acceptance of the evaluation system once it is implemented.

SUGGESTED EXERCISES

1. Bring together some teachers and some administrators to discuss what is necessary to include in an evaluation form. Define what quality teaching is and use those items to set standards in the instrument.

2. What questions might be used to develop an open-ended evaluation form? What *words* in the instrument questions might cause the evaluator to carefully observe behavior of both the instructor and students during a classroom observation?

Accountable Teacher Evaluation

CHAPTER 3

TOWARD AN *ACCOUNTABLE* EVALUATION SYSTEM

Accountability.... t*he responsibility for implementing a process or* procedure, for justifying decisions made, and for results or outcomes produced.

Responsibility: *that which a person is expected and obligated to do* and for which he/she is accountable.
Teacher Evaluation Kit Glossary (2003), pp. 1 and 27

It has been my experience that the best source for assisting faculty in their developmental needs, as well as a means of making both formative and summative evaluation decisions, are highly qualified instructional administrators and division chairpersons.

Community colleges usually make a choice of an administrative, peer, or student evaluation system or a combination of the three. The *choice* of a faculty evaluation method and evaluation system of policies and procedures is crucial if a school wishes to have *quality control* and keep teachers accountable for the instruction within the school system. In the K-12 system the administrators are usually assigned the responsibility of evaluating teachers.

Stufflebeam (2003) outlined what he calls the conceptualization of evaluation, which includes a shared and strong understanding between the clients (teachers) and stake-holders (administration, governing board, students, parents, and taxpayers). The elements of his conceptualization of evaluation includes the following:

1. **Definition**: How is evaluation defined?
2. **Purpose**: What purpose(s) will be served?
3. **Values**: What values will undergird this evaluation?
4. **Questions**: What questions will be addressed?
5. **Information**: What information is required?
6. **Audiences**: What persons and groups will be served?
7. **Agents**: Who will do the evaluation?
8. **Process**: How will the evaluation be conducted?
9. **Standards**: By what standards will the evaluation be judged, i.e., utility, propriety, feasibility, and/or accuracy? (p. 1)

These nine components of evaluation provide for a *process* of formulating an evaluation system that will be effective and acceptable to schools and colleges. Stufflebeam offered a cautionary statement that these components should be adapted to fit the individual needs of each system using them.

Contrary to popular myth, research has supported the fact that teachers do welcome supervisory evaluation as long as they perceive it to be fair. Mary Futrell, past executive director of the National Education Association (NEA) found administrative or supervisory evaluation processes acceptable when they are carried out professionally:

> Most teachers agree that they should be evaluated, but teachers do not want evaluations done by someone standing outside the classroom door or by someone who turns on the public address system and listens in a classroom, or by someone who steps into a classroom to deliver a message and later calls that stopover an evaluation. Teachers want to know what evaluation instrument will be used. They want the evaluators to come into the classroom for at least a full class period of time and

within five days, they want feedback—in writing and orally—and a chance to respond (1986, p.58).

Anastasi and Urbina (1997) referred to the concern of "error of central tendency" which occurs because evaluators tend to avoid the extremes in their ratings. They also pointed out that there is a "halo effect" that occurs when raters are influenced one way or another "generally" about a person who they are evaluating. In this case the evaluators do not make good differentiations between a teacher's strengths or weaknesses.

Marshall (2003) referred to the practice of principals rarely getting into classrooms as Hyperactive Superficial Principal Syndrome (HSPS), which includes:

1. The principal being trapped in the office dealing with one crisis after another;
2. Each day is so chopped up by interruptions that it's very hard to focus on deeper stuff;
3. Teachers are rarely observed in a thoughtful way and almost never get feedback;
4. Evaluation visits happen only when they are absolutely required, which is usually once every year or two;
5. Evaluators often see "glamorized" lessons that aren't very representative of daily practice;
6. Evaluations are sometimes based on rumor, gossip, and innuendo and are not very deep;
7. There are few authentic teaching/learning conversations between teachers and principals;
8. Teachers are mostly on their own and get used to working in isolation; and
9. Starved for feedback, many teachers stagnate, and mediocrity flourishes (p. 702).

Marshall also suggested that the effective "leader" must push against these type of forces and get into the classroom, observe, and offer every instructor verbal feedback. His method concentrates on visiting classrooms for five-minute intervals. This author and many others disagree on the length of time in classes that he promotes. Much of what is taking place in organization, interaction, testing, and other activities planned for a full class period have to be overlooked and missed in his five-minute interval evaluation system.

EVALUATION SYSTEMS CURRENTLY IN USE

Supervisory evaluation continues to be the primary system used in elementary, middle and secondary schools. This is the system, combined with student or peer input, which was reported by faculty leaders and administrators to be used by the largest number of community and technical colleges responding to the national survey by Andrews, et al. (2002a). Many colleges reported using student evaluations in combination with supervisory ones. A small number selected student evaluation as their sole method of evaluation. The two types selected most often in this national study were:

1. Student and administrative
   input combined   208

2. Student, peer, and administrative
   inputs combined   195

The results showed that most community colleges used multiple sources of input in their evaluation systems. This information came from 655 respondents out of 930 colleges contacted (a 71 percent return). How much weight was given to each of the two or three sources of input utilized was not documented (p. 96).

A previous study with 250 respondents was conducted of community and technical colleges in the 19-state North Central Association (now The Higher Learning Authority) region of the United States. In this first study Andrews and Licata (1988-89) reported the following types of evaluation systems:

1. Administrative evaluation   33%
2. Combined student and administrative   33%
3. Combined student, peer and administrative   16%
4. Student evaluation only   7%
5. Not reported   11%

The university system, by contrast, has largely focused upon student evaluations and to some degree upon peer evaluation (faculty evaluating one another). The university evaluation emphasizes research and publication output rather than classroom teaching.

In his analysis of the use of student ratings Erwin (1994) confirmed their limited usefulness in decisions for tenure, promotion, and salary decisions. He did, however, suggest their usefulness in providing valuable information on the positive or negative impressions students have of the teacher's instructional approach (p. 51). This was supported by Ghorpade and Lackritz (1991) who found that teachers gained the most from student ratings in terms of what would help in redesigning their methods of teaching in their courses.

Cashin (1995) suggests the term "student ratings" is more appropriate as an identifier of what students are doing in completing student survey forms than "student evaluations" which is the term normally used in the field and also used as an ERIC descriptor in the research. Cashin has been consistent in his position that student ratings need to be combined with other data about teaching in order to make good judgments about the quality of college teaching (pp. 1-6).

Another evaluation option, *self-evaluation*, is used by a

---

number of colleges. In his study of evaluation systems Centra (1977) found self-evaluations were given little value by division chairpersons in their tenure and promotion decisions. He found in his study of 343 teaching faculty from five different colleges that self-evaluation outcomes when compared with student ratings had a median correlation of only .21 (1973). Teachers doing self-evaluations were even more generous in rating themselves than were students. Centra found 30 percent of the teachers in the study ranking themselves higher than the ratings given by their students. In summary, Centra determined that the faculty, who felt the ratings would be used in determining promotions, would rate themselves even higher. Self-evaluations were considered useful for an individual who is serious about improving his or her instruction, but they have been found of "limited use for administrative purposes" (p.71).

The present chapter focuses on the research behind student and peer evaluation systems, with respect to their impact on the quality of instruction in the community and technical colleges. These systems are seldom used in the K-12 schools. Further, these types of evaluations have limited use in the legal system. Each of these systems is promoted as having the goal of helping to improve instruction. In some colleges they are used in place of an administrative or supervisory evaluation system. Yet there is much concern as to whether they provide the type of input necessary to help boards and administrators improve instruction.

STUDENT EVALUATION

Research continues to focus most of the studies of teacher evaluation on student evaluation. The reason is that most of the research is conducted on senior college and university campuses. The university researchers, when focusing upon the type of evaluation present on their campuses, end up with

---

student and some peer and self-evaluation systems in place and available for their research.

Such evaluation usually yields numerical outcomes that make it appear much less subjective than written narrative reviews by supervisors. This numerical data makes it easy for researchers to make comparisons, to rank and to analyze reports for administrative personnel to review. According to Cashin (1988), there were over 1,300 published articles and books on student evaluation. This number is now much larger with the increase in the number of studies over the past fifteen years.

Stodolsky (1990) expressed a concern that too much emphasis has been placed on trying to ensure reliability and objectivity, at the expense of attention to validity and definitions of teaching. She held that "selection of a system should be determined by the match between the school district's view of teaching and the adequacy with which the instrument reflects that view" (p. 181).

SOME RESEARCH ON STUDENT EVALUATION

Cashin (1983) listed several defects in the utilization of student evaluation ratings. He did not see students as qualified to be curriculum experts and felt they were not able to judge the knowledge level that a teacher has in his or her field of study. He also found students tend to be quite inflexible in their ability to accommodate a variety of teaching methods and approaches (pp. 60-61).

Centra (1979) had conducted the most comprehensive reporting on student ratings at that time. He concluded: (1) students seem to rate elective courses or courses in the major area more highly than courses taken to fulfill a college requirement; (2) students are generally lenient in their judgment; therefore students' ratings may be misleading regarding the effectiveness of some teachers (pp. 152-153). The following limitations of student ratings were cited by Centra:

1. Because most student rating instruments elicit numerical responses that can be scored and quantified, it is easy to assign them a precision they do not possess.
2. Student ratings may be given too much weight in relation to other criteria.
3. It may be possible for teachers to influence ratings but not student learning. the teacher who is lenient in assigning grades and out-of-class work is not improving learning, yet may be better rated by some students.
4. The manipulations of ratings by teachers must be considered when ratings are used for personnel decisions.
5. Student ratings have misled some institutions into thinking that nothing more is needed to upgrade instruction. While some teachers can use the rating information to make needed changes, others need faculty and instructional development services.
6. Because of the positive bias in student ratings, teachers who need to improve may not realize their weaknesses (pp. 44-45).

Two important studies in the late 1990's raised more doubt about the validity of student evaluations (Wilson, 1998). Both studies concluded that teachers had a tendency to "teach to the evaluations." This article quoted information from studies originally presented by Williams (1997) in *Change* magazine and by Greenwald (1997) in *American Psychologist*. It was determined that those instructors who want to receive higher ratings started "dummying down" their teaching materials in addition to raising their grade levels and working to keep the students entertained.

Anthony G. Greenwald, a psychology professor from the University of Washington worked with Gerald Gilmore, director of the university's Office of Educational Assessment to develop the information for the *American Psychologist* article. Their approach was to study ratings from hundreds of courses. One of their findings was that those instructors who became easy graders were receiving higher evaluations from students than those professors who were tougher in their grading practices.

Both of these studies found "enthusiasm" by teachers also improved student ratings. This was true even where there was no improvement in the students' learning. These studies raise many questions relative to the validity of hundreds of research studies on student evaluation conducted over the years.

Wilson (1998) quoted Paul A. Trout, an associate professor from Montana State University, as saying, "most professors have learned how to get good ratings from students. Some professors stick to their guns and get punished. But an awful lot of people have figured out how to get their numbers high enough so that the evaluations are not a liability to them. People are changing their teaching, the rigor of their courses, to insure they get tenure" (p. A14).

Spencer and Flyr (1992) sent a random sample questionnaire on the effects of evaluation to 250 tenured faculty from five colleges and universities. They received a 58 percent response. In regards to student evaluation as a stimulus to making changes in teaching, classroom management or basic philosophy of education, 77 percent responded that they *did not* use student feedback as one of their impetuses for change. They were, however, used by some in specific areas such as in altering handout materials, changing the number of assignments, and changing the pacing of lectures.

Spencer and Flyr had only two-percent of the tenured faculty reporting they had used administrator evaluation feedback as a stimulus for making significant changes in their teaching. Seventy-three percent indicated that the formal evaluation process never did, or only occasionally, lead to significant instructional improvement. Sixty-four percent reported that follow-up support from administrators was never provided to help make changes.

This is very much in line with the findings of Andrews, et al. (2002a) that faculty development is greatly neglected as an outcome of evaluation procedures. It is also an indictment of the many administrators who go through the motions of evaluation and then neglect making significant suggestions and do not follow up on faculty development needs.

Personnel Decisions Using Student Evaluations

Even with the limitations that have been presented many colleges and universities use student evaluation for both tenure and promotion purposes. Student evaluation has also moved into the community and technical college systems and, in some instances, into secondary school faculty rating systems. Centra's research (1979) found two-year colleges using student ratings almost as much as the four-year colleges (p. 9).

Some 70 percent of American colleges and universities Selden (1984) surveyed were collecting student ratings of their faculty members (p. 48). Ory and Parker (1989) surveyed 40 large research universities and found all 40 of them using student ratings as their evaluation process. What once started as a process to help students select courses more effectively has now become "a powerful source of information that is consistently used by administrators to make personnel and program decisions" (p. 383).

Ory (1990) found research studies on student response information on teachers as far back as the 1920s. This early information was used in the selection of courses and instructors. In the 1960s, students were demanding greater participation in all areas of college life. Some of the extremely low ratings by students were all of a sudden being considered in decisions of promotion, teaching assignments, and tenure. In the 1970s, this type of data became part of the accountability tools used by administrators (pp. 63-64).

Legal actions: Using student evaluations for support

In a review of the literature available on faculty termination cases over the past 38 years in this country, I have been *unable to uncover any court cases* where student evaluation led to termination of any faculty member who was performing poorly. On the other hand, faculty evaluation conducted by supervisory administrators has become a subject of much research and there are now many legal cases that have supported well-documented administrative evaluation decisions in faculty dismissals.

A major problem with the *anonymously* written student evaluations is that they do not stand up in court. Anonymous evaluations means that there is no one who can be called to testify in a governing board hearing, in an arbitration hearings or in subsequent court case. In addition, students are not trained to evaluate teacher knowledge or techniques. They also do not have any responsibilities in follow-up evaluations to check up on areas that need remediation. In most instances a student may never again enroll with and have the same instructor.

When a student complained about a course not matching up with the course description in the college catalog, in *Ianello v. The University of Bridgeport* (1979), it was found that the student's complaint had provided minimal substance. The case was subsequently lost when the court determined the student lacked sufficient evidence to support her claims against this particular instructor. This case helped prove that it is rare, indeed, that a student could win such a case. Students usually do not have the resources available and are not able to collect relevant evidence that would hold up in arbitration or court cases.

STUDENT EVALUATIONS AND ACCOUNTABILITY

Andrews' (1986b, p. 6) chart, presented as Table 2 below, is a capsule summary of the differences that exist in accountability between administrative and student evaluation systems.

The differences between administrative and student responses are significant in a school's or college's efforts to improve the instruction of each teacher in their institution. The administrators are responsible for evaluating the total job of the teacher. Students will write responses relating to one class. The administrators conduct follow-up visitations to the teacher's classes. If there are deficiencies in the teaching review by the administrator they may lead to a number of follow-up classroom visits.

Administrators, unlike students, have no expectation of a grade following an evaluation. Students have no responsibility or expectation of having a follow-up visit with a principal, superintendent or college administrative official. Administrative evaluators have such responsibilities and accountability to a governing board. The major differences are in terms of accountability for the improvement of instruction and in provision of a legally defensible system of evaluation.

STUDENT REVIEWS: NEGATIVE RESPONSES

Holcutt (1987-88) raised some strongly worded questions concerning the movement he termed "student poll of teaching" (SPOT). Universities were asked to look at what

TABLE 2: Administrative vs. Student Evaluation in Accountability and Professionalism

Professional Administrative Evaluation	Student Evaluation
1. Evaluation of the total job of the faculty member (in-class and other professional responsibilities). Follow-up to other classes may be made.	1. Evaluation of one class only.
2. Evaluators are grounded in teaching techniques, teaching experience, educational psychology, learning theory, observational techniques, etc.	2. Students are evaluating with no experience in teaching, educational psychology, or training in classroom observational techniques.
3. Evaluators enter the classroom to observe good teaching and learning techniques and and environment.	3. Students are in the classroom for subject matter and learning needs. The need to evaluate is thrust upon them with no prior preparation.
4. Evaluators will be following up classroom evaluation with both written and oral evaluation reports to the faculty members.	4. Student evaluation is a one-time event. There is no follow-up by students following their written report or in sebsequent semesters or terms.
5. Evaluators expect no rewards from the instructors.	5. Students often evaluate prior to their expectation of a grade for the course.
6. Evaluators have job responsibilities to the board of trustees to guarantee that quality instruction is taking place in the classroom. Accountability is made directly to the instructor and to boards.	6. Students have no responsibilities to anyone relative to their evaluations. They will remain anonymous and not be subject to account for the remarks.

they were accomplishing with the SPOT movement: "Was the SPOT's rise merited?" "Has it proved its worth?" "Has it provided the universities with a good measure of teaching?" "Has it helped to improve teaching?"

Hocutt defined a good teacher as "simply someone from whom students learn." He added a simple clarification to his definition with the example of, "The best teacher of algebra is the one whose pupils learn the most algebra" (pp. 58-59).

In looking at how SPOT can be misused, Hocutt continued his criticisms to include the following: (1) SPOT gives the appearance of providing objective, factual information. Worked out to two decimal places, it looks very scientific, and many people think it is. (2) SPOT does not yield an objective measure of the teacher's performance but a subjective index of the student's satisfaction. (3) No matter which study you pick (regarding SPOT), there is another on the same issue to contradict it. (4) A professor who does his own grading is in a position to use grades to influence his ratings on SPOT. Yet, once again, most universities let instructors do their own grading, so it becomes impossible to separate the part of an instructor's rating that is due to his teaching effectiveness from the part that is due to his grading policies. (5) There *seems* to be a weak relation between learning and ratings on the SPOT, but much of the research has been so flawed that nobody can legitimately claim to know what this relation is or reliably estimate its strength (pp. 58-59).

Hocutt became even more critical when reviewing his research on grading practices. He saw cynical professors thinking that that they could buy themselves higher ratings with the grades they gave. Part of it has to do with encouraging professors to adopt grading practices that he says have no relationship to learning. He believes that it is "no accident" that the greatest "grade inflation" in educational history has paralleled the increasing use of SPOT. He pointed out that the average grade today is a "B", as opposed to a "C" during the previous two or three decades. Holcutt further saw SPOT detrimental to teaching by encouraging professors to give up the teaching of complex concepts and replacing them with simple facts and figures.

STUDENT LEADERS: SOME STRONG WORDS

A survey by Andrews and Erwin in 1993 of student leaders in Illinois community colleges was conducted for a state-wide workshop (Andrews, 1995). The students identified *teacher quality and evaluation* as their *number one concern* that year. They wished to explore what could be done to improve teaching through faculty evaluation in their colleges.

The survey was conducted with the student advisory committee members of the Illinois Community College Board prior to their meeting. It was surprising to see how *highly critical* of the teaching these students were in a significant number of their classes. The questionnaire asked to report how many *high quality* and *poor quality* teachers they felt they had had during their college time (the first two years of college).

The following is a *sampling* of individual responses to this first question. Some gave specific numbers and others gave a percentage of high quality or low quality teachers:

1. How many *high quality* faculty have you had in college?
   12, 6, 7, 6, 3, 3, 6, 5, 6 / 70%, 90%, 25%
2. How many *poor quality* faculty have you had in college?
   3-4, 4, 5, 10, 1, 1, 1, 7, 1 / 33%, 10%, 30%

The second question asked the student leaders what they felt were the *best teaching methods* and practices they had

---

observed as students. The following responses are not in any specific order:

1. Hands on experimentation;
2. Fun/sense of humor;
3. Stuck to the syllabus;
4. Explained exactly what is expected;
5. Giving encouragement;
6. Gathering outside sources;
7. Interaction between students;
8. Treats everyone on the same level;
9. Asks questions and has interaction with students;
10. Open mindedness of teacher.

The next question asked the student leaders to identify what they considered to be the *worst teaching methods* they had experienced. The following methods were reported:

1. No organization;
2. No complete knowledge of the material;
3. Difficult to contact;
4. Lack of sense of humor in classroom;
5. No enthusiasm for the material;
6. Does not stay current with new information;
7. Hides behind tenure;
8. Lectures strictly from the textbook;
9. Not present during office hours;
10. Constantly late for class;
11. Leaving a matter that is complex at a level that cannot be understood;
12. When an instructor does not leave his/her personal life out of the classroom;
13. Tests that have information not discussed in class or in the book;
14. Obscenities;
15. Repeating the same material.

Another question asked was, "What do you believe your college should do to improve the poor teaching practice you have experienced?" It brought the following reactions:

* I feel the selection process of an instructor should be taken more seriously than in the past.
* Reevaluate tenure.
* Actually pay attention to teacher evaluations.
* Require teachers to attend refresher sessions.
* Confront teacher with problems.

The student leaders were asked to express the personal feelings they had when they learned they had a poor teacher for a class. The following are direct quotes from the students:

* I feel outraged and upset since I am paying for the class and the college fails to provide a qualified instructor for the class.
* I feel that I am cheated out of an opportunity along with my college education.
* Worse than that (losing the money) is when you know that another class you have to take is taught only by a poor instructor.
* I am disgusted that I wasted my time and money on this class.
* *Mad as hell!* Not only is it a waste of my time, money, and efforts, it is a rip-off of students who do not have the money to lose.

The next question, "Have you discussed your concern with an administrator?" revealed more frustration:

* They cordially take notes and say that they will speak to that instructor and then nothing happens.
* As a result that particular instructor was dismissed from the college and the renewal of the contract was denied.
* He said he couldn't write a teacher up for the same charge

twice...but I think that is stupid when you consider a class of 25 dissatisfied students (pp. 25-27).

This forum presented an unusual opportunity to ask community college student leaders, ranging in age 18 to 50, to react to instruction they had been receiving. Most research had been limited to students' responses on a single course. Assuring confidentiality of the responses helped make the exercise meaningful and open.

Bonato (1987) presented some legal considerations to be addressed about the time that student evaluations are obtained: "The weight afforded student ratings is likely to be greatly diminished if, for example, they were solicited at a time the students knew there was administrative dissatisfaction with the teacher's performance and a desire to fire the teacher" (p. 25).

PEER REVIEW

Research on peer review has provided results that are very similar to that found on student assessment of teaching. As mentioned above, Centra (1979) found that "colleague evaluation" was even more generous than student evaluation. He summarized that 94 percent of peers judged the teaching of those evaluated as "excellent" or "good." He also found peer evaluations to be statistically unreliable. The highest correlation he could find in the research among ratings by different colleagues was .26 for each item. He concluded "this low reliability casts doubts on the value of colleague ratings as they were collected in this study" (p. 75).

Most researchers agree that division or department chairpersons are in a position to be competent peer evaluators of faculty under their supervision. Chairpersons are regarded as peers in most university settings, and it varies as to whether they are considered peers or supervisors in community col-

TABLE 3: Comparison Summary of Types of Evaluation Systems

Type of Evaluation	Outcome Orientation	Accountability Role	Quality Factors
ADMINISTRATIVE EVALUATION	For positive reinforcement	Professional responsibility of administrators	Professionalism Experience
	For identifying improvement needs For developing remediation processes	Required for all faculty and academic support personne	Knowledge of teaching/ learning process
STUDENT ASSESSMENT OF INSTRUCTION	For assessment of major strengths and personal development needs	Anonymous— no accountability Optional for most tenured faculty	Amateur status Lack of experience in professional assessment
	For student input into weaknesses from a learner's viewpoint only	Required for non-tenured faculty	"Halo" effect
"PEER" ROLES IN EVALUATION	For assessment and improvement suggestions in content, organization and depth	Non-job responsibility of peers Optional, or as suggested by administration	Tendency to resist providing negative evaluation of peers

leges, elementary, middle, and secondary school settings. The legal distinction between whether a division or department chairperson is an administrator or a peer is that to be an administrator the supervisory responsibilities must be at least 51 percent of the chairperson's work.

The above discussion may leave the reader in a quandary as to which method or methods of evaluation to select when setting up an evaluation system. A comparison chart (Table 3) has been prepared to show how administrative, student and peer evaluation differ in relation to outcomes, accountability and quality factors.

Table 3 shows that accountability is lacking in both student and peer evaluation. Evaluation is considered as one of the most important components within job descriptions for elementary, middle or secondary principals, assistant principals, or college deans or division chairpersons. The administrators are by training and experience professional evaluators versed in curriculum, teaching methodologies and techniques of instruction.

SUMMARY

The focus of the chapter has been on the various systems of evaluating teachers. Research presented shows student assessment of faculty is able to provide some useful feedback materials for teachers. There is, however, little to no evidence that such evaluation leads to improved teaching. Student evaluation does not allow for face-to-face meetings between students and teachers to discuss findings and recommendations.

The literature summarized by Centra and others points to a generous positive skewing in the outcomes of student ratings. Students are not inclined to cause faculty problems, prevent tenure from occurring, or influence pay increases to be withheld for poor performances.

Peer evaluation has been found to have low reliability as have student ratings. Centra's research found peer evaluations more generous than student ratings. Peers seldom actually visit a faculty colleague's classroom or conduct professional reviews of what takes place there. Peer evaluation in university settings is primarily comprised of a review of research and publishing success. Community colleges and secondary schools using peer evaluation are more likely to identify a "peer" as a person in a role of chairperson or a department or division chairperson.

Research presented supports the view that student ratings should not be used by educational institutions as the sole type of teacher evaluation. There are some areas that students can legitimately help assess. Those areas were presented by Selden (1989) as (1) the teacher's ability to communicate at their [students] level, (2) professional and ethical behavior of the instructor.

Student ratings have not been found to lead to the remediation or dismissal of incompetent faculty members. The student evaluation systems lack credibility in arbitration hearings. They are of little to no value in court hearings as they are almost always carried out as anonymous reviews. There are no students able to appear, speak, or face cross-examination in such hearings.

Governing boards, administrators, and faculty need to be aware of these limitations when establishing effective evaluation systems. It is not yet clear whether, and to what extent, student or peer evaluation systems can be used in improving instruction. The uncertain efficacy and reliability of these systems have made them of little value in the institutions' need to make summative evaluation decisions.

SUGGESTED EXERCISES

1. Outline components of an evaluation system for a secondary school or community college. What weight might be properly given to supervisory, student and peer input?

2. What concerns or fears might students have when they are asked to fill out a faculty-rating sheet? Are students you know honest in rating teachers? Ask some students about their feelings about filling out such ratings at the end of a semester.

3. Identify some of the feelings and considerations a teacher may have when rating a "peer" or colleague in the same department.

CHAPTER 4

SETTING QUALITY TEACHING STANDARDS FOR EVERY TEACHER

> Effective teaching methods hardly seem a mystery… the mystery seems to be why such principles are not already in place.
>
> Walberg, (2002), p. 72

The following definitions are taken from the *Teacher Evaluation Kit Glossary* (2003) to provide a basis for "standard setting for teachers" as presented in this chapter:

Standard Setting: The determination of the teaching performance level considered acceptable in terms of the purpose of the evaluation.

Standard: The level of performance on the criterion being assessed that is considered satisfactory in terms of the purpose of the evaluation. The three major categories of standards are: (1) **Developmental standards** specify improvement levels to be attained and may be used for professional development and self-assessment. (2) **Minimum standards** designate the level below which performance is not acceptable and are used for such purposes as licensure and job assignments (pp.29-30).

Defining and knowing *quality teaching* is the first step in the appraisal process of teachers. This is necessary if administrative evaluation is going to be effective. In the

---

research literature there is no one source that has been found that captures all of the effective characteristics of teachers.

Every schoolchild in America needs and deserves teachers of the highest quality this nation is capable of producing (American Council on Education, 1999). The *need* for quality standards and the enforcement of them, which is part of the *No Child Left Behind* legislation, was identified in a U. S. Department of Education report several years earlier (U. S. News and World Report, 1996a). It was reported that almost one third of the mathematics teachers in high schools across the country did not have a college major or minor in the subject of mathematics.

Rice (2003) reported that the National Center for Education Statistics 2000 had recorded close to 2.9 million teachers educating over 46 million public elementary and secondary school students (p. 2). Keller (2003) summarized that thirty-three states had reported, that on the average, there were highly qualified teachers in 4 out of 5 classrooms. Twenty-eight states indicated these figures were the same in their high-poverty schools. Eight of the states did, however, show at least a 5 percent difference in numbers of quality teachers between their statewide averages and their high-poverty schools (p. 1).

A wide variance between states came out of this report. Alaska announced only 16 percent of their teachers were in the "highly qualified" group, meaning a baccalaureate degree major or minor in the courses that the teachers were teaching. Wisconsin, at the other extreme, reported 98.6 percent of their teachers fit the "highly qualified" guidelines. Kansas reported 80 percent of their teachers as "highly qualified" in all schools including the high-poverty schools. California did not fare well, showing only 48 percent of the classes being taught throughout California had "highly qualified" teachers as identified by the *No Child Left Behind* legislation (pp. 2-3).

Education Week (2003, Jan. 9) summarized some of the

problems that exist between low poverty and high poverty schools relative to the recruitment and placement of "high quality" teachers. The material came from *Quality Counts (2003)* which focuses on teacher problems, the teacher gap, and an analysis of its causes and possible solutions. It provided a summary of the data as reported by Richard M. Ingersoll, an associate professor of education and sociology at the University of Pennsylvania:

- Almost one quarter (22 percent) of the secondary school students take at least one class with a teacher who did not even minor in the subject he or she teaches. In the high poverty schools this jumps to 32 percent;
- The high poverty school secondary students were found twice as likely as those in the low-poverty schools (26 percent vs. 13 percent) to have a teacher who is not certified in the subject taught;
- Approximately 70 percent of secondary students in the *low-poverty* schools have teachers who have both majored in and become licensed in their subjects. Only about half of secondary students in *high-poverty* schools can say the same.
- Students in high-poverty, high-minority schools also are more likely to be taught by inexperienced teachers (pp. 1-2).

This report states that twenty-two states require the schools to post report card information relative to teacher characteristics. Included in the report is the percentage of the teachers who teach in each school district with emergency credentials. Only five states, California, Indiana, Kentucky, Louisiana, and Tennessee, provide information about credentials of every public school teacher in their states' systems to parents via a web site. "Signing bonuses" to attract new teachers were provided in five states, but only California and Massachusetts geared their bonuses to those teachers willing to work in high-need schools.

Gewertz (2003) found urban schools improving in the hiring of "highly qualified" new teachers during the 2003 school year. Los Angeles reported that only 6 percent of their new hires lacked the credentials for being "highly qualified." This was a marked improvement over previous years. The "less than qualified" number hired was 59 percent in 2001. Philadelphia reported hiring 6 percent "less than qualified" in 2003 compared to 10 to 12 percent the previous year. New York reported all 9000 of their new hires in 2003 were certified by the state. Gewertz pointed out that state-certification may or may not be equal to the "highly qualified standard" in federal legislation (p. 1).

The research data reported by Ascher and Fruchter (2001) found that while poverty and minority status has some negative influences on student achievement there were other strong factors involved. Those schools having larger percentages of less than fully qualified teachers, teachers not permanently assigned, or teachers lacking in teaching experience had lower academic performances recorded for their students.

Quality Counts '99 was a thorough survey of all 50 states on their policies relating to school accountability. The study found only two states had attempted to tie evaluation of individual teachers to how well students perform (p.2). This is quickly changing in the years since 1999. The study further found that "most rewards and sanctions are focused primarily on schools and their performance, rather than on individual educators" (p. 2). In Education Week (2003, Jan. 9) it was reported in the *Quality Counts, 2003* research that little is being done by school districts or states to overcome the problem of less qualified teachers being assigned to students in the high-poverty and high-minority schools (p. 1).

CHATTANOOGA REVERSES THE PATTERN!

Benton (2003) described how Chattanooga, Tennessee, has worked to upgrade its inner-city schools teaching staff. At one time the district had much difficulty recruiting and retaining highly qualified teachers in the inner-city schools. Recognizing that the teacher's quality is the most important element in its classrooms, the new mayor, elected in 2001, and school officials set out to change this past history. This decision followed receiving statewide data identifying that nine of the twenty lowest performing Tennessee elementary schools were in the Chattanooga system. All were put "on notice" by the state education officials.

The school district eventually moved 100 of the weaker teachers in the Benwood elementary schools into suburban schools. Identifying better teachers was, in part, accomplished by using the state data on which teachers had been making the largest gains with their students. The incentives used were $5,000 bonuses for those teachers in the Benwood School whose students scored high in the state testing program. Loans of $10,000 toward purchase of a home were made by a local foundation. Teachers staying in the Benwood schools for five years were to have the loan forgiven. The third incentive was $2,000 to each teacher in any of these schools that showed overall student improvement. Applications for positions in the Benwood schools increased significantly over previous years.

What has been the outcome to date? Student performance on the Tennessee state tests in 2003 showed a marked improvement. The passing rate *increase* for the Benwood schools was three times the passing rate increase for students in the suburban schools in the district. Every school improved in the number of third graders reading above grade level with most of these students scoring more than ten percent above grade level.

THE CERTIFICATION ISSUE

Tirozzi (2002), Executive Director of the National Association of Secondary School Principals, highlighted the significant problem facing schools relative to teachers not being fully certified. Nearly 20 percent or 58,000 of the California teachers lacked full certification. Keeping certified teachers is a vast problem that Tirozzi related to deteriorating school facilities, depressed salaries, safety issues, overcrowded classrooms, budgetary limits, and other frustrations facing schools. These problems are magnified in the high-poverty schools (p. 1).

Tirozzi suggested calling the federal and state legislators to task. He saw their lack of commitment in areas of increasing compensation for teachers, giving more prestige to teachers as professionals, and increasing incentives for those willing to teach in high-poverty schools warranted a "call to action" (p. 2).

Hart and Teeter (2002) discussed in detail the political debate revolving around whether teachers need to be "highly qualified" only in subject matter or also in their "teaching skills." They referred to "the bottom line"—and the area of disagreement—is that, "while teachers' strong content knowledge and verbal skills have demonstrated links to higher student achievement, they may be necessary but not sufficient conditions for high-quality teaching and learning" (p. 688). They went on to say, "while content knowledge is unarguably essential, knowing how to teach content—whether learned in pre-service training or on the job—makes a measurable impact on student achievement" (p. 690).

Bradley (1999) found that legislators, governor candidates and the general public took notice when nearly 60 percent of the teachers in training at the universities in Massachusetts flunked the first-ever licensure exam. Bradley quoted columnist Robert J. Samuelson, who had responded to these results by suggesting, "some of the nation's teachers belong elsewhere" (p. 1). Bradley also found some states are now holding their principals and teachers accountable for student success results. Some principals have lost their jobs due to low student success. There are now laws in ten states that allow for principals to be removed. The same holds true with similar laws for teachers.

Bradley mentioned that the concern for quality in teaching would become even more acute as some 2 million new teachers will need to be prepared in the next decade. The shortage of qualified principals at the beginning of the twenty-first century will continue to be a concern in the years ahead, especially if they are held accountable for student success (p. 4).

Secretary of Education Rod Paige (U. S. Department of Education, My.ED.gov, 2003b) called it a "watershed moment" when he announced on June 10, 2003, that all 50 states, Puerto Rico, and the District of Columbia had approved accountability plans under the *No Child Left Behind* legislation (p. 1). He announced that the funding of programs for improving the quality of teachers had increased 45.8 percent for a total of $1.02 billion.

The funding available under this act, for tutoring and other supplementary services for students who come from low income families, will assist students in every state in those schools identified in need of improvement. It is this author's concern that these *tutoring funds* do not replace the need to improve the individual classroom teachers who are not producing acceptable student results. The school administrators' responsibility for improving or removing these teachers must remain paramount under this act.

New York will hold school districts accountable for

evaluating their teachers through their report cards. Beginning in 2001 these report cards had to show how many teachers were dismissed and how many were rated as "unsatisfactory" (Bradley, p. 6). The First Vice President of the New York State United Teachers, which represents 400,000 affiliate teachers to the American Federation of Teachers, stated it is "humiliating to teachers" to be characterized like this (p. 6).

Quality teachers are the number one factor in a child's success at learning. This fact was reinforced in the summary of a comprehensive review of the empirical evidence presented to the *American Council of Education Presidents Task Force on Teacher Education* (American Council on Education, 1999). The main recommendation of this task force to college and university presidents was to move the education of teachers to the center of their professional and institutional agendas (p. 1). The task force found evidence that effective teachers need (1) firm command of their subject matter, (2) receive sound professional preparation, and (3) demonstrate a high overall achievement (p. 2).

Rivers and Sanders (2002) found that regardless of ethnicity, children with similar previous achievement levels tend to respond similarly to an individual teacher (p. 17). It is important, therefore, to define what *quality teaching* or the *desired performance* expected is within the specific setting where the teaching is taking place. The settings may be in an elementary school, middle school, senior high school or a community college.

Hanushek (2002) referred to the good teachers as "those who get large gains in student achievement in their classes; bad teachers are just the opposite" (p. 3). He pointed out that the good teachers near the top of a faculty group can get gains of one and a half grade level equivalents in one year of instruction. On the other hand, the poor teachers will gain only about one half of a year in the same time period (p. 3).

The standards in each school or college should be defined using a combination of excellent faculty and administrators who will be involved in the evaluation process, according to Conley (1988). The job of the evaluator will be to hold the faculty members to the standards that have been jointly developed. Conley suggested the local committee that formulates the teaching standards for a school should use the research available on defining effective instruction and effective schools. The standards committee, while using research, should also utilize the committee's expertise. He concluded: "Performance standards, when they are accepted as valid and fair, provide a valuable tool for adding precision to the process of determining a teacher's level of performance" (p. 82).

Well-defined behavioral expectations will be needed for both the supervisors and the teachers involved with the evaluation process. Such standards will provide a clear frame of reference from which to promote the *desired performance standards* established for all teachers in the system.

Wheeler et al. (1993) defined *effectiveness* as "an attribute of those schools, teachers, programs, and approaches that meet the needs of students and their society" (p. 12). Rivers and Sanders (2002) pointed to the consistency of the findings from the University of Tennessee Value-Added Research and Assessment Center:

> Teachers who are relatively ineffective tend to be ineffective with all student subgroups across the prior achievement spectrum, whereas teachers who are highly effective tend to be very effective with all student subgroups across the same spectrum (p. 17).

CLEAR STANDARDS: INCREASED FACULTY SUPPORT

In a longitudinal study presented by Rosenholtz (1985) highly dissatisfied faculty were identified as those unaware of the criteria used for evaluating them. These faculty members felt they were at a disadvantage not knowing where they might direct their energies in trying to improve their teaching.

Peterson (1995) expressed concern that "administrators may not have been selected for their role because they were themselves the best classroom teachers" (p. 169). This adds to the faculty's caution when attempting to give evaluation practices their trust.

Rosenholtz also found that the teachers having the greatest satisfaction were those most frequently evaluated. He identified the "vital functions" found in active supervision were accomplishing the following:

1. It furnishes teachers professional development.
2. It sends a continuous academic signal to the faculty, administration, and board about the priorities of the school and the importance of everyone's individual contributions toward achieving them.
3. It provides a clear basis for organizational decision-making, such as tenure, promotion, dismissal, and leadership roles.
4. It establishes criteria for knowing when goals have been attained.
5. It informs all who work within the school precisely what constitutes acceptable performance (pp. 368-369).

Rosenholtz's study centered on the importance of a continuing commitment promoting teaching standards with all faculty.

IMPROVING QUALITY BY *FOSTERING GROWTH*

Duke and Stiggins (1986) reported that, if done well, "teacher evaluation can lead to improved performance, personal growth, and professional esteem. If done poorly, it can produce anxiety or ennui and drive talented teachers from the profession" (p. 5). These same authors conducted an in-depth study of 30 teachers who had experienced positive growth. They found that no small part of their success was attributed to effective evaluation. The following are characteristics of effective evaluation identified by these teachers as the "keys to growth" in their careers:

- There is a system-wide commitment to the evaluation process by the school board, administration, and teachers.
- Administrators and teachers are full partners in the design and monitoring of the evaluation process.
- Necessary resources—staff, materials, funds, and training—are available.
- There is a clear sense of the goal or purpose of the evaluation process.
- Teacher evaluation takes into account the individual teacher's competence, personal expectations, openness to suggestions, orientation to change, subject knowledge and experience.
- Regular review of existing procedures, improvement of the teacher evaluation environment, and upgrading of the evaluators' skills occur on an ongoing basis.

- Persons responsible for teacher evaluation have credibility, patience, trustworthiness and good supervisory track records as well as the ability to persuade those being evaluated of the need to change.
- Recommended and required evaluation procedures are carried out to the letter.
- Carefully planned procedures for feedback which is delivered, rich in specific suggestions, for change by the individual teacher, are in place (pp. 5-6).

STUDENT PERFORMANCE AND EVALUATION OUTCOMES

Schwartz (1997) offered the following as basic fundamental beliefs in teacher evaluation.

No. 1: At some level, a relationship must exist between student performance and the instructional competence of classroom teachers. If you agree, then move to the next basic belief.

No. 2: We should be able to improve student achievement by improving or removing teachers whose instructional skills are less than adequate. If that is the case, then the third basic belief logically follows.

No. 3: The performance evaluation or appraisal system should be used as a tool to help improve instruction. If it is not, then we are negatively impacting student achievement (p. 2).

Schwartz went on to ask what percentage of inadequate teachers a school system could tolerate or find acceptable, "Fifteen percent? Ten percent? Five percent?" He said the percentage varies "as long as one of them is not teaching your own child" (p. 2). Allowing these poor instructors to continue to teach is an indictment of the administration and is viewed as an abandonment of both professional, moral, and ethical responsibilities of the administrators.

SETTING HIGH STANDARDS

Roueche (1983) said that a good teacher knows how to get students excited about learning. Successful teachers hold high expectations and motivate students to fulfill them:

> You've got to expect a lot, demand a lot, insist upon a lot, or you are likely never to be very successful, in parenting or in teaching. Those standards have to be clear; and, folks, that's not conservative. That is an absolute essential, time-honored value. If you don't insist upon quality, you will surely achieve mediocrity (p. 31).

The two parts of the equation he defined were as follows: (1) to provide structure, demand the best, and use tasking and (2) nurture and support students as they strive to accomplish the objectives that have been set. He concluded: "the genius in teaching is in our abilities to excite students to want to learn what we have to teach. Expect a lot, demand a lot, and then help them achieve" (p. 34).

Good teachers set high standards for their students and help them to reach or exceed those goals. Good administrators and faculty should, together, set high quality standards for teachers, and use an effective evaluation system to motivate teachers to that level of excellence.

TEACHER EFFECTIVENESS: ELEMENTARY

The development of a "prescription" for successful management of elementary school classrooms was presented by Evertson and Holley (1981). They observed effective teachers on their classroom organization beginning with the first days of a school year and included 16 observations during the year. The classrooms were characterized by (1) high levels of student cooperation; (2) success; (3) task-involvement; and (4) good achievement gains during the school year.

On the basis of these observations, a manual was developed entitled *Organizing and Managing the Elementary School Classroom* (Evertson et al. 1981). It was pilot-tested and then used with 41 teachers, from grades one through six, in 14 schools. The teachers chosen had taught for two or fewer years, or they were in their first year at their present school. A group of 23 of these teachers were given the manual before the school year began and were given an orientation workshop. The remaining teachers received the manual later in the year. The results of this study showed the manual to be of significant help in establishing classes with higher levels of (1) student task-engagement; and (2) appropriate behavior.

The manual prescribed the following:

Prescription 1: Reading the classroom

Be certain your classroom space and materials are ready for the beginning of the school year. *Rationale:* The first days are crucial to the rest of the year. Advance planning can lead to avoidance of problems which result in 'dead time' for students (p. 18).

Prescription 2: Planning rules and procedures

Decide before the year begins what behaviors are acceptable or unacceptable in your classroom. Then think about what procedures students must follow in order to participate in class activities, to learn, and to function effectively in a school environment. Develop a list of these rules and procedures. *Rationale:* Children readily accept the idea of having a uniform set of rules and procedures (p. 31).

Prescription 3: Consequences

Decide ahead of time the consequences of appropriate and inappropriate behavior in your classroom, and communicate these to your students. Then be sure to follow through consistently when a child behaves appropriately or inappropriately. *Rationale:* If the teacher plans ahead of time what rewards and punishments will be used, and when they will be used, then the teacher will have more confidence in his/her ability to control the classroom (pp. 61-62).

Prescription 4: Teaching rules and procedures

Include in your lesson plan the sequence in which rules or procedures will be taught on each day, when and how they will be taught, and when re-learning or practice will occur. Plan to teach those rules and procedures first that are needed first. Teach your rules and procedures systematically (p. 70).

Prescription 5: Beginning of school activities

Develop activities for the *first few days* of school that will involve the children readily and maintain a whole group focus. *Rationale:* During the first few days of school, your children will begin to form work habits, attitudes, and behavior that will shape the rest of the year (p. 76).

Prescription 6: Strategies for potential problems

Plan strategies to deal with the potential problems, which could upset your classroom organization and management. Be especially aware of things, which could interfere with your monitoring or otherwise teach students bad habits. *Rationale:* Unexpected problems are especially likely at the beginning of the year, when you have least time for them (p. 92).

Prescription 7: Monitoring

Monitor student behavior closely. Look for:
a.   students who do not follow procedures or do not finish or even start assignments;

b.   violations of rules or other uncooperative or deviant behavior;

c.   appropriate behavior.

Rationale: Careful monitoring helps detect problems before they become critical (p. 104).

Prescription 8: Stopping inappropriate behavior

Stop inappropriate and disruptive behavior quickly; it won't go away by itself. *Rationale:* This establishes your system of rules and procedures as well as your credibility. Inappropriate behavior thrives when ignored. Monitoring is crucial to stopping inappropriate behavior; you can't stop what you don't see (p. 107).

Prescription 9: Organizing instruction

Organize instruction to provide learning activities at suitable levels for all students in your class. *Rationale:* One of the biggest challenges teachers face is providing instruction at appropriate levels for all their students. One characteristic of effective teachers is their ability to diagnose students' academic needs and adjust instruction accordingly, within practical limits (p. 112).

Prescription 10: Fostering responsibility

Develop procedures that make the children responsible for their work. *Rationale:* Early in the school year, the teacher will be arranging learning activities and giving assignments requiring students to produce something (p. 132).

Knowing and using the above prescriptions was shown to significantly improve instruction in the 23 out of 41 elementary school classrooms where the teachers received the manual *before* the start of the school year. These prescriptions also provide an administrative evaluator some excellent guides for classroom evaluations.

An inner-city elementary model

Mason (1993) presented some facts about an inner-city elementary school, New York's East Harlem Public School 171, which was very successful in getting its 536 African-American and Hispanic students to perform at an outstanding level. The students ranked first in their district in standardized reading scores. Some 77 percent scored above grade level in mathematics, again placing them first in the district. In all, they were ranked in the upper 30 percent of New York City elementary schools. The principal, Lorraine Man Skeen, has identified 10 factors that she feels have contributed to the "chemistry" of excellence in teaching at her school over the past 16 years:

- Top-notch school management;
- Excellent classroom management by teachers;
- School-wide discipline;
- Teachers' high expectations of students;
- Willingness to try new ideas, for example: reading non-fiction books, giving sustained silent reading time, allowing students to take reading books home, and focusing on problem-solving in math;
- Teachers devoted to teaching and children;
- Well prepared and detailed lessons;
- Good student-teacher relationships;
- Support from supervisors;
- Communication with parents through monthly report cards and orientation meetings.

Report cards are only required to be sent out three times during the year. This school, however, has found the monthly report to greatly improve communications with parents (pp. 1-4).

Additional effective methods

Important changes in the 1990's and 2000's included the ability for using school and state data to make decisions, determining *individual needs* of students and tailoring instruction to meet those needs. These have become especially important in meeting the intent of the *No Child Left Behind* legislation. They are also important in working with students in urban schools and in the schools now assisting hundreds of thousands of immigrant children.

One other area of importance as each school attempts to achieve total school improvements in student outcomes is the ability of teachers to work cooperatively on teacher teams. These teams work with both teachers and with administrators who have overall responsibility to deliver the *improvement goals* of the school and to meet demands from both state and national legislation.

TEACHER EFFECTIVENESS: MIDDLE SCHOOL MODELS

Evertson and Emmer (1982) found that for it to be effective, it is crucial to establish good classroom management at the beginning of the year. They further found that investing time in planning and decision making before the school year starts strengthens classroom teaching. In their review of Moskowitz and Hayman's work from 1976 they found the "best practices" of teachers included them having (1) a more successful first day; (2) using that time [first day] to establish control; (3) exhibiting more orienting and climate-setting behavior, and (4) experiencing very little off-task behavior from students. The more effective teachers also monitored pupil behavior before it became disruptive. Evertson and Emmer studied the behaviors of "effective managers" versus "less effective managers" in mathematics and English classes during the first three weeks of the year. They found that, in contrast to the "less effective managers," the more "effective managers":

1. Describe objectives clearly;
2. Use materials effectively to support instruction;
3. Present information clearly;
4. State desired attitudes/behaviors;
5. Have a high degree of pupil success;
6. Experience less disruptive behavior;
7. Stop disruptive behavior quickly;
8. Give rules or procedures to stop disruptive behavior;
9. Display listening skills;
10. Have a task-oriented focus in the classroom (p. 490).

In comparison to elementary teachers these middle school teachers placed less emphasis on teaching the rules and procedures since middle school students have had more school experiences in these areas. Evertson and Emmer summarize that "the teacher's task (at this level) is essentially one of communicating expectations clearly, monitoring subsequent behavior for compliance, and providing corrective feedback, rather than providing extensive instruction and rehearsal of correct procedures. At the middle school level, the procedures and behaviors for maintaining student responsibility for work were more dominant than in elementary school classrooms" (p. 497). Both elementary and middle school studies of faculty have concluded that the level of preparation before school starts and the early patterns of behavior established will set the tone for the school year.

TEACHER EFFECTIVENESS: SECONDARY SCHOOL

Rice (2003) noted that the research on teacher quality characteristics identified frequent differences between elementary and secondary school teachers. The difference in grade levels, subject area and student populations also was found to make a difference. Some of the highlights in Rice's empirical study of research on teacher quality differences between elementary and secondary schools included:

- "Learning by doing" in the early years was deemed as an effective technique.
- Teacher coursework in both the subject area taught and pedagogy contributes to positive education outcomes.
- The importance of content coursework is most pronounced at the high school level.
- Tests that assess the literacy levels or verbal abilities of teachers have been shown to be associated with higher levels of student achievement (pp. 2-3).

Mayer et al. (2000) reported that research of teacher characteristics conducted by the National Center for Education Statistics related school quality affecting student learning was concentrated in the areas of (1) training and talent of the teaching force, (2) what goes on in the classrooms, and (3) the overall culture and atmosphere of the school. Teachers with high academic skills teaching in those subject areas relating to their college degree areas of specialty were found able to teach more effectively for student learning than those teachers with lower academic skills teaching outside of their major and minor areas of training.

Inner-city adolescents were asked to identify *qualities of good teachers*. Corbett and Wilson (2002) reported the following results from these interviews: (1) they push students;

(2) maintain order, (3) are willing to help, (4) explain until everyone understands, (5) vary classroom activities; and (6) try to understand students.

TEACHER EFFECTIVENESS: COMMUNITY COLLEGE

Traditional v. nontraditional (adult) student needs

Keller et al. (1991) surveyed 316 traditional aged (17-19) and 278 nontraditional aged (27-65) college students in a small southeastern university. They completed a questionnaire that identified items that they considered the *most effective* teaching techniques.

The traditional students listed "review before an exam" and "available to students outside of class" as their top two choices. The nontraditional students selected instructor techniques using "practical applications to real problems" and "showing enthusiasm/love for the subject" as their first and second choices. Keller, et al. concluded that instructors, by being aware of the behaviors that seem important to these groups, might do well to adjust their teaching to accommodate the learning needs of each group. The two groups did select a number of items in which they were in agreement.

In eighteen years as a dean of instruction I found a number of community college teachers to be negligent in keeping their course syllabi and reference reading lists up-to-date. The department chairpersons agreed to conduct a review of all syllabi within their divisions every three years. The syllabi were returned if there were outdated or incomplete areas. While this procedure took some time it was invaluable in keeping teachers up-to-date. The more outstanding faculty didn't have this problem of outdated course materials.

Centra (1979) warned about using people who were not particularly effective teachers themselves to conduct the evaluation. He pointed out that a school could not expect improvements to take place when poor evaluators, who do not know what quality classroom instruction looks like, are used (p. 84).

Interactive teaching

Baker et al. (1990) found exemplary teachers to be actively involved in the teacher-learning process:

> We can say without hesitancy that effective teachers are conscious of their critical role in the learning process and their responsibilities and obligations to students. Moreover, we have demonstrated the classroom teacher's cognizance and understanding of student readiness. This factor is crucial to the ability of excellent instructors to perform as situational teachers, altering their teaching style based on student needs (p. 28).

Establishing classroom climate early

Opening day for each community college course is very important for students and instructors. The importance of the *first class meeting* was highlighted by Wolcowitz (1982). It is here that instructors fulfill the obligation of telling students what to expect in the course, regarding content and mechanics. The first class also sets the atmosphere for the entire term. A "student-teacher contract" should be made explicit in the opening session through the written course syllabus and supported further with statements by the instructor. Wolcowitz stated that the good instructors use the first class to accomplish the following:

1. Tell the students as specifically as possible what material will be covered in the course and why.
2. Provide students with a well-constructed syllabus that outlines the major and minor subdivisions in order to serve as a framework for organizing their thoughts about the course.

3. Try to convey enthusiasm about the course material, as well as provide information.
4. Explain the workload (length of the reading list, number and timing of exams and papers, etc.) so students can assess the amount of time involved in the course.
5. Explain how grades will be computed (pp. 11-14).

Wolcowitz saw the first meetings of classes as the chance to "define the atmosphere that the instructor would like to create in the classroom" (pp. 11-14). He also said it is important for teachers to know something about their students as well as their names. A good instructor will find out what prior knowledge and preconceived ideas his or her students bring to the class as well as what they expect from the class. With the advent of internet courses in the 1990's and early 2000's for community college and secondary school students it has become important that written communications are very clear and thoroughly outlined. Instructors must make themselves available to students via e-mail address and chat rooms for classes on the internet. Both students and instructors have to be highly motivated to pursue this avenue of instruction.

Defining "exemplary" community college teachers
Questions were asked of 30 teachers who had been defined as "exemplary" in the City Colleges of Chicago, Illinois. The following responses were used to define those characteristics that made these teachers effective (Guskey and Easton, 1983):

1. All of them were highly organized, planned carefully, had unambiguous objectives and high expectations for their students. Each class had a clear design:
   (a) an introduction at the beginning;
   (b) a summary at the end; and
   (c) a clear sequence of development in between.

2. All of them emphasized the importance of expressing positive regard for their students:

(a) Most used some time during their first class session to become familiar with their students and continued to exchange personal information throughout the semester.

(b) They generally learned their student's names very early in the semester and addressed them by name.

3. They had an emphasis on encouraging student participation:

(a) They consistently asked questions during class to stimulate involvement.

(b) They also monitored student participation at frequent intervals to gain information as to whether the class was going well or if a change was needed.

4. In addition, they strongly emphasized the importance of providing students with regular feedback on their learning and rewarding learning successes:

(a) Feedback was generally provided through written comments on tests or papers.

(b) They frequently asked their students to see them after class to discuss learning problems.

(c) Written comments were also used to praise students' efforts and to make special note of improvements (pp. 3-4).

SUMMARY

This chapter has presented a variety of material to help establish clear standards for quality teaching. It further emphasized the importance of a joint effort between administrators and teachers to establish local quality standards that incorporate findings from research on effective teaching. Clear and explicit standards are crucial to gaining support from teachers for the evaluation process.

Good evaluation systems clearly communicate the standards to which teachers will be held. In addition to quality standards an evaluation system must have: a system-wide commitment to the process; availability of necessary resources; a clear understanding of the goals of evaluation; ample provision for feedback to teachers; scrupulous adherence to evaluation procedures; and well-trained evaluators.

Effective teachers set high standards for their students. A good evaluation system holds teachers to these high standards and motivates them to achieve a high level of performance. Effective elementary teachers prepare their work environment in advance for the beginning of a school year; plan in advance what behaviors are unacceptable and what the consequences will be; teach rules and procedures; monitor student behavior and promptly stop inappropriate behavior; and develop clear, and organized instruction.

It becomes more important at the middle school level to make students responsible for their work. Less emphasis is placed on teaching middle school students procedures that they should already know.

High school teachers need more depth in the subject matter areas. It is important to have subject matter qualifications with majors or minors. The *No Child Left Behind* legislation puts a strong emphasis on the need to be *highly qualified* with these qualifications.

Characteristics of effective college teaching include an emphasis on motivating students; establishing rapport; using a variety of techniques; and keeping materials up to date. The first class meeting was presented as important in establishing a climate for the class and for informing students. College instructors encourage student participation; acquire basic information about their students; give each class a clear structure; interact with students through questions; test students regularly; and give students feedback on their progress.

SUGGESTED EXERCISES

1. In small groups, define ten to twelve teaching qualities that you feel are important in providing for excellence in teaching. Secondly, place them in some form of priority order.

2. The teaching qualities reported in exercise one should now be placed in a single taxonomy of *effective teaching*. Each participant should select and explain why a teaching quality is considered important.

Section II

ESTABLISHING TEACHING AND EVALUATION STANDARDS

Accountable Teacher Evaluation

CHAPTER 5

EFFECTIVE EVALUATORS AND THE EVALUATION PROCESS

Evaluator: A person who assembles data and information collected about a teacher, analyzes them, makes judgments as to whether that teacher's performance level meets the pre-specified standards, prepares a summary report, writes recommendations, and may provide feedback to the teacher, directly or through another person.

Teacher Evaluation Kit Glossary, (2003), p. 12

The elements necessary for a successful administrative faculty evaluation program are as follows: governing board involvement, chief administrator (superintendent or college president) leadership, faculty support, well-trained administrative evaluators, and a well-defined evaluation process.

The administrative evaluators have key roles in the quality control of faculty development. The quality of the institution depends to a large extent upon the effectiveness of the evaluators and how well they carry out their roles in the evaluation process.

Well-prepared administrative individuals are necessary to conduct in-class observations and evaluation of the other aspects of a teacher's work within a legally defensible framework. Courts have been found to support evaluators' efforts when poor teaching practices are properly documented and legally sound procedural guidelines are followed in cases of teacher dismissal.

A number of researchers over the years have agreed that the evaluating of teachers had been ritualistic and largely a waste of time (McLaughlin 1990). They have not seen teacher evaluation practices improving accountability or making improvements in the educational practices of teachers (p. 403).

EVALUATOR EFFECTIVENESS

Wise et al. (1984) believed, "the judgment of excellence in teaching must be based on superior standards of practice. Thus, the evaluator must have a high level of expertise to judge excellence" (p. 93). In addition, they found many teacher evaluation processes focusing only on assessing *minimum* criteria. The absolute minimum requirement they described as acceptable in a teacher's classroom was "a non-disruptive classroom" (p. 93). Mastery of subject matter presented through a variety of teaching methods was also seen as necessary. Unless these criteria are met, Wise et al. suggested the evaluators should *not certify* the teacher as acceptable.

Effective evaluators motivate teachers to change and improve their instruction. The success of this depends in large part on how open the teacher is to it.

Stiggins and Duke (1988) identified several teacher characteristics linked to the level of *receptivity* teachers would have to suggestions being made for their improvement:

1. Strong professional expectations;
2. A positive orientation to risk taking;
3. Openness to change;
4. Willingness to experiment in class;
5. Openness to criticism;
6. Strong knowledge of technical aspects of teaching;
7. Strong knowledge of subject matter; and
8. Some positive prior experience with teacher evaluation (p. 94).

The characteristics *evaluators* should possess to be successful motivators of teacher change and growth were identified as follows:

1. Credibility as a source of feedback;
2. A helper relationship with teacher;
3. Trustworthiness;
4. A nonthreatening interpersonal manner;
5. Patience;
6. Flexibility;
7. Strong knowledge of the technical aspects of teaching;
8. Capacity to model suggestions;
9. Familiarity with teacher's classroom students;
10. Teaching experience;
11. Useful suggestions;
12. Persuasiveness of rationale for improvement (pp. 94-95).

Faculty leaders, discussed in Chapter 2, had voiced a similar need for high-quality, credible evaluators and for a process that provides feedback and allows for disagreement when necessary. These faculty leaders also discussed how an evaluation system can be perceived favorably as a means of improving instruction, or negatively as a tool to "get someone." The quality of evaluators will highly influence the acceptance of the system in the eyes of faculty.

Leas and Rodriguez (1987) reversed the process and hypothesized the *ineffective* characteristics of college deans that they felt would be predictive of *failure to an evaluation process:*

1. Ineffective deans are poor communicators who are unable to listen effectively or assert themselves fairly.
2. Ineffective deans are closed, impersonal, and unattuned to the social nature of their jobs.

3. Ineffective deans are less conscientious regarding follow-up actions, are less than honest, and are often unwilling to support their faculty.
4. Ineffective deans are easily angered and are more prone to seek retribution.
5. Ineffective deans will be threatened by differences and be less objective about human situations.
6. Ineffective deans will be unsure and uncomfortable with the politics of their positions (pp. 97-101).

Leas and Rodriguez suggest that turning these factors around can help develop a climate for a successful evaluation process. These same factors could just as easily be applied to school principals.

Bridges (1990a) presented a list of "special knowledge and skills" that he felt administrators need to in order to become effective evaluators:

1. The ability to describe and analyze what is happening in a teacher's classroom.
2. The ability to provide an unbiased rating of a teacher's poor performance.
3. The ability to diagnose the cause(s) for a teacher's poor performance.
4. The ability to prescribe remediation that is appropriate to the teacher's classroom deficiencies.
5. The ability to conduct conferences with teachers regarding their instructional performance.
6. The ability to document matters related to 1 through 5.
7. Knowledge of the legal bases for evaluating and dismissing incompetent teachers (p. 41).

DEVELOPING CREDIBLE EVIDENCE

An evaluation system needs to be fair, the source of credible evidence, and legally defensible in those faculty cases where remediation or termination may be sought. Cases going forward on appeal from a principal to a superintendent, or a dean or vice president to a college president, and then forwarded to a governing board, arbitrator or a court of law must be able to withstand close scrutiny at every level. Bridges (1990a) stressed the need for this type of credible evidence:

> To justify its decision, the administration must be able to establish through its written records that a *pattern* of poor performance exists in relation to the district's criteria for evaluating teachers. Because there are no clear-cut standards or yardsticks for determining whether a teacher is meeting a particular criterion, administrators must accumulate numerous examples of the teacher's shortcomings and use these specific instances to verify that there is a pattern of unsatisfactory performances (p. 154).

Bridges cited the case of *Board of Education v. Ingels (1979)* in which an appellate court judge noted, "Proof of momentary lapses in discipline or a single day's lesson gone awry is not sufficient to show cause for dismissal of a tenured teacher. Yet, where brief instances and isolated lapses occur repeatedly, there emerges a pattern of behavior that, if deficient, will support the dismissal of a tenured teacher. Where the school board fails to show examples of conduct constitute a pattern of deficiency, then dismissal cannot be permitted" (p. 154). It is the pattern of behavior, properly documented, that will assist administration and governing board efforts to improve or remove poor instructors.

The courts were found by Rebell (1990) to tend to "defer to the administrators' 'expert' judgment and accept the results of their evaluations without undertaking any independent analysis" (p. 345). It is most important in cases of remediation or termination that evaluators follow proper procedures and collect sufficient documentation to prove incompetency or deficient behavior.

Administrative evaluators must stand behind their written statements. This is in contrast to the use of student evaluations which assure students' anonymity. How would one receive testimony or be able to cross-examine students who have participated in these systems? The student evaluation process, by design, makes it virtually impossible.

The burden of proof, in proving incompetence in order for a tenured faculty member's termination to be properly processed, is on the administrators. Piele (1981) showed use of expert testimony by administrators as being advantageous in winning cases in the courts. Dismissals overturned in the courts often have been found to lack defensible data from administrators' evaluations of teachers' performances (p. 69).

COURT SUPPORT

Courts have been found to be supportive of boards and administrators in their efforts to dismiss incompetent faculty. Strike and Bull (1981) showed why policies of a school can help to protect administrators. One example they presented was when an administrator is accused of being "capricious" in a decision to terminate a teacher. Board policies, if properly followed, can support the administrators' actions by providing the following documentation: (1) grounds for termination are contained in written school policy, (2) all other teachers in the institution have been submitted to the same review process, and (3) other teachers have been terminated for similar evaluation-related shortcomings (p. 313). Strictly following the procedures and documenting the process provides for the due-process rights required for the teacher involved.

Rebell (1990) cited a Pennsylvania court that applauded the "model" evaluation procedures used in *Rosso v. Board* (1977):

> The evaluations occurred at two levels. At the first level is the principal; if he rates a professional employee unsatisfactory, the matter is referred to the second level, the superintendent, for further evaluation. While a teacher might object to being rated so often in a short period of time by different persons, such a procedure is clearly in the employee's best interest since it brings into the evaluation different viewpoints, thereby lessening the influence, personal bias and prejudice with respect to teaching methods one evaluator can have. We are particularly impressed with the ratings . . . [on] what was going on in the classroom at five-minute intervals. This method of evaluation has given us the best picture of the learning atmosphere in a classroom that we have seen to date in an anecdotal record (p. 345).

The court was also impressed with the fact that the evaluations, in this case, were conducted over a two-year period.

TRAINING FOR ADMINISTRATORS

Andrews' and Licata's research (1990a) found only 28 percent of faculty leaders reported evaluation results were shared with faculty members and that plans for improvement were developed. Over 61 percent of the faculty leaders reporting stated that the number one purpose of evaluation should be "individual faculty development." Only 27 percent of the faculty leaders rated evaluation in their college as "very effective" or "effective."

Areas of training needed for administrators to become effective evaluators were listed by Hammons and Wallace (1977) as follows (pp. 62-66):

1. Evaluation of instructor (73 %);
2. Techniques of motivating faculty/staff (72 %)
3. Conducting performance appraisals (66 %)
4. The law and higher education (62 %)

Administrators continue to ask where they can obtain experience and training in effective classroom observation techniques. University researchers and evaluation practitioners have developed few helpful models to meet the needs of administrators who conduct faculty evaluations.

McLaughlin (1990) saw the need for evaluators to be properly trained in the job of evaluating faculty. In addition to learning proper legal procedures he felt their training should include: (1) observation; (2) recording classroom activities; and (3) conducting pre- and post-evaluation conferences with teachers (p. 408).

EVALUATION AS A *PROCESS*

It is important to view effective administrative evaluation as a process involving several key assumptions. Some assumptions are:

1. A process is agreed upon with the administration and faculty, and governing board;
2. The main intended outcome of evaluation is improvement of teaching;
3. Evaluators who have been teachers, or presently teach, and are respected as knowledgeable about teaching will conduct the evaluations;

4. Faculty has opportunity to discuss their written in-class evaluations;
5. Faculty has the chance to disagree both orally and in writing;
6. The opportunity for remediation, if necessary, is available;
7. Recognition is given for outstanding teaching performances.

Table 4 presents a flow chart of the evaluation process.

Table 4: Faculty Evaluation Flow Chart

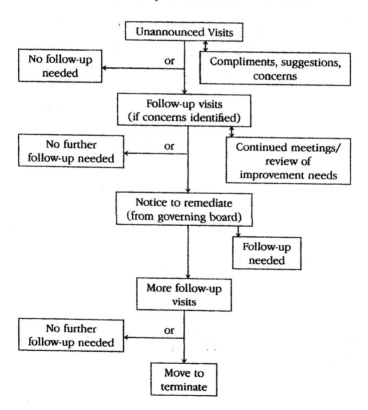

Unannounced visitations

The practice of unannounced classroom visits elicits many different responses from faculty and administrators. It has been my philosophy and practice over the years that evaluation of faculty should start with the *assumption* that *faculty will come prepared to teach during every class period*. With this expectation communicated to all faculty in any given school or community college, an evaluator should, therefore, feel free to observe classroom instruction at any time. A scheduled visit may be appropriate when a faculty member is trying a new method of teaching or is involved in the early stages of a remediation process.

Meeting with teachers... following classroom visits

The in-class evaluations must be in written form. It provides information on the specific strengths and weaknesses that were observed and that will be discussed with the teachers in the follow-up meeting. Faculty should expect a meeting a short time after the classroom visit in order to alleviate anxiety of the teacher. Such a meeting can take place immediately after the visit, the same day, or within a few days. Such a feedback timetable can be included in the written evaluation procedures of the school or college. Faculty will respect and appreciate those evaluators who give quick feedback.

Teachers should be allowed to explain how and what they feel about the in-class evaluation visit, review what was expected to be accomplished, and explain how they felt their class was conducted. Evaluators need to explain their overall impression of the class, identify both strengths and weaknesses that were observed. Faculty members should be encouraged to respond and agree or disagree and to clarify what they feel might have been missed by the evaluator. This review should include *compliments on the strengths of the teaching observed, suggestions for improvements,* and clearly stated *concerns* that must be remediated prior to further classroom evaluations. A time frame to allow for needed improvements should be given to those teachers who are in remediation.

The large majority of teacher evaluations will be positive. These evaluations offer an opportunity to recognize large numbers of faculty for the good job they are doing both in and out of their classrooms. Quality teaching needs to be recognized and praised. Earned praise will do much to improve morale and instruction within a school, as will suggestions for improvement given by competent and trusted administrative evaluators.

Necessary follow-up visits

It will be necessary to conduct follow-up visits with those faculty members receiving recommendations to make needed changes in their teaching. Appropriate changes must be documented. Those faculty members not making the required changes will need to have further documentation to support that remediation efforts are being attempted. It is also important to let these faculty members know of the possibility of dismissal if remediation is not completed satisfactory. The next step is progressive remediation on those defects and deficiencies in the teaching processes where changes were not made. Documentation should be made of the follow-up class visitations and one-on-one meetings held to review the written evaluations. The evaluator's meeting notes are most important in impressing upon the teacher that the outlined changes need to be made. The evaluator must make clear that both the follow-up evaluations and review sessions are to review and document that such changes are being carried out in a timely manner.

Remediation

Remedial action may become necessary when needed changes and improvements are not made. Remediation actions need to be clearly spelled out by the supervisor(s) and may involve the instructors in some of the following activities: (1) developing daily course outlines; (2) publishing and disseminating daily course objectives to students; (3) disseminating course requirements and the grading system to students; (4) visiting other teachers' classes; (5) consulting other professionals in the field within the same school or at other elementary or secondary schools, or colleges; (6) doing course work or readings in the methodology of teaching and psychology of learning; (7) participating in professional workshops or meetings; (8) improving testing and grading practices; (9) providing for appropriate methods of instruction depending on the teaching lesson to be presented; (10) improving supervision of laboratory students and/or maintaining equipment and supplies; (11) keeping current on articulation matters with other faculty, schools, or colleges; (12) updating course syllabi and(13) attending meetings as required.

The formal notice to remediate

Lack of improvement by an instructor may lead to a *formal notice to remediate*. This formal step will require action from the governing board. At this step the evaluators must provide a well-documented case showing "lack of improvement" as required and expected in the less formal remediation outlined above. It is most important that the superintendent of the school or the president of the college support this action going to the board. These top level administrators are the professionals who must seek the formal remediation notice approval from the governing boards.

After a governing board approves the notice to remediate

more follow-up evaluations will need to be conducted with those teachers cited for deficiencies in their teaching. If improvement is not forthcoming, further due process action becomes necessary. Such due process action might include termination by the board followed by arbitration with an outside hearing officer. If the teacher continues his/her appeal it would enter the court system.

Tenure and non-tenured evaluation processes

Andrews and Licata (1991) documented that most faculty leaders and administrators felt that the evaluation process should be the same for both tenured and non-tenured faculty. The non-tenured faculty will in most institutions be evaluated several times a year during their *probationary* or non-tenured years. Tenured faculty, unless documented for deficiencies, may not need to be evaluated more than two or three times during a five-year period.

SOME ADMINISTRATIVE STRESS

Spitalli (2003) encouraged administrators to stay positive when trying to remediate a poor teacher. He mentioned the need for the evaluator to have "thick skin." The teacher may try to make others think the administrators are not competent, that they are biased or have other negative characteristics. Yet Spitalli sees this stress can become a positive and can prove to be motivational. Having supportive colleagues in the administration and a competent attorney with school law background are also helpful and necessary.

Andrews (1988c) provided a list of key points in the

evaluation processes that can lead to stress for administrators involved in conducting effective evaluation of teachers:

1. Reporting negative or weak performances on written reviews;
2. Meeting the teacher face-to-face reviewing the negative performance;
3. Follow-up meetings to discuss progress or lack of progress;
4. Making the decision that not enough progress is being made to remediate the problems;
5. Going to the president (or superintendent) and board of trustees to support the need for a formal *notice to remedy* from the board;
6. Discussing the notice to remedy with the faculty member after board action is approved;
7. Continuation of several evaluations of in-class and other job responsibilities;
8. Having union and/or faculty association personnel involved in the case;
9. Feeling negative responses from other faculty members in the college who may not fully know the facts of the case;
10. Making a final determination to move toward termination of the faculty member if sufficient progress is not forthcoming (p. 63).

SUMMARY

The role of evaluator has been described as one of the most important elements in an effective evaluation system. Obtaining proper training and gaining on-the-job experiences as well as understanding the importance that faculty evaluation plays in the improvement of instruction are paramount in this job.

Universities should be modeling and teaching these skills in their educational administrative degree programs. It is, however, very difficult to find programs that teach the importance of, and system of, evaluation. Teacher evaluation and development are possibly the most powerful tools available for improving instruction in our K-12 and community college systems.

Professionally trained and experienced teacher evaluators can do much to improve teacher-administrator communication, motivate teachers in the process of improving classroom instructional practices, "counsel out" incompetent teachers and, as the *number one outcome*, improve student learning and achievement.

Evaluator's credibility and trustworthiness depend upon careful and thoughtful observation and unbiased feedback to each teacher. Effective evaluators must also be open, personable, and persuasive in assisting faculty needing help to become highly competent teachers.

The evaluator must carefully document all classroom visits and follow-up meetings with the faculty member. The teacher should receive prompt feedback and have an opportunity to respond. If evaluation efforts find that those teachers who are not working at a quality level will not, or cannot improve, remediation must be initiated. It is the responsibility of the school superintendent or college president to request an official "notice to remediate" from the governing board.

Credible evidence needs to be documented for those faculty cases that are in need of remediation and/or possible termination. This evidence will become the proof that is necessary for supporting the charge of incompetence in termination cases. Courts have proven to be supportive of the administration and governing boards when cases have been adequately documented and due process procedures have been properly followed.

The evaluation process should also provide opportunities to give recognition to those teachers who are doing well in their teaching. Recognition is a major motivator and is one of the strongest tools that the evaluator can use to reinforce and/or change teacher behavior.

The administrative evaluation process necessarily puts the administrator in stressful situations. However, faculty evaluation by effective administrative evaluators can do much to achieve the improved instruction and quality in teaching expected from teachers in their schools and colleges.

SUGGESTED EXERCISES

1. Define some personal and professional characteristics that you feel administrative evaluators of teachers should possess.
2. Define some ways that new administrators can gain experience and skills in teacher evaluation practices.

CHAPTER 6

DEFINING QUALITY STANDARDS FOR THE EVALUATION FORM

Desired Standard: The level of performance on the criterion being assessed that is considered satisfactory in terms of the purpose of the evaluation.

Teacher Evaluation Kit Glossary (2003), p. 29

Quality standards need to be developed in an evaluation system in order to determine quality outcomes of the process. The outcomes need to include improved instruction, formative teacher development, positive recognition, tenure decisions, remediation, and termination if necessary.

The quality of these outcomes depends upon the data gathered and weighed against expectations in a school's or college's evaluation process. These expectations can be converted into an evaluation form that will become a critical component of the overall system.

Developing a meaningful evaluation form will assist in the objective and informed assessment of teacher performance, based upon agreed standards of teaching. Defining quality teaching techniques and outcomes and converting them into an evaluation form is a foremost early step in developing an effective evaluation system.

DEFINITIONS OF QUALITY TEACHING

Faculty and administrative evaluators should work together and agree on definitions of quality teaching techniques and processes as a first major step in developing the in-class evaluation instrument. The process will take weeks or months but will help to obtain the necessary support from the faculty members, who will know that the standards were decided upon as a result of their own or their representatives' participation.

The audiences of a school need to know that the school or college has set high quality standards for classroom teachers in their institutions. The Teacher Evaluation Kit Glossary (2003) defines the audience as follows:

> Those individuals who have a potential interest in the results of teacher performance assessment and evaluation and in the quality of teaching (p. 29).

The audience is often referred to as stakeholders and includes teachers, principals, school and district staff, students, parents, school board members, future employers, taxpayers, and community members. When one looks at the impact teachers have on so many people and groups it becomes evident why a school should not settle for less than the highest quality of instruction and outcomes that can be obtained from every teacher in the school or college.

The characteristics of effective teachers using successful teaching methodologies were presented in Chapter 4. This chapter focuses on faculty and administrative groups working together to convert quality-teaching characteristics into a workable evaluation form. If it has been determined that good teaching requires a faculty member to be prepared for every class period, then all faculty within that institution should be evaluated against that standard. If learning the names of students and their interests is considered an important motivator in the learning process, then it should also be included as an evaluation criterion. In short, the qualities of excellence in teaching as defined by teachers, administrators, and researchers, needs to become the measuring stick within the evaluation process. These criteria should become the substance for the evaluation instrument to be developed.

Sample evaluation questions are presented in this chapter and are open-ended. They require evaluators to write narrative responses on the quality of teaching observed for each teaching criterion. Each of the criterion of teacher effectiveness listed below has been converted into an evaluation question.

Poole and Dellow (1983) identified one measure of teaching effectiveness as that of "presenting material in an orderly and preplanned method compatible with the stated objectives of the course" (p. 20). A second measure would be the teacher's preparedness for every class period.

Sample observations will follow each of the evaluation questions listed below. Some will be observations of quality teaching followed by observations of teaching needing improvement. While these are presented in the third person to serve as objective samples, actual evaluations will be more personalized.

Converting the expectation that "a teacher should be totally prepared" into an evaluation form question might look as follows:

1. What evidence is there that the teacher is or is not prepared for this class?

Quality teaching:
    The lecture was on the admission procedures for nursing homes. The instructor passed out an outline of these procedures at the beginning of class. She related

---

the need for the procedures as well as how to complete the process. The topic was covered with a good blend of the instructor presenting new material and students contributing their knowledge and clinical experience to the discussion. She answered students questions respectfully and checked student's understanding of the answers. She was prepared for this class.

Teaching requiring improvement:

While the instructor had previously produced a complete course outline, he was not prepared for this class session. He announced the incorrect date for the final exam (corrected by a student), spent the full hour attempting to review the previous exam (reviewing only 8 of the 15 questions), offered no new course content, announced plans to repeat the same test in two days and left no time to review for the final exam scheduled for two class meetings from that time.

Guskey and Easton (1983) found quality teachers to be highly organized and to have high expectations for their students. Converting this into a question one might ask:

2. What evidence is there that the teacher is organized and has appropriate expectations of his/her students (i.e., homework, class participation, etc.)?

Quality teaching:

The instructor's course outline included a specific schedule of outside assignments (both reading and written exercises) and class discussions. Due dates and other responsibilities were clear. The lecture portion of the class was sequential and clear. One half the period was devoted to small group discussions on the current topic which allowed all students to participate. Students were involved and had lively discussions based on an issue at the core of today's lecture material.

Teaching requiring improvement:

The instructor gave no evidence of clear expectations of his students. No homework was turned in, and no assignment was made for the future. He lectured the entire class period with fewer than one half of the students taking notes. No time was allowed for questions or checking student understanding of the lecture.

In terms of utilizing good teaching techniques and presenting a positive learning environment the question might be stated:

3. How effective are the techniques used and how does the instructor provide for a positive learning environment?

Quality teaching:

The instructor used the discussion method with this class, which required extensive student participation and student-instructor interaction. Students appeared motivated and very responsive. The instructor also outlined conclusions of the discussion on the board and students took notes on them.

Teaching requiring improvement:

The instructor did not establish a positive learning environment during this class period. There was no interaction or involvement of students. Although he provided a list of questions pertinent to the topic noted on his weekly plan, the students were asked to "find" the answers in their textbooks and complete the questionnaire. The directions were to do this quietly, with each student working independently. There was no interaction and no time allocated to ask questions on the material. A number of students appeared bored, and several became disruptive to the class.

Knowledge of the subject matter was mentioned in several faculty descriptions of quality teaching. It is the basis for all teaching:

4.   How does the instructor demonstrate an *adequate knowledge* of the subject, activity, or skill?

Quality teaching:

It is obvious that the instructor is knowledgeable about the teaching of nurses aide material. Her experiences in the field greatly contribute to her knowledge of the course content. She was able to cite field examples for each of the key points being presented during the lecture.

Teaching requiring improvement:

The instructor appeared unsure of the information he was presenting. Any knowledge of the subject was lost due to a lack of structure in the lecture. He "followed" the textbook, at times reading long passages (up to two pages) verbatim to the students. Some factual mistakes were made in answering student's questions, once with a student correcting him.

Classroom activity needs to correspond to the course syllabus. The following two questions deal with the course syllabus. In question 5, a quality expectation is that the instructor is on schedule or very nearly on schedule with the student course outline, syllabus, or lesson plan previously developed:

5.   How closely does the discussion or activity follow the course syllabus?

Quality teaching:

The topic covered today, procedures relating to death and dying, was planned for this day on the student course outline. While this subject is to continue for two more days, the instructor completed material planned for this day.

Teaching requiring improvement:

When asked where today's topic fit into the course outline, the teacher was unable to find the topic on the outline. He suggested it might be on another outline (which he was unable to produce).

In question 6, the expectation is that the teacher will complete the course material necessary for this class. This is essential for any class that is a prerequisite for subsequent courses in the students' curriculum. It is also important to those high schools and community colleges that are preparing students for the next articulated level of their program.

6. What evidence is there that the course syllabus will be completed as required?

Quality teaching:

The instructor is up-to-date with the syllabus. Her syllabus includes the required course material, by date, for her students. Her student course outline is an excellent guide. Today's lesson was the one scheduled for this date on the course outline.

Teaching requiring improvement:

Absolutely none. The test material discussed was related to information which should have been covered five weeks ago and prior to the mid-term of the class, according to the student course outline.

Nash (1982) suggested that testing dates and types of testing to be used should be presented clearly in the class syllabus when it is distributed the first day of class. He also expected testing to be used at key points throughout the course (p. 84). An expectation is that evaluation of student learning is done early in the semester and that student feedback is given often enough to measure learning and to allow for adjustments in teaching methods to meet the student needs.

7. How frequently and effectively does the instructor evaluate student progress?

Quality teaching:
Four unannounced quizzes have been given as of the tenth week of the course. Major exams are scheduled on four dates throughout the semester and two have been completed as of this evaluation.

Teaching needing improvement:
No testing has taken place as of this evaluation on November 2 (class started in August). Neither of the two written assignments made during this period have been returned to the students.

Learning students' names early (if classes are small enough) helps to facilitate student participation. Knowing the students, holding high expectations for their preparation prior to each class meeting, giving meaningful homework and reviewing it in class, and encouraging collaborative learning within the classroom, are methods to motivate students to participate to increase student learning.

8. How has the instructor encouraged student participation in the class?

Quality teaching:

In today's class, students were asked several times to answer the questions as a result of the group process. The teacher also asked questions of individual students, calling on them by name. His rapport with his students was clear as they were motivated and ready to respond to his questions and requests. He also asked for and responded to questions from the students.

Teaching needing improvement:

The instructor did not encourage student participation during this class. I would suggest that the instructor review through examples some of the concepts discussed this hour to see if students understand them. This would give students a chance to ask questions. This would also increase interest, make the learning an active process, and give the instructor an opportunity to evaluate student progress and understanding.

Additional questions can be developed from the list of quality teaching standards that are established by the faculty and administration. They can be used to evaluate both classroom and other job responsibility areas. Some additional questions that may be included on evaluation forms follow:

9. How effective is the teacher in "getting the materials across" and in answering student questions clearly?
10. How does the teacher make effective use of audio-visual, multi-media, or other technology in the classroom?
11. In what ways does the teacher participate in faculty meetings, division meetings, and school committees?
12. How does the teacher keep current on the latest developments in his/her field of study?
13. How would you describe the type of working relationship the instructor has with his/her colleagues and the administration?

14. How well does the instructor meet time requirements? (i.e., deadlines for school and state reports?)

Two sample evaluation forms with open-ended questions are found at the end of this chapter. The first one is suggested for elementary and middle school teachers. The second form is developed to meet the requirements for secondary school and community college evaluation.

DOs AND DON'Ts IN WRITING EVALUATIONS

Conley and Dixon (1990) suggest some "do's and don'ts" in writing faculty evaluations. These items will enhance the feedback process with teachers after classroom observations have been made:

1. Don't write the report the day before the evaluation conference. Do it as soon as the observation is completed.
2. Don't write all your evaluations at once.
3. Don't expect teachers to read and react to the report in the conference.
4. Don't be afraid to change items in the report as a result of the conference.
5. Don't write in the third person; personalize the report.
6. Do make certain that there is nothing in evaluatees' personnel files related to the evaluation process that they have not seen and/or signed (pp. 12-13).

Conley and Dixon described what must be done differently when dealing with a candidate for dismissal: "Basically, a well-written evaluation report will provide you with the documentation you need if it becomes necessary to pursue dismissal. The act of offering help to a teacher will not be held against you in court" (p. 13). Conley and Dixon make it clear that it will be more effective for evaluators to design evaluation forms or reports toward growth and improvement of teaching since the percentage of incompetent faculty will be low.

Isenberg (1990) made the following suggestions about improving methods of appraising teacher effectiveness:

1. Being objective helps make the evaluation process more consistent.
2. The principal is in a unique position to stimulate and motivate staff to achieve maximum performance.
3. An administrator who has a solid foundation in evaluation and appraisal will help his or her staff accomplish their goals.
4. A strong, fair evaluation offers the teacher the opportunity to explore personal educational philosophies and compare them with actual classroom practices (p. 17).

Making sure a school or college has clear and consistent standards and a corresponding evaluation form that reflects these standards is important. These items will allow evaluators to gain support and recognition for identifying good teaching efforts. They will also provide necessary and effective tools for identifying less effective teaching efforts.

The East Richland Community Unit District #1 in Olney, Illinois, utilizes an outline of expected "observable teacher behaviors" that they share with all teachers in the district. It refers to the "effective teacher as one who will: (A) initiate, (B) develop and sustain, (3) and summarize the content students are to learn." These three areas are detailed so the teachers will have clear ideas of what will be looked for in the supervisor's evaluation of their classes. A partial listing is presented here:

A. Initiating the Lesson:

1.01   The teacher relates new content to material presented previously and to students' prior knowledge;

1.02   The teacher specifies lesson purposes, learning objectives, and activities to follow;

1.03   The teacher provides efficient and smooth transitions between lessons and activities;

1.04   The teacher introduces a learning activity using language and concepts that students understand;

1.05   The teacher communicates expectations for high levels of learning by all students.

B. Developing and Sustaining Learning:

Effective teachers distribute their attention fairly, speak fluently and precisely, adjust the pace and difficulty of the lesson for students, keep the students' attention focused on the activity and present and ensure comprehension of concepts and skills.

1.06   The teacher speaks clearly, audibly, precisely, and fluently while keeping to the topic of the lesson;

1.07   The teacher provides explanations that are adequate to helping students understand the content of the lesson and their tasks;

1.08   The teacher moves the lesson along, adjusting its pace and difficulty to assure students' understanding;

1.09   The teacher presents new material with various pre-identified methods, such as lecture, modeling, demonstration, experiment, and role playing;

1.10   The teacher asks questions that students can successfully answer and that require students to recall, explain, compare and contrast, and evaluate information;

1.11   The teacher pauses after each question to allow students the opportunity to reflect or respond;

1.12   The teacher makes sure that all students have opportunities to ask questions and to contribute to and participate in class activities;

1.13   The teacher provides guided practice, circulating to check students' progress and provide assistance. Independent practice follows guided practice.

Summarizing the Lesson:

During and at the conclusion of the lesson, an effective teacher summarizes what has occurred, brings closure to learning, and forecasts upcoming activities.

1.14   The teacher summarizes the main points of the lesson by presenting or eliciting a restatement of the content or activity;

1.15   The teacher brings closure to the completed lesson and forecasts what will be learned next.

Category 2: Classroom Management

Effective teachers assure that classroom activities occur in an environment that promotes and encourages learning. They manage routines, establish and communicate expectations and consequences, and promote beneficial interpersonal relations among class members.

Managing Routines:

2.01.1   The teacher has all necessary materials ready and distributes materials in an orderly manner and in a small amount of time;

2.01.2   The teacher starts students at tasks quickly and assures efficient transitions between activities;

2.01.3   The teacher maintains a high level of time-on-task for all students and redirects students who are off task;

2.01.4   The teacher continuously monitors student behavior, encourages appropriate student behavior, and promptly stops inappropriate behavior;

Expectations and Consequences:
2.01.5   The teacher establishes rules and procedures for routine administrative matters and for student behavior during whole class and group   instruction;
2.01.6   The teacher communicates expectations, rules, procedures, and consequences of infractions.
2.01.7   The teacher checks student understanding of expectations, rules, procedures, and consequences;

Interpersonal Relations:
2.01.8   The teacher interacts with students in a mutually respectful and friendly manner;
2.01.9   The teacher expresses verbal enthusiasm for the lesson and student participations;
2.01.10 The teacher praises students for on-task behavior, appropriate conduct, and learning accomplishments.

A third major category including "assessment of learning" and "feedback to students" is also part of the evaluation process considered in each teacher evaluation by the administrators. These items allow the evaluator and teacher to both be working from the same expectations of what is expected for this school district (East Richland Community Unit District #1, 2003). They also relate directly to the evaluation form used by the school district.

SUMMARY

This chapter reviewed quality-teaching standards and translated them into questions that might be used in an evaluation form. Successful instructional methodologies as well

---

as desirable personal characteristics were considered. Providing a well-designed evaluation form, developed jointly by teachers and administrators, helps to measure teachers' performances against the agreed upon standards for teaching excellence and will help raise the teaching quality of faculty members.

Information gathered and recorded on the evaluation form provides the basis for decisions on faculty development needs, recognition, tenure, remediation, or termination. Questions and responses presented in this chapter give the practitioner examples of the kind of comments that can be written on faculty evaluation forms for clear feedback to the teacher evaluated. There are two sample evaluation forms—one for elementary/middle school and a second one for secondary school/community college—provided at the end of this chapter.

SUGGESTED EXERCISES

1. What demonstrates that a teacher has prepared properly to teach a class? Identify what you know a teacher needs to have done to be prepared in advance.
2. How might a teacher assure that students will become involved in active learning processes within a class?

Sample Form
EVALUATION FORM FOR TEACHERS
(Elementary and Middle School)

_____Tenured   _____Non-Tenured   _____Part-Time

Name of Person Evaluated:_____

Date:_____   Building/Room Number:_____

Class, Lab, Counseling Session Observed:_____

Name of Supervisor Making Evaluation: _____

No. of Students Assigned____

No. of Different Teaching Preparations___

Section I: Planning and Preparation

1.   What evidence was there that prior planning was accomplished?

COMMENTS:

2.   What evidence was presented to show the teacher knowledgeable about the material being presented?

COMMENTS:

3.   How well did the teacher stay within the pre-planned time frames for subjects or activities?

COMMENTS:

4.   Describe the room organization for teaching effectiveness. Include use of bulletin boards, reading areas, etc.

COMMENTS:

5.   What was the range of activities presented by the teaching during this observation?

COMMENTS:

6.   Describe how well the teacher maintains "time on task."

COMMENTS:

7.   What evidence was there that the teacher communicates clearly with the students?

COMMENTS:

8.   What teaching techniques were observed that stimulate student participation?

COMMENTS:

9.   What feedback activities or actions to students were utilized?

COMMENTS:

10.   What individualized student activities and techniques were observed being used?

COMMENTS:

11.   How does the teacher relate new ideas and materials to previous or future learning activities?

COMMENTS:

12.   What level of student active participation was observed?

COMMENTS:

13.   How were instructional media, audio-visual materials, or computers utilized to enhance in-class learning?

COMMENTS:

Part III: Organization and Management

14.   What evidence was there that the teacher has or has not achieved a level of discipline necessary for maximum learning?

COMMENTS:

15.   How well does the teacher accept and set goals and move toward class and overall school outcomes?

COMMENTS:

16.   What evidence was there that the teacher is effective in correcting inappropriate student behavior?

COMMENTS:

17.   How well does the teacher maintain and turn in required planning materials, grades, and other reports?

COMMENTS:

Part IV: Other Responsibilities

18.   Explain in what ways this teacher supports school policies, participates in pertinent school activities, communicates with parents (individual student concerns and parent conferences), selects appropriate textbooks and teaching materials.

COMMENTS:

19.   How does the teacher relate to other teachers, supervisors, and other school personnel?

COMMENTS:

20.   In what ways does this teacher maintain professional upgrading?

COMMENTS:

SUMMARY COMMENTS AND RECOMMENDATIONS FOR IMPROVEMENTS:

Remediation Concerns and Plan:
Problems/Concerns:

Expected Outcomes:

Target Dates:_____

Signatures of Appropriate Administrator(s) and Teacher

_____
Building Principal   Date

_____
Teacher   Date

_____
Assistant Principal   Date

_____
District Superintendent   Date

Sample Form
EVALUATION FORM FOR FACULTY
(Community College or Secondary School)

_____Tenured   _____ Non-Tenured   _____Part-Time

Name of Person Evaluated:_____

Date: _____ Building/Room Number:_____

Class, Lab, Counseling Session Observed: _____

Name of Supervisor Making Evaluation: _____

1.   What evidence is there that the teacher is or is not prepared for this class?

COMMENTS:

2.   What evidence is there that the teacher is organized and has appropriate expectations of his/her students (i.e., homework, class participation, etc.)?

COMMENTS:

3.   How effective are the teaching techniques used and how does the instructor provide for a positive learning environment?

COMMENTS:

4.   How does the instructor demonstrate an *adequate knowledge* of the subject, activity, or skill?

COMMENTS:

5.   How closely does the discussion or activity follow the course syllabus?

COMMENTS:

6.   What evidence is there that the course syllabus will be completed as required?

COMMENTS:

7. How frequently and effectively does the instructor evaluate student progress?

COMMENTS:

8. How has the instructor encouraged student participation in the class?

COMMENTS:

9. How effective is the teacher in "getting the materials across" and in answering student questions clearly?

COMMENTS:

10. How does the teacher make effective use of audio-visual, multi-medial, or other technology in the classroom?

COMMENTS:

11. What evidence is there of sound testing and review techniques being used?

COMMENTS:

12. How would you describe the interaction that was observed between the teacher and students?

COMMENTS:

17. What evidence is there that the teacher has appropriate grading standards?

COMMENTS:

OTHER PROFESSIONAL RESPONSIBILITIES

13. In what ways does the teacher participate in faculty meetings, division meetings, and school committees?

COMMENTS:

14. How does the teacher keep current on the latest developments in his/her field of study?

COMMENTS:

15. How would you describe the type of working relationship the instructor has with his/her colleagues and the administration?

COMMENTS:

16. How well does the instructor meet time requirements (i.e., office hours, deadlines for school and state reports?

COMMENTS:

SUMMARY EVALUATION STATEMENTS AND RECOMMEN-DATIONS FOR IMPROVEMENT:

- -

Signatures of Appropriate Administrator(s) and Instructor

_____

Chief Academic Officer / Principal

_____

Division / Department Chairperson

_____

President / Superintendent

_____

Instructor

CHAPTER 7

CASE STUDIES: FORMATIVE TO SUMMATIVE

Formative Teacher Evaluation: An evaluation conducted for the purpose of improving the teacher through identifying that teacher's strengths and weaknesses.

Summative Teacher Evaluation: An evaluation conducted primarily for the purpose of making personnel decisions about the teacher (e.g., merit pay, reassignment, promotion, dismissal, tenure).

Teacher Evaluation Kit Glossary, (2003), pp. 14 and 31

There has been considerable debate about whether an evaluation system can be both formative and summative in nature. A number of writers, Popham (1988) and Hunter (1988b) included, describe an inherent conflict between the formative and summative functions. They argue that defensiveness and self-protective behaviors are brought out by summative evaluation activities, while it is important to have candor and cooperation for staff development to be successful in the formative process.

Barber (1990) sees assisting teachers to improve their own teaching as the purpose of formative teacher evaluation. To improve, the teacher must be able to admit that his or her teaching may be less than perfect and can be improved through the changes that are outlined in the formative evaluation process. Barber views evaluation systems as being inherently neither formative or summative. He says that it depends upon how the data obtained is used. If the process never deals with judgments, salary, status, tenure, or working conditions, the system is considered formative. If evaluations are used for any of the above purposes, then it is considered a summative system. There is no room for compromise in his description (pp. 216-217).

Licata and Andrews (1990) argued that both formative and summative results are necessary if an evaluation system is to be considered effective:

> It is our further belief that one system should be set up and both outcomes should be possible, but not until after significant efforts at formative help are attempted. Furthermore, institutions and evaluation experts must be ready to reckon with the fact that there will occasionally be negative outcomes from any evaluation system, whether it is set up to be formative or otherwise. Theorists who insist on dual systems are not dealing with the reality that those who work in the trenches and administer such evaluation systems are working toward formative evaluation outcomes. Having dual systems ignores the fact that formative attempts may, indeed, end in summative decisions that have to be made. Such evaluation outcomes are part of a continuum rather than separate system (p. 48).

Licata and Andrews argue further that even the action to bring a faculty member before a governing board for a formal "notice to remedy" is part of the continuum; the remediation process is still an attempt to obtain "formative changes" without having to move for a dismissal. This argument goes against the pure separation of formative and summative evaluation that most four-year college theorists have promoted.

Wise and Gendler (1990) suggested that the procedures in an evaluation system assume most teachers, prior to tenure, will need evaluation to identify improvement needs. In this way the system provides for formative results. They suggest that "management-by-exception" should be used when handling cases of candidates for dismissal (p. 393). Wise, et al. (1984) supported procedures which provided for dismissal as an exception and, which procedures have been jointly designed and implemented as a cooperative effort of administration and teachers (p. 111).

The preparation of principals and college deans and division chairpersons to conduct meaningful and quality evaluations needs to continue to improve. Schwartz (1997) summarized how Project Helping Evaluators Lift Performance (H.E.L.P.) in the Guilford County, North Carolina, schools was developed for this purpose. Goals are to:

1. Establish procedures and train administrators for documenting performance in providing written plans of improvement;
2. Identify staff who can give and who need help;
3. Develop and implement action plans for those teachers most in need of help, specifically defining problems and prescribing strategies to demonstrate improvement; and
4. Assist principals in removing employees who cannot or will not meet performance expectations (pp. 5-6).

Schwartz also presented a clear case that, "Principals need detailed instruction on how to effectively document poor performance. Effective documentation, not just more of it, is what we are after" (p. 6).

The following are samples of two faculty evaluation cases that lead to very different outcomes. The first led to a recommendation for tenure. The second led to the teacher's resignation—at the board's request. Both cases were drawn from professional evaluation records, and have been changed to some degree to protect confidentiality.

FORMATIVE ASSISTANCE FOR A NON-TENURED TEACHER: A POSITIVE CASE

The first case presents feedback given to a non-tenured faculty member. Concerns were identified early in the evaluation process. A total of three evaluators were involved in classroom assessment of the teacher's ability to carry out quality teaching processes throughout each of her first three years teaching at the community college. The following written comments were given to the instructor at different times during the three-year probationary review process. They were also discussed with her within days of each evaluation:

First evaluation, first year:
1. Be careful about moving through the lecture material too rapidly. Give students a chance to digest the materials and to clarify any misunderstandings.
2. Speak loudly and distinctly. Be careful about lowering your voice too much as it sounded like you were mumbling.
3. Try to lessen your dependency on notes, and try not to read from them in future classes.
4. Spend more time questioning your students to see if they are understanding the material. Give examples and discuss experiences from your personal work-related activities and readings. Take time to summarize important points after covering each specific topic.
5. Try to relax. Perhaps practicing your lecture prior to class may help. When you become more relaxed, your lectures will flow more freely.

Summary of first evaluation:
This instructor needs to outline the key points in her material for a lecture class as well as pace the presentation

better. Students need to be asked throughout the lecture to contribute and ask questions for clarification. By stepping away from her notes she can keep better eye contact and help assess which students do not grasp a concept. Speaking distinctively will help show command of the material.

Post evaluation meeting with instructor (first evaluation):

The instructor has become very frustrated teaching this course. She tries to cover too much material in each lecture. We discussed her need to plan her lesson to present "highlights" of the main concepts supplemented by examples from experience in the field. The pace needs to be slowed down for students to take notes and get involved in interaction with the teacher. Some of the students have had experiences in hospital and nursing home work and could add examples to a number of the lecture points. She was very open to suggestions during the post-evaluation meeting and plans to work on presenting her upcoming lessons in a different way. She will work with her direct supervisor and visit classes of other nursing teachers in order to observe and improve upon her own teaching methodologies and use of audio-visual technology support.

Follow-up in-class evaluation several weeks later:

The instructor began the class by mentioning the objectives to be covered for today's class. The instructor appeared nervous, possibly somewhat due to the two evaluators presence. There was still more dependence on notes than should be necessary.

Two students were involved in a demonstration. This is a good technique to use. The instructor appears to be gaining more confidence in her teaching. She knows her students' names now and appears to relate well with them.

Second follow-up in-class evaluation notes:

During this class the instructor used a brief amount of lecture, carried on discussion interaction with students, continually asked for and received student responses, brought into the discussion a recent television documentary on the topic, and used transparencies that illustrated each of the main discussion points. Students were attentive and were involved with small group presentations. Student interest was evident. The instructor illustrated confidence and knowledge of the topics during this observation.

Summary: This class was well presented. You have worked very hard on your teaching techniques, and it is paying off. Your listing of the goals for the class period on transparencies and then reviewing them at the end of the class was very good. It is obvious that you now are able to "draw" many of your students into the lecture discussion. Your ability to let students respond to your questioning and still keep on schedule was commendable. Keep up these methods of teaching.

Third follow-up in-class evaluation notes:

It was a pleasure to observe the vast improvements in teaching techniques this instructor has mastered since her initial semester. The confidence in herself, material presented, and her ability to "teach" and motivate her students were all much stronger during this evaluation.

She called on her students and expected them to be ready to respond. They took notes, listened carefully and participated during questioning several times during the hour. The instructor used notes to guide her lecture material but was not dependant upon them. She used the overhead to highlight key points, and paced herself so everyone could keep up with her.

This was a well-prepared and taught lecture. Keep up the good work. Your contributions to this program will be felt by all your students.

Fourth follow-up in-class evaluation notes:

Every time I observe this instructor I am impressed with her improvements in her teaching techniques. During this session, she exhibited the following quality teaching techniques:

1. Use of well developed transparencies with a few key words to guide the lecture;
2. Involving students in the discussion;
3. Lecturing without a reliance on notes;
4. Calling upon students by name;
5. Not being "tied" to the podium;
6. Telling the students what they were responsible for;
7. Relating the topic to live laboratory problems and future experiences the students will have during their clinical practice.

I do not feel I can help you improve much more. You have taken our suggestions and you have been evolving into a quality teacher. It is a pleasure working with someone who is willing to take suggestions and then watch as you effectively implement those methods. Keep it up.

Last evaluation prior to tenure recommendation:

This instructor has made great strides in her teaching techniques over her non-tenured period. She has been open to suggestions, sought out assistance and has developed from an inexperienced classroom teacher into a quality, experienced teacher. Her involvement of students in her lecture material is one outstanding example of her improvement.

The lecture during this visit was well paced, clearly presented, and reviewed throughout by questioning of her students. The positive feedback the instructor gives to the students reinforces their willingness to contribute. This instructor has used her three non-tenured years to strengthen many aspects of her teaching and has become an excellent instructor. She should continue to improve and contribute to her profession and to the college for years to come.

Final observation before tenure decision

The above non-tenured instructor was hired as a teacher immediately after obtaining her master's degree in nursing. She had been an excellent student but had never had previous teaching experiences. With some early intervention from her administrative evaluators, she was able to turn around what may have become a very negative and tragic teaching experience. The first post-evaluation conferences brought out her concerns. She discussed her high level of frustration that led her to put into far too many hours and still not feeling successful. She was willing, however, to work closely with her direct supervisor over the next few weeks in areas that were targeted for improvement. With an open mind and an attitude of wanting to do better, and with continued in-class follow-up evaluation, improvements were being made and reinforced through subsequent evaluations over a several week period. The reinforcement led to continuing improvement and helped to build the personal confidence the instructor needed to try out other teaching methodologies. Formative evaluation proved very helpful throughout this instructor's non-tenure years.

FORMATIVE ASSISTANCE: A FACULTY MEMBER'S VIEW

The following is an interview with the non-tenured faculty member above who received the formative assistance through the evaluation system. This interview highlights how the evaluation process worked for her as she saw it:

Interviewer: How did the evaluation system assist you?
Teacher: The evaluation system assisted me by making me

---

aware that the student is responsible for part of the teaching-learning process. I had been giving so much information in lecture that the students were not able to take notes and were frustrated.

I learned how to prioritize the material and cut down on the amount given to them. I also learned to use audio-visuals to assist me. I did not even know, prior to the evaluation process, what resources were available to assist me at the college. I also learned what was expected of me. I feel this is an important aspect of the evaluation process. As an instructor, if I don't know what is expected of me I will not be able to do the kind of job expected of me.

Interviewer: What did you feel about teaching prior to receiving assistance?

Teacher: I was frustrated, exhausted, and overwhelmed. I was unhappy about the job I was doing and so exhausted from the work load that I could not see the light at the end of the tunnel. I was trying to teach the students too much. As a recent graduate with an M.S. degree I was trying to tell students everything I knew. My expectations of the students were too high. I was determined to do a good job, but the more I worked the more exhausted I became. I believe this cycle could have led to failure for me without some assistance.

Interviewer: How did you feel when supervisors offered to assist you?

Teacher: I was relieved. I did not do any student teaching or have course work on how to teach in my degree program at the university. My supervisors informed me of their expectations of my work. This gave me guidelines and ideas on how to improve my teaching. I used these ideas and guidelines and now feel good about what I am doing. After recommendations were made, I knew what I needed to do to improve my teaching. I welcomed those recommendations because I was trying to do my very best but I was sinking.

Interviewer: What do you remember about how the assistance began? When did you feel it was starting to make a difference in your teaching?

Teacher: Two of my supervisors met with me after sitting in my classroom. They discussed what they saw as problems and suggested I talk with the director of the program. They also made recommendations on how to improve my teaching; for example, use audio-visuals and have overheads typed with key points in large print; move around, don't stand behind the podium; SMILE! Ask questions of my students, and so forth. I realize most of this is common sense, but I was so exhausted from the extensive preparation I was doing I did not put this together on my own. I needed to hear it from someone else.

My program director explained I was teaching in too much depth for the level of my students. He told me to "skim" the chapters to find important subject areas and discuss what was important for students to know in class. The students were expected to read the rest. Again, this seems like such common sense now.

Interviewer: What steps did you take to change your teaching and try different strategies and teaching methods?

Teacher: After my supervisors confirmed my feelings that things were not going well I had to change what I was doing. I had lost weight and was exhausted doing it my way. I knew I was capable and decided to change my strategy. After getting some rest, I put to work what my supervisors recommended. I prioritized the main concepts of my lecture on typed transparencies. I tried to lecture on the important aspects of the content. I moved around the room more and became more relaxed as my confidence grew. I was so determined to prove to myself, and my supervisors, that I could do a good job as an instructor that I would have tried almost anything. My supervisors believed in me. I felt they cared enough to take time to help me and it was up to me to take it from there. I am happy the evaluation system worked for me. Without the assistance I received, I might not be teaching today.

Interviewer: Does the college's evaluation system act as a formative (assisting) system for faculty?

Teacher: I feel the college's evaluation system keeps instructors on their toes. It demands certain expectations from faculty, which is important to maintain excellence in education. It is a way to inform faculty of expectations in the educational milieu.

FORMATIVE ASSISTANCE: A NEGATIVE OUTCOME

The next case describes a second non-tenured faculty member's evaluation history. This instructor was advised about some early classroom teaching concerns identified through the in-class evaluations by three administrators. Improvement was noted in some subsequent evaluations but then strong evidence was documented later that the instructor returned to his previously identified poor performance. He started showing a lack of preparation and an almost total lack of student involvement during his lectures and other class activities.

First evaluation:

The test was passed back but not reviewed except for one question. Students were raising their hands to ask about other questions but the instructor indicated his short review had ended. You need to spend more time in future test reviews. You also need to pace your material and start having

---

student involvement in the lecture material. They became very passive as the lecture progressed with you doing non-stop lecturing. Work to draw out your students' experiences on various lecture points. This would have enriched the lecture as well as motivated students to participate.

Suggestions: Why not use the corrected test as a learning device? It appeared your students missed, or did not understand, more than just the one question you reviewed. You should use prepared visuals on the overhead for both your outline and the diagrams you referred to. Keep your lecture moving and include your students more in the discussion. A number have worked in related job settings and could have added to the lecture from their experiences. At times you "lost" students as you lectured. Identifying some examples of the various components you discussed would have been helpful.

First in-class follow-up evaluation notes

From what I observed today there was some improvement in the instructor's advanced preparation for the class as well as his presentation. I encouraged him to:

1. Continue to specifically spell out what each student is expected to do to prepare for each class and what skills he/she is to develop.
2. Consciously make an effort to ask specific students questions in order to check the students' understanding. I suggested that he work to draw all students into the discussion.
3. Continue to summarize as he did by asking questions and referring to the handout materials.

Second in-class evaluation notes

Get your class started on time. Five to six minutes wasted during each one-hour lecture adds up to hours during the semester. By starting late it took you several more minutes to

---

get your notes organized. This should have been done before your students arrived. You also need to remember to include your students in the lecture. Your lack of enthusiasm in the material was prominent. It appeared that you were just going through the motions of getting the material presented. You need to work on:

1. Motivating your students to come to class on time or set up some penalties, i.e., loss of points and/or, having student sent to the dean of student's office after three recorded tardy appearances.
2. The class moved too slowly. Step up the pace to keep students interested.
3. Work at generating enthusiasm by modeling and by involving students.
4. In order to check the students understanding I suggest that you make them more a part of the class session by asking them more questions.

Third in-class evaluation notes

Be prepared with an active lecture that takes you away from your overlays and notes. There are several ways to present this material with much more appeal and interest. Student involvement needs to be actively pursued to assess their learning.

What was important on the power point slides? All of it? Parts of it? I was not sure after observing your presentation of so much material.

Review of tests is a good learning device. The review could have been shortened to focus on those questions that were most misunderstood by the largest number of students.

How do your lab assignments relate to where you are in the lecture? Your lab schedule indicates that student labs have little to no relationship and coordination to the lecture material you presented. They should be closely coordinated and outlined in your student syllabus in a much more organized fashion.

Based upon the division chairperson's recent complimentary evaluation, I believe we caught you on a less than fully prepared lecture hour. I will be interested in another classroom visit in the near future and will look for improvements in the areas of concerns documented in this last evaluation document.

Fourth in-class follow-up evaluation notes

The more involvement and participation you can get from the students, the greater their interest will be and the more effort they'll make to learn the material.

Is time being used efficiently in lecture to cover the material required in this course? Your lecture lasted 25 minutes of the 50 minutes scheduled for this class.

It appears to me that this instructor is not making a conscious effort to do the best possible job that he can in teaching his automotive mechanic courses. A quality teaching effort needs to include good preparation and organization, knowing the subject matter thoroughly, involving students in the lecture material, and presenting that material in the best possible manner for student understanding.

You need to make arrangements with your division chairperson to visit experienced faculty members classes in the immediate future.

Fifth in-class follow-up evaluation notes

The first part of this class was a review of questions on the test given the previous week. The review was helpful in clarifying misunderstandings from various questions.

This was a definite improvement over evaluations of the instructor's teaching last year. He has implemented some teaching techniques in his presentation that were suggested at that time. As suggested on previous evaluations, I am still asking that the instructor sits in on lecture classes taught by senior instructors noted for their teaching ability and effectiveness.

Sixth in-class follow-up evaluation notes

The instructor appears to be well versed in the topic of brakes. His students took notes from the overlays projected on the screen. However, the overlays were wordy and not to the point. The instructor apologized twice that he had not updated the overlay being used and commented they were "too wordy." You need to improve your lectures by using brake parts and brake models for demonstration. Some clear overlays with pictures would also clarify and supplement your lecture.

I do not see the improvements in your lecture presentations that was expected by now.

Seventh in-class follow-up evaluation notes

I was disappointed in your lecture. Many of these present suggestions are the same as those made in your previous evaluations:

1. Come to class prepared! Have your transparencies prepared with much less detail. Bring tools and equipment (models, parts, mock-up, etc.) to supplement your lecture material.
2. The class moved too slowly. Try to "speed" things up and make them more interesting through proper planning and organization. You must motivate your students by involving them.
3. Try some new methods in your class.

I did not observe any constructive changes in your teaching methods from last year. There is a lack of making consistent changes over the three-year period. To improve you must work to make the changes we have discussed over the past three years. You need to review carefully and follow-up on the suggestions and directives you have been given through the evaluation process.

Final observation

This instructor tendered his resignation, effective May 30, 20XX. Much effort was put forth during the three-year period trying to assist him in making adequate quality and effective improvements in his preparation, organization and classroom delivery. He showed some threads of improving during his second year but relapsed back to his old bad habits during his third year. The necessary effort to prepare properly for his classes was never evident. This instructor was given the option of resigning or being terminated by the board of trustees. He elected resignation.

MOVING TO A RECOMMENDATION FOR TENURE

A third case involving a non-tenured instructor led to a recommendation for tenure. A total of twelve classroom evaluations were conducted during the three-year probationary period. The following recommendation was prepared for the college president for presentation to the board of trustees for awarding of tenure to a community college art faculty member. It highlights the instructor's strengths in his evaluations over the three-year non-tenure period.

Recommendation from the Division Chair:

During the probationary period this instructor taught courses in the art history sequence, and studio courses in drawing, design, visual communication, life drawing, and painting. His experiences have been broad as he has taught in the extension program, the college prison program, day, and evening, and summer sessions. He has also accommodated the increasing number of art students by assuming some over-load teaching.

Comments from evaluation reviews:

The following excerpts are taken from written evaluations of his supervisors throughout the last three years and attest to the high quality of this instructor's teaching:

1. The instructor presented the material in a clear, well-paced manner. The explanations and descriptions were understandable, and the instructor interacted well with the students. The students were attentive and took notes or responded with questions and comments during the instructor's presentation.

2. There was enough questioning to and by students to maintain an on-going communication and to check on students' understanding.

3. This instructor's course in art history, as represented by this class, was a positive exercise in learning. All discussion and activities were focused on goals indicated in the lesson plan.

4. The instructor's studio class is not an area where students' creative juices flowed forth in an uncontrolled stream; rather, the evaluator observed that students worked carefully under the influence of proven theories and systems relative to this particular art form.

5. New terminology and concepts are introduced and explained well. The instructor demonstrates enthusiasm in the subject matter, and it is obvious that he enjoys teaching.

6. Good study guides and vocabulary lists are prepared and distributed by the instructor to help guide student study. Overall, this was a well-conducted lecture hour.

Summary:

I would describe the commentary from all thirteen of the evaluations of this instructor as noting the progressive improvement of his competence in the classroom and the studio. At this point, in a relatively brief teaching career, he has taken command of his courses organizing the material and presenting it clearly to his students. All activities go forward smoothly and with efficiency.

Throughout his probationary period, this instructor has demonstrated a willingness to work with his students, his colleagues, and his division chair to provide strength and growth in the art program. I am confident that the attainment of tenure will allow him to develop more fully and demonstrate the leadership that the program needs to reach even higher levels of stability and success.

I remain hopeful that you, as a board of trustees, will support this recommendation for a tenure appointment.

ONE EVALUATION SYSTEM: FORMATIVE AND SUMMATIVE OUTCOMES

The three evaluation examples above were drawn from non-tenured faculty evaluation files. These examples are representative of the different kinds of outcomes experienced in an evaluation system with a continuum resulting in both formative and summative outcomes.

These examples provide the reader some samples of evaluators' efforts to motivate teachers to improve the quality of their teaching. They also show the necessity and importance of conducting numerous follow-up in-class evaluations in order to continue the formative process.

The instructors in all three examples were given a full three years of non-tenure evaluation experiences to reach the

---

level of teaching expected by the college administration and board of trustees.

FORMATIVE TO SUMMATIVE: REMEDIATION

What happens when a tenured teacher is evaluated over a period of time and continues to demonstrate deficiencies in his/her teaching and other job responsibilities? When a lack of progress in remediating those deficiencies is documented through follow-up in-class evaluations, the school or college has the option of seeking board action for an official 'notice to remedy.' This is a difficult position for a teacher since this action, in most states, will be taken in an open session of the board.

Formative evaluation, as defined by Licata and Andrews (1990), requires improvement suggestions from evaluators and help for both non-tenured and tenured faculty. These improvement efforts continue throughout the process of administering the "notice to remedy" to a tenured faculty member. An administrator's request to remediate current deficiencies is, in fact, an offer to the faculty member of a last chance opportunity to make the requested improvements and changes in their teaching and other job responsibilities (p. 48).

THE 'NOTICE TO REMEDY'

The fourth example will present what might be said to a teacher in summarizing the problems that will lead to a request for a 'notice to remedy' from the governing board:

> In our meeting in my in office on June 2, 2003, I summarized and clarified the severity of our concerns about your classroom teaching and overall job performance.

The evaluators presented you with major concerns relative to your teaching in the two courses in which we recently evaluated your performance:

1. In the morning class you showed little rapport and minimal communication with the students. While you indicated that this was possibly a very poor group to work with, out observations of them in other classes in the program showed them to be a very responsive group.
2. Your failure to produce an updated, meaningful, and completed course syllabus for this course was inexcusable after having over a two-year period in which to prepare it. This was a prime example of your lack of preparation and organization.

In your afternoon science course the following observations were made by the division chairperson and myself:

1. Students arrived in this class without any expectation of needing to take notes. Note pads were not even brought to the class.
2. You gave no review of previous lecture material, asked for few or no responses from the students in the class, and completed the hour without announcing an assignment for the next class period.

You told us much of your testing comes directly out of the textbook. I suggested that you needed to make key points in your lecture and have students be responsible for this material on tests. It is possible, under your testing system, for a student to be absent from your lecture classes and not miss out on any material that will be found on your exams.

Significant changes must be made to demonstrate that you can bring your instruction and related job functions up to the level expected and asked for in your recent evaluations. These changes include improving your organization, your communications with students, and updating your course materials to meet the level of our expectations at this institution.

We will, in the meantime, recommend that the governing board, at their June 20, 2003, meeting formally issue you a letter of remediation for the defects and deficiencies that have been cited to you over the past twelve-month period. The board is very concerned with inadequate teaching performances and expects faculty here to continue the tradition of high quality instruction. A vote on the "notice to remedy" will be taken in the open session of the board meeting.

It should be obvious to the reader that this is a serious step to take in a comprehensive evaluation program. Where does formative evaluation end and summative evaluation toward termination begin? Licata and Andrews (1990) argued that formative evaluation efforts should continue through a time period that is considered reasonable for a teacher needing to make improvements. If, after a three-year probationary non-tenure period, progress is still lacking, it becomes imperative for the administrators to move toward a summative decision of termination.

The ripple effect of this action will be felt throughout the institution. Teachers identified as needing to make improvements will see the institution is serious about making improvements in its teaching. The action may also provide an incentive to those teachers, who have been accustomed to "just getting by," to work for improvement. The message that *quality is expected in all classrooms* should become the driving force for the institution's faculty, administrators and governing board members.

SUMMARY

Formative and summative evaluation have traditionally described the type of outcomes expected from a teacher evalu-

---

ation system. Formative evaluation has been considered as the attempt to improve teaching while summative has been used to describe the type of decisions that are made relative to continued employment, tenure, salary, probation and termination.

Some writers have argued that there is an inherent conflict between the two functions as outcomes of a single evaluation process. Licata and Andrews argue, however, that the two functions are not mutually exclusive. They described the evaluation process as being part of a continuum of formative actions and suggestions for improvement that may become part of needed summative outcomes and decisions. They further included the process of remediation as being part of the continuing process of formative evaluation assistance. During remediation teachers are still being offered assistance and suggestions to improve their teaching prior to any decision to be removed from remediation and to being terminated.

This chapter presented four examples of the use of formative and summative evaluation. Praise and positive reinforcement were given when improvements were observed, and when the teachers made progress in those areas needing improvements. Each of the cases led to a different outcome. In the first case, the teacher was documented making significant progress throughout her three-year non-tenured period, and raising her teaching to the level expected by the institution. She was recommended for tenure at the end of the three-year probationary period.

The teacher in the second example was documented as continuing his pattern of inadequate preparation and using poor teaching techniques and processes over the three-year probationary period. It was the decision of the administrative supervisors that this teacher's behaviors proved to be irremediable, and he was asked to resign or be terminated by the board of trustees.

The third example summarized a series of classroom evaluations leading to a recommendation for tenure of an art teacher. The fourth example showed how an administrative request for remedial action was used to give a tenured teacher a final opportunity to make the required improvements before a formal "notice to dismiss" was sought.

SUGGESTED EXERCISES

1. There is an assumption that defining quality teaching and using it as the foundation in an evaluation system can improve instruction. How might this happen?
2. Discuss how a notice to remedy can be considered as formative evaluation.

CHAPTER 8

RECOGNITION: A NEED UNFULFILLED!

> Teachers who elicit academic gains from their students are not rewarded for their achievements. Most teachers are hard working and doing the best they can, but in the absence of incentives to improve, additional resources are not directed to maximizing student output.
>
> *Hanushek, (2002), p. 1*

Giving special recognition for outstanding teaching efforts should be an easy task. Wrong! It has been documented that this is not the situation across the country.

An editorial in the Chicago Tribune (2001, October 1) lauded the rewarding of modest $300 bonuses in the suburb of North Chicago to teachers based upon performance. The editor expressed pleasure that the faculty union was supportive of the plan. He used the term "no-brainer" to highlight the fact that outstanding teachers need to be recognized more than mediocre ones (p. 10, Section 1).

The practice of giving special recognition and rewards to faculty for outstanding work in the field of education continues to be neglected. In addition, there are few studies assessing what recognition practices are being utilized and to what extent. There is, however, evidence that teachers in all levels of education feel neglected when it comes to receiving recognition for outstanding teaching as well as performance in other job responsibilities.

Recognition for outstanding teachers should be a part of

---

every community college and every elementary, middle and secondary school's process of improving instruction. This is far from the case, however.

Andrews and Erwin (2003) found administrators reporting that only approximately 55 percent of the community colleges in their national study have faculty recognition programs. In addition, only 19 percent reported recognition programs for part-time faculty.

REVITALIZING AND MOTIVATING TEACHERS

During the course of a teaching career, faculty members need to be "revitalized" to keep them up-to-date and motivated. Taking additional course work, travel, sabbatical leaves, and recognition for work that is appreciated by the college and board of trustees or board of education are some of the ways to achieve revitalization.

"Revitalizing" appears to be the key word in the faculty members' reactions to receiving recognition for a job well done. Andrews (1987a) had several faculty recognition award winners, from a survey of 31, use the word 'revitalize' in expressing their reaction to their recognition. One teacher commented:

> I believe support from colleagues and supervisors is vital if one is to 'revitalize.' Encouragement from others adds to one's sense of value to an organization and its members. Often times it is the word of praise or encouragement that is more motivating than financial rewards (p. 2).

A second response spoke to how recognition can keep teachers motivated and keep them from 'burnout' in their work:

In the most self-actualized moments, one feels, 'I don't care what others think, I know this is good and I'll continue to give my all.' Many of us can work with that attitude, but only for a period of time. Lack of recognition - - emotional, financial, etc. - - eventually evokes 'burnout' from very talented and conscientious individuals. The small doses of sincere recognition along the way keeps one interested and eager to continue to improve oneself and the institution (p. 2).

This instructor's response followed a personal merit recognition she had received for the first time after having taught for over 20 years. The college's recognition program had been recently instituted.

It is important for evaluation systems to accurately discriminate between exceptional and poorer performances of faculty members, according to Cashin (1996). He also pointed out that faculty must feel that these discriminations are accurate and that the results must go to those considered more effective, in terms of rewards, from those deemed ineffective (p. 5).

Weld (1999) focused his doctoral dissertation research on the effects monetary awards had on science teachers. He conducted numerous interviews and received hundreds of completed questionnaires. The two groups he studied were (1) those teachers who had been granted monetary awards and (2) those science teachers who had not been granted any such awards.

Winners had won recognition awards ranging from $25 to $1,000. Weld found that most of them were motivated to continue their teaching until retirement years. One winner made the following comment:

Winning the award was a boost to my self-esteem. Instead of feeling burnt out, it provided me a much-needed motivation. It was great to know that you are doing something right (p. 2).

Winners were supportive because they saw this as a way to enhance the teaching profession, highlight successful teaching practices, while also projecting a positive image to the public. There was a mixture of resentment as well as support among non-recipients.

Some of the negative aspects of these awards came from teachers who felt themselves to be doing an excellent job but who had not won a recognition award. These responses point to the need to have an ongoing program so other excellent teachers will subsequently be recognized.

In a random national sampling, Weld found non-recipients to be supportive of the idea that they might someday be awarded such an honor. They did, however, have some doubt about the chances of this happening.

A review of the literature on faculty awards by Frase and Piland (1989) pointed to the use of such rewards for motivational purposes. They cited studies and articles by Cohen and Brawer (1982), Baker and Prugh (1988), Andrews and Marzano (1983), and Filan, Okun, and Witter (1986), as centering on the motivational value of faculty rewards (p. 25).

MONEY: IS IT A MOTIVATOR FOR TEACHERS?

In studying merit pay programs for teachers Deci (1976) concluded that merit pay, as an incentive for teachers may be ineffective. He summarized that money, as the major incentive in trying to improve teaching, is likely to fail no matter how well such a program is designed by the school district. His research findings led him to the following conclusions:

1. Positive feedback can, under certain circumstances, increase intrinsic motivation (one's feeling about his/her own competence and effectiveness).

2. Schools could adopt merit praise plans. Such a plan recognizes that intrinsic satisfactions cannot be manipulated by material rewards, but can be complemented by the right kind of feedback;

3. Superior teachers should be rewarded with various types of praises and recognition. Evaluations should be descriptive rather than judgmental, focusing on what teachers do rather than how one teacher's performance compares with that of another;

4. All teachers should be provided with honest, positive feedback about their accomplishments in the classroom. If this is done properly, it can increase each teacher's sense of satisfaction about the kind of job he or she is doing (61-72).

The focus of Deci's suggestions is on the "intrinsic satisfactions" that teachers seek. A main sense of satisfaction comes from helping their students to learn. The recognition system he proposes can motivate teachers by appealing to their "intrinsic satisfactions" as opposed to a merit pay system that is driven by pay increase incentives.

Frase and Piland (1989) found that the altruistic motive "to help others learn" was prevalent at all levels of entry into the teaching profession. They summarized a large number of studies and concluded that "the intrinsic drive to help others learn has repeatedly been shown to be the primary motive" (p. 25). These researchers also pointed out how, even though research results and empirical evidence have consistently pointed to intrinsic incentives as being the most effective motivators for teachers, the 1980's reform movement turned to financial incentives to try to effect change. Career ladders and merit pay were the two largest changes sought, and Frase and Piland felt it should have been predicable that they both would fail.

Some merit pay myths

Dunwell (1986), in his position paper, listed five myths about merit pay that are widely believed:

Myth 1: "Teachers favor merit pay."

This statement contrasts with a number of findings in other studies and surveys. Teachers have been found to favor rewards other than merit pay.

Myth 2: "Money is a motivator—more money produces more work."

Research studies did not support this. Money was found to motivate some people whose salaries were below market value, in some circumstances.

Myth 3: "Merit pay will persuade highly qualified people to enter teaching."

There is no research to support this. Teachers do not enter into teaching primarily to make money. On the other hand, money is a "dissatisfier." Many people do leave teaching because of low salaries.

Myth 4: "Merit pay promotes competition and competition promotes excellence."

The paper asserted that competition will not necessarily promote excellence but cooperation probably will.

Myth 5: "Motivating teachers is a simple matter of offering an extrinsic reward."

The researcher documented that motivational needs vary from one individual to another. Merit pay can actually depress the intrinsic motivation of some teachers (pp.7-21).

The NEA position on merit pay

In a *National Association of Secondary School Principals(NASSP) Bulletin* (1986) interview with Mary Futrell, who was president of the National Education Association, Futrell addressed the issues of the newly created career ladder program options and merit pay systems:

> Teachers are rather apprehensive about differentiated staffing plans. They are opposed to merit pay systems, but are seemingly more willing to look at career ladders. Again, I think that implementing a plan like that requires working with teachers.
>
> We oppose merit pay because it has not worked and is discriminating. Let's face reality—the teaching profession is similar to other professions. We have some people who do an outstanding job. We have a few who are not doing a good job. The bulk of people are in the middle. The profession is made up of a solid core of people who are doing a good job. If I am one of those teachers doing a good job, are you going to say to me that I don't get a pay raise?
>
> We propose that everybody be given a pay raise so that the teaching profession can compete with other professions. Some people will say, 'What about the people who are not doing a good job?' Let's go back to our discussion of evaluation procedures that enable everyone to grow professionally. For the few who are not doing a good job, you use the summative evaluation to say either you shape up or you ship out. You protect their due process rights, but if they don't improve, a procedure for removal should be started (pp. 59-60).

Futrell clearly articulated the NEA's stand on merit pay. In addition, this stand provided support for administrators in their need to improve instruction through evaluation as well as by suggesting that administrators should move toward removal when it is necessary. It was clearly pointed out that such action would be acceptable as long as the due-process rights of the teachers are respected.

Lewis (2000) reported on the Douglas County, Colorado, schools' pay for performance plan. Teachers and persons from the community and businesses were included in the development of the plan. The superintendent cited a "key factor" was the involvement of the Douglas County Federation of Teachers. The two elements necessary in this plan were teacher appraisal and the district's goals. If teachers were rated by the principals as outstanding, a one-time bonus was to be awarded. If rated proficient, regular pay increases would be given, and if rated unsatisfactory the person's pay would be frozen.

It is possible for all the Douglas County teachers in any of their schools to receive a bonus if the individual school's goal of improving student achievement is met. Long-range follow-up will be needed to document the success of this program.

Some strong motivators (other than money)

Scherer (1983) summarized faculty needs in his research at Teachers College, Columbia University. He studied why veteran teachers had positive feelings about their teaching jobs. In order of importance they were as follows:

1. Receiving respect;
2. Receiving recognition;
3. Receiving reinforcement;
4. Participating in research studies;
5. Being a member of a teaching team;
6. Earning grants for curriculum development;
7. Being encouraged by principals, parents, colleagues, and students (pp. 22-25).

The research concluded that merit pay was not effective as a motivator in education.

MOTIVATIONAL THEORIES

One should be able to conclude, after several decades of developing motivational theories and testing such theories through empirical investigations, that educators would know specifically which rewards reinforce teachers' behavior and provide them with the desire to continue to improve and become master teachers. This does not appear to be the case in the majority of elementary, middle, or secondary schools and community college districts.

Abraham Maslow and Frederick Herzberg, theorists of the Human Potential Movement, are often cited in educational and psychological literature. In moving from theory to practice, a major concern of educational leaders is identifying the conditions that will motivate individual teachers to achieve excellence in instruction. Both Maslow (1954) and Herzberg (1966) perceive motivation as essentially an internally driven force in individuals. Maslow has identified the "need for self-actualization" as being the internal drive that one uses to strive to be the best one might become.

Maslow (1954) described a "hierarchy of human needs", which he sees as necessary in understanding human behavior. The basic needs of humans have to be satisfied first before the higher level needs, such as working toward excellence and self-actualization, can be met. These basic requirements are described as survival needs, which include adequate pay to secure the essentials of living. He sees this as the most primary concern of workers. Once this first-level need is addressed satisfactorily, the second level, which includes job security and safety, can be secured. The third level includes seeking to establish a congenial work group and to have the feeling of being needed. Once satisfied on all three of the

---

above levels, an individual is free to focus on fulfilling the higher-level needs of esteem, recognition, and self-actualization (pp. 105-107).

Herzberg's (1966) theory of worker motivation is based on two different levels of motivators. His Motivation-Hygiene Theory point to two sets of factors as being paramount in influencing workers' morale. The 'hygiene' factors within a work environment include: (1) pay, (2) working conditions, (3) relations with co-workers, (4) competence of supervisors, and (5) company policies. These can be compared to Maslow's lower level or basic needs. These must be adequately addressed, according to Herzberg, in order to prevent worker dissatisfaction. Even if these are met, he points out, it may not be enough to insure a worker being highly motivated. He addresses this concern with what he refers to as "motivation" factors, which also must be satisfied. These factors include: (1) achievement, (2) responsibility or autonomy, (3) recognition, (4) opportunities for advancement, and (5) enjoyable and challenging work-assignments (p. 266). One can see how these later factors relate closely to the higher-level needs in Maslow's theory.

Steinmetz (1979) showed how both theories proposed a two-stage approach to motivation: first, adequately satisfying basic levels of human needs leads to the possibility of freedom; second, fulfilling the higher-level needs that can unleash greater productivity and the striving for excellence.

APPLICATION OF MOTIVATIONAL THEORIES

Moving toward a practical implementation of these two theories, first, one must see if indeed the basic needs of faculty are being met. Questions such as, "Is the salary adequate?" "Does the working environment produce a feeling of trust between teachers, and between teachers and administrators?"

and "Are administrators honest and competent?" all need to be addressed and answered. An inventory needs to be taken to see if there are adequate "hygiene" factors in the institution.

Next, there needs to be individual motivation towards excellence, self-improvement, and providing a better climate for student productivity. In this case both Maslow and Herzberg identified esteem and recognition as important motivational factors. This places the burden on governing boards and administrators to provide an institutional climate that leads teachers to excel and have their higher level needs met. Educational institutions that provide formal recognition and rewards for excellence in teaching will be creating the proper condition for fostering and promoting motivation in their teachers.

A NATIONAL STUDY OF RECOGNITION PRACTICES

A national survey of community college chief instructional administrators was conducted by Andrews and Erwin (2003). The chief instructional administrators responded to several questions relative to recognition programs on their campuses:

1. Does your institution have a recognition program for full-time faculty?

   Yes: 353   No: 280

The "yes" responses of 353 represented 55.7 percent, while 44.3 percent of the colleges reported having no plan in place.

2. Does your institution have a recognition program for part-time faculty?

Yes: 92   No: 290

Only 19 percent reported recognition programs for part-time faculty with 81 percent of the responding colleges having no recognition programs for the same group.

In an earlier study Erwin and Andrews (1993) surveyed recognition programs for the part-time faculty in the North Central Association region (19 states) and found 33 of the 250 responding colleges had recognition for part-time faculty. This was only 13.2 percent as compared to the present study showing 19 percent.

Success and acceptance

The administrators in the 2003 study were asked the following question relative to success and acceptance of their recognition systems:

3. Is your recognition program successful and accepted by your faculty?

Yes: 284 (89%)   No: 35(11%)

The overwhelming response was "yes." This was interpreted to mean that the large majority of recognition programs had meaning for the faculty. This response spoke to programs that have been developed with support of both faculty and administration groups and are considered fair in their administration.

Types of recognition

The follow questions were asked about the components involved in the recognition programs:

4.   What are the components of your recognition program?

Component	Number of Responses
Plaque	240
Monetary Award	228
Special Occasion	200
Special Travel Monies	73
Equipment for Classroom	14
Supplies for Classroom	14

It became obvious that plaques, small to medium monetary awards and "special occasions" such as a supper, recognition at a board meeting, etc., were by far the types of recognition most often awarded teachers.

5.   What is the amount of your monetary award?

Amount	Number of Responses
$ 1,000	43
$ 500	30
$ 2,500	8
$ 1,500	8
$ 2,000	6
$ 5,000	4

The awards of $1,000 and $500 dominated the amounts of the recognition stipends. Faculty unions have, over the years, been much more receptive to these one-time recognition awards than to merit pay plans.

---

6. How many awards in a year are given?

Number of Respondents	Number of Awards
60	1
14	2
19	3
7	1-2
5	3-5
5	5-10
4	2-4

By far the largest number of colleges awarded grants to only one teacher in any given year. This was a major and highly disappointing finding. When there are large numbers of faculty who are considered outstanding in some school systems, it would seem like a pretty remote possibilty to be one of those recognized when only one award per year being granted.

DEVELOPING A RECOGNITION SYSTEM

Administrators and faculty need to cooperate in developing a recognition system. Both parties need to discuss and agree upon the major tenants of such a plan within each school system. McMillen (1984) suggested that if a recognition system is to work well, first there must be agreement on what constitutes meritorious performance in teaching. Second, there must be a mechanism to appraise what has been agreed upon. It helps if both parties understand that there are these two distinct elements to a system. Agreement needs to be reached on the desired outcomes and the theoretical base of such a plan. The emphasis can then shift to deciding on a reward system that will be acceptable to both parties and that will meet the higher-level needs of esteem and recognition. Meeting these needs should provide the motivational factors necessary for obtaining and maintaining a high level of teacher performance and student outcomes (p. 27).

Cheshire and Hagemeyer (1981-82) suggest that a successful recognition system must have the following three elements: First is faculty and administration identification and agreement to what they consider criteria for outstanding job performances. The second component is the development of a fair, objective, and effective system of evaluating the job performances of faculty. The third component is the stipulation of the actual award.

It is clear that developing a recognition system is no easy task and has several complex features. With such uniqueness in American educational systems, whether at the elementary, middle and secondary schools, or at the community college level, it would be naive to suggest there is one best system of recognition. Rather, each institution needs to make an assessment of the "motivational" factors of achievement, responsibility, recognition, etc., presently at play within the school or district, adopt an appropriate theory, and apply it in developing a recognition system. It is only after these factors are determined that a recognition plan will have a chance of success. Follow-up surveys of the recognition recipients need to be conducted at a later date to see if, indeed, the system is working as planned.

PUTTING THE SYSTEM INTO PRACTICE

The recognizing of excellence in the teaching profession is a complicated process. Sbaratta (1983) said that encouraging teachers to strive for excellence is, "maybe the most critical task," but "rewarding excellence is the trickiest" (p. 27).

Frase et al. (1982) stated that it is crucial to have "competent administrators who are capable of identifying excellent teaching" (p. 266). They also point out that principals are legally responsible to carry out the evaluation.

Two institutions that put recognition systems into practice were the Catalina Foothills School District in Tucson, Arizona, and Illinois Valley Community College in Oglesby, Illinois (Frase et al., 1982b; Andrews, 1988a). Both systems saw their programs as alternatives to merit pay. Both systems included faculty evaluation and offered positive feedback for excellence in teaching. Both systems also relied heavily on Herzberg's Motivation-Hygiene theory.

The Program for Excellence was Catalina district's reward system for excellent teaching. It drew upon Herzberg's theory in that it attempted to identify those factors that motivate people to achieve high level of performance. It identified achievement, recognition for achievement, intrinsic interest in the work, and meeting growth and advancement needs of its faculty. This system depended upon a reliance and trust that the administrators were competent and capable of identifying excellent teaching within the district. Catalina recognized its principals as also being legally responsible for the evaluation of instruction (pp. 266-267).

The recognition system at Illinois Valley Community College paralleled the Catalina system. It provided recognition of outstanding teaching and excellence in overall job responsibilities and was based upon an in-class evaluation system administered by instructional administrators. It also placed strong emphasis on competence in classroom instruction.

Both of these systems, in addition to drawing much of their philosophical basis from Herzberg, also drew from Maslow in recognizing that the lower- level needs of their faculty must be met before launching into a program of recognition. Adequate base pay, a professional work environment, and trust between faculty and administration are fac-

TABLE 5: Summary of Faculty Reaction to Recognition for Excellence Reward Programs at Catalina Foothills School District and Illinois Valley Community College

Faculty Responses to Objectives	Catalina Foothills N = 27		Illinois Valley C.C. N = 31	
	YES	NO	YES	NO
1. Teachers receiving awards view the recompense as special recognition for teaching excellence.	24	3	31	0
2. Faculty members who have received the rewards are motivated to continue to excel.	21	6	30	0
3. Teachers receiving awards value highly the recognition they received.	22	5	30	0
4. Faculty receiving awards believe they will continue to receive special recognition if they continue excellent teaching.	19	8	21	8
5. The merit recognition system is viewed as an outcome of the faculty evaluation at IVCC.	—	—	22	7
6. The faculty view the evaluation system as "fair."	—	—	23	5
7. Is the 'publicized' system the college uses preferred to a secret reward system?	—	—	29	1
8. The college should continue to recognize outstanding faculty performances with a merit recognition system.	—	—	31	0

tors both programs felt had been met prior to the implementation of their recognition programs.

DOES RECOGNITION WORK? ASK THE FACULTY

Do recognition programs achieve their intended goal of satisfying the higher-level needs of the faculty? Do faculty feel that they will continue to be motivated to provide quality instruction? These were some of the questions Frase et al. (1982b) asked the faculty in the 'Program for Excellence' in the Catalina Foothills School District. Andrews asked similar questions of the faculty who had received merit recognition at Illinois Valley Community College. The results of both surveys are summarized and presented in Table 5 above.

Both groups of teachers overwhelmingly accepted their rewards as the schools had intended, that is, as special recognition for teaching excellence. Both teacher groups also felt that receiving the rewards motivated them to continue to excel, and that they highly valued the recognition they received. There were, however, doubts in both groups when asked if they expected the recognition to continue if they continue excellent teaching.

Several additional questions were asked only of the college faculty. Over 75 percent of the faculty saw the recognition as an outcome of the college's evaluation system. An even higher percentage reported that they felt the evaluation system was 'fair.' All but one of the 30 respondents preferred that the college continue to publicly announce the recognition winners. All 31 respondents said 'yes' to the question of continuing formal recognition of outstanding faculty performances.

Non-monetary rewards as motivators

Early in the developmental stages of the recognition program it was decided that the Catalina district rewards must conform to Herzberg's theory. Frase et al. (1982a) stated that the district expects each recognition award should be an experience or reward that the teacher values highly. It should also affect the work content or the "teacher's ability to assist children in the classroom" (p. 267).

Herzberg's theory stated money is a motivator only in meeting a lower level need and can, in fact, become a 'hygiene' factor (or dissatisfier). It was with this in mind that the Catalina district focused on rewards other than merit pay as motivators. Some of the rewards given to teachers were: (1) attendance at professional conferences held outside the state; (2) computers; and (3) classroom instructional or enrichment materials.

Responses from reward recipients and non-recipients

There was a second-stage evaluation conducted at the Catalina school district, which included six of the recipients in the program, and six faculty who were not recipients. The following were studied.

1. Importance: Are the rewards valued?
    "Yes," was the reply, and attendance at conferences was highly rated. Money as a reward was the least valued by both the recipients and non-recipients. Both groups saw it as being a non-professional reward.

2. Flexibility: Can the reward be individualized?

    This brought a strong positive response; both groups saw their system as giving adequate flexibility.

3. Visibility: Is a secret reward system preferred to a publicized one?

    This brought a mixed response. There was some feeling the non-recipients would feel hurt, while others felt it was fine to publicize the names.

4. Frequency: How often can rewards be given?

    One award was provided an individual in any one school year. It appeared that the same teachers could receive additional awards in subsequent years.

5. Cost: How much does the program cost?

    The district considered the outlay small but very beneficial (p. 258).

The Catalina study concluded that the Program for Excellence did indeed accomplish its goal in recognizing and motivating their best teachers. It also appeared to influence other teachers in the system as a secondary benefit. A third conclusion was that Herzberg's Motivational-Hygiene Theory provides an adequate foundation for a program designed to reward excellence in teaching.

Faculty mandate for merit recognition

The Illinois Valley Community College rewards began as a publicly announced award, which included a plaque and a one-time $500 check. Recipients were later selected to attend national master teacher conferences or state and national meetings in their fields. Being honored at a regular board meeting with the board of trustees was an additional means of providing public recognition. Table 5 showed that the publicized part of the program was strongly favored with a 29 to 1 response. Recipients replied "yes" with a 31 to 0 response, when asked whether the college should continue to recognize outstanding faculty performance with the recognition program. With such a mandate one might reasonably conclude that the recognition program was indeed meeting the motivational needs, postulated by Herzberg, of the Illinois Valley faculty.

CASES OF PEER REJECTION

In a few cases it had been reported that recognition for some teachers has resulted in negative reaction from peer teachers and administrators (McCormick 1986). This negative reaction was described as an attempt to reject or "punish" the teacher, especially when it came from the principal or another supervisor. In one case an outstanding teacher who gained national recognition for her ability to encourage children to write was "stunned" by her peers' reaction to her success. She did not receive one positive reaction within the system to her success, even though she had been in the system for 20 years. Another teacher reported that a teacher friend said her colleagues stopped speaking to her after being named a finalist in the New York Teacher of the Year program. McCormick concluded: "The message is clear: Do meritorious work and you risk being misused by administrators and ignored by colleagues—or worse" (p. 14).

Another case involved a teacher who was asked by the State Department of Education to give two workshops. The teacher said, "Even the most adversarial administrator will have to be pleased about this. I mean, the State Department of Education! And it's only 17 miles away, so I'd be crossing no frontiers." After her request for leave was denied, she addressed her concern with the superintendent. She was granted one day of leave—if she paid for the substitute teacher. No one ever offered a "congratulations."

McCormick concluded that it is no wonder we have had mediocrity in our schools because "it is the only road to professional survival" (p. 15). Such examples, although rarely reported, do have a chilling effect on the teaching profession. Administrators must be sensitive to these possible reactions and work to provide an environment that stimulates recognition and growth for all faculty. There is much at stake. Allowing faculty to be thwarted in their desire for excellence, due to lack of attention and/or rejection by peers and supervisors, can cause the institution to sink into or to continue in mediocrity.

RECOGNITION PROGRAMS GROWTH

The State of Virginia established $5,000 recognition awards for faculty in both public and private colleges. They are awarded to faculty based upon their "outstanding teaching, research, and public service" (Chronicle of Higher Education, 1987). Thirteen faculty, of 108 who were nominated during the first year, received the awards. "It's a great award. I feel the many years I've put into this have paid off," stated Daisy B. Campbell, a teacher of English at Southwest Virginia Community College (p. 16).

A major finding in a 1991 study of recognition programs in two-year colleges in the 19-state North Central Association (Andrews 1993) was a significant increase in colleges moving to recognize outstanding faculty. The results of this study were compared to a previous study in 1984 of the same two-year colleges by Andrews (1987c).

A total of 166 of the 278 colleges in the 1991 study reported they had recognition programs for faculty. This was an increase of 111 colleges when compared to the 55 colleges reporting recognition programs in the 1984 study. These numbers represented 60 percent of the colleges having recognition programs in 1991 compared to 20.1 percent in the earlier study.

The states showing the greatest number of increases were Illinois (+21), Michigan and Colorado (+11), Wisconsin (+10), Arizona (+8), Minnesota (+ 7) and Ohio and Missouri (+6). Seventeen of the 19 states in the study reported increases in college faculty recognition programs between the 1984 and the 1991 studies. Most of the recognition programs in community colleges were reported to have been in place fewer than 10 years.

SUMMARY

Teacher recognition programs continue to be absent in many schools and colleges. Teachers often find that their efforts and outstanding performance go unrecognized. Teachers who have received merit recognition rewards say that the awards have had a revitalizing effect on them and rescued them from becoming "burned out."

What motivates teachers? Contrary to popular myth, merit pay is very low on the list, if it appears at all. Administrators, teachers, and faculty unions have not favored merit pay as the answer as to how to reward outstanding faculty. According to the motivational theorists of the Human Potential Movement, money may well become a "dissatisfier." The "intrinsic" motivators are professional recognition, esteem, challenge, and autonomy.

It is important for boards and administrators to be sure that basic-level needs, including adequate pay, a congenial work environment, and an atmosphere of trust have been satisfied. Once these needs have been met, the recognition system has a chance of success. The important steps in developing a recognition system are: (1) agreeing on the definition of excellent teaching; (2) establishing a fair and objective system to evaluate teacher performance; and (3) deciding on the type of awards to give.

There is evidence that using recognition to motivate teachers can work to improve instruction. Those teachers who have received recognition awards have said that they value the recognition they received, and both reward recipients and non-recipients say that such recognition programs act to motivate them to excel. There have been cases, however, of some meritorious teachers who, having been recognized for their outstanding performance, found themselves rejected by their peers. If administrators don't move quickly to strongly discourage this sort of behavior, it will surely stifle the drive for excellence and sanction mediocrity.

There has been a significant increase in the use of recognition programs. One of the most discouraging factors from the research presented was that the majority of the community colleges reporting recognition programs for their faculty had only one such recognition award a year. Many more excellent teachers need the opportunity to receive this type of recognition.

The use of recognition as a motivator for improving instruction is gaining in popularity and is becoming much better accepted as an alternative to merit pay systems. There are, however, schools and colleges needing to consider such programs for their highest performing teachers.

SUGGESTED EXERCISES

1. Why should governing boards consider recognition programs for their outstanding teachers?
2. Why do teachers find recognition awards to be acceptable and how important will they be in the No Child Left Behind movement?

CHAPTER 9

TYPES OF RECOGNITION PLANS

> Develop a system that will reward and honor good teachers. Given the job they do, these teachers deserve as much praise, thanks, and honor as any American citizen.
>
> *Hanushek, (2002), p. x.*

Quality teaching performance has been defined as meritorious performance (Teacher Evaluation Kit Glossary, 2003), and as "a level of performance that well exceeds the standard for [what is] minimally acceptable, and that may be worthy of professional recognition, career ladder advancement, or merit pay" (p. 19).

OBJECTIVES FOR RECOGNITION PROGRAMS

One of the main objectives in implementing a recognition program is to encourage and then reward excellence in teaching. Another objective may be to comply with mandates for recognition by the state governing board, board of trustees, board of education, superintendent, president or chancellor, or the faculty contract.

Hanushek (2002) focused on having the government provide incentives for teachers who are doing the job effectively. His recommendation was that, "if one is concerned about student performance, one should gear policy to student performance" (p. 8). In short, recognize what teachers achieve with the students they teach.

Dr. Eugene Hickok (2002) was Pennsylvania's Secretary of Education for a six-year period. He worked to improve choices for students in failing school districts and to entice school districts to develop better student outcome plans with rewards for teachers who were improving student performances (p. 30).

Andrews (1993) listed a number of influences that have led community colleges in the North Central Association's 19-state region to initiate faculty recognition programs (See Table 6). The number one response, listed by 45 colleges, was the "desire to recognize extra efforts and excellence." The second, third, fourth, and fifth influences listed by far fewer colleges were: (1) legislative mandate or state governing board; (2) board of trustees (local); (3) president or chancellor; and (4) a desire to improve teaching quality within the college (p. 55).

Table 6: Summary of Influences on Colleges to Initiate a *Faculty Recognition* Program

	Influence	Number of Responses
1.	Desire to recognize extra efforts and excellence	45
2.	Legislative mandate or state governing board	16
3.	Board of trustees (local)	13
4.	President / Chancellor	11
5.	Desire to improve teaching quality	9
6.	Faculty	7
7.	Others: Faculty morale, faculty-administration-board committee, basic need for recognition, grant to college, negotiated into contract, long-range plan, and consortium of local colleges	16

The National School Boards Association (NSBA) (1987) concluded that existing pay structures didn't give outstanding teachers any special incentives or rewards. Those teachers working the hardest were not differentiated from those who were doing the least amount of work (p. 9). The NSBA suggested that a major challenge exists in motivating those many faculty presently in the system to become better teachers. Boyer (1983) observed, "Whatever is wrong with America's public schools cannot be fixed without the help of those teachers already in the classrooms. Most of them will be there for years to come, and such teachers must be viewed as part of the solution, not the problem (pp. 154-55)." The NSBA summarized that school boards nationally have always supported good teaching and good teachers. They also saw the need for boards to continue that support and to offer recognition and incentive programs, based on strong evaluation processes, as ways to improve teaching and the image of teachers.

DESIRED OUTCOMES

The main concept of a teacher recognition program is that rewarding excellence in teaching should produce desired outcomes, such as increased motivation and improved instruction. In the workshops on recognizing quality instruction mentioned earlier (Andrews 1988b), over 140 Central Illinois elementary and secondary school superintendents and principals were asked to identify the quality outcomes their schools might achieve from a teacher recognition program. The following are some of the potential outcomes these administrators agreed upon:

1. Positive public relations for the school;
2. Faculty motivation;
3. Maintenance and reinforcement of quality teaching;

4. Increased feeling of ownership in the school;
5. Improved teacher performance and, thus, student performance;
6. Improved image of teaching profession in eyes of students;
7. Improved morale, improved instruction;
8. New and creative efforts;
9. Higher quality students entering the teaching profession;
10. Retention of talented teachers in your district;
11. Excellent instruction promoted in the school;
12. Decrease in marginal teaching;
13. Enhanced teaching climate;
14. Rewards that provide a milestone in professional growth;
15. Overall instructional improvement by students and staff.

These responses were summarized in the following categories to identify the benefits of a teacher recognition program: (1) improvement in the quality of teaching; (2) improvement of the teaching environment for teachers; (3) improved public image of the teaching profession and schools; and (4) a caring attitude toward faculty to let them know that outstanding teaching performances do not go unnoticed by administrators and governing boards.

HOW TO MAKE THE PROGRAM WORK

How do administrators and faculty prepare a school or college district to accept a faculty recognition program? First, there needs to be an understanding of the motivational or human potential theories, such as those of Maslow and Herzberg identified in the preceding chapter. The governing board of a school or college needs to be appraised of how recognition programs can and should lead to improved instruction. At the same time there must be an evaluation system with one of its goals being a recognition program for the most outstanding faculty within the school or college.

Importance of establishing values

Andrews (2000a) pointed out that governing boards should first agree on the educational philosophy that will underlie their recognition programs. Clarifying values for an elementary, middle, secondary school or college provides a framework for developing quality control in teaching. Some suggested values, and a plan to implement them, are listed below:

Value 1:

The Governing Board values quality teaching in every classroom.

Plan to Implement Value:

A plan of evaluation will be developed to guarantee that quality instruction exists in all classrooms:

A. A plan for classroom evaluations will be developed.
B. All teachers will be informed concerning their performance.
C. Good teachers will receive appropriate positive feedback.
D. Average teachers will be given suggestions for improving.
E. Poor teachers will be given specific directions for immediate improvement efforts.

Value 2:

The Governing Board values individual development needs of its teachers.

Plan:

The administration, working with the teacher organization and individual teachers, will support faculty growth opportunities.

A. Teachers will receive reasonable financial support to attend appropriate professional meetings and conferences.

B. Teachers will be encouraged and sometimes directed to attend specific types of training. "Directed" opportunities will be developed with persons who have a less than satisfactory job performance or lack of subject matter background as cited through evaluation and the No Child Left Behind legislation.

C. Curriculum development or improvement projects, and other well-defined job-related growth opportunities, will be supported.

Value 3:

The Governing Board supports a recognition program for outstanding teacher and administrative accomplishments.

Plan:

The administration will recommend a recognition plan that will include the following:

A. Recognition for outstanding efforts by teachers in the classroom as determined through the school's in-class evaluation program.

B. Recognition for outstanding efforts by teachers in other areas of the job performance, such as student outcomes, curriculum development, student club experiences, and work with business, industry, or social agencies (pp. 28-29).

The above set of values places the recognition program within the framework of faculty evaluation, with clearly defined outcomes.

Importance of a fair evaluation process

In the NSBA Monograph (1987) on teacher compensation and incentive plans mentioned above, one point of general agreement from all the programs reviewed was that it is important for the evaluation process to be perceived as being fair, objective, and comprehensive by each of the participants. The items listed as most frequently used in evaluation were: (1) classroom observations; (2) measurement of student achievement; and (3) examination of records. Classroom observation was found to be used most often (p. 24).

Savage (1983), in speaking about the Charlotte, North Carolina, school district, saw the need to have an effective evaluation system to help determine which faculty should be promoted in the career ladder program or within the district. He concluded:

> It is not hard to think of the pitfalls inherent in evaluation programs; it is also true that some teachers are outstanding and some are barely passable, and a good evaluation can help reward the first-rate and improve the mediocre. If we want to change the system, and many of us do, we must develop evaluation systems that truly identify quality teaching. We must also develop payment and promotion systems that reward outstanding performance and encourage teachers to excel (p. 56).

Educational Research Service (1978) surveyed over 1,000 schools to learn about their teacher evaluation systems. They found classroom observation used in almost all of the districts surveyed. In a later study by Educational Research Service (1983) it was found that the main reason merit incentive plans had been dropped between the years of 1978 and 1983 was due to difficulties with evaluation procedures. Difficulties, according to respondents, included difficulty in avoiding subjective evaluation, inconsistency among evaluators, and difficulty in devising a satisfactory evaluation instrument.

In Fairfax County, Virginia, the teachers' union voted overwhelmingly (4,275 to 748) to withdraw its support from the performance-based merit pay plan (Olson 1989). The plan had received favorable faculty support in three prior votes and had been given national recognition. The district felt the plan needed the support and cooperation of teachers to be successful. The vote to withdraw support followed a move by the governing board to reduce the percent of pay increase that had been agreed upon previously.

MONETARY AND NON-MONETARY INCENTIVE PROGRAMS

The National School Board Association (1987) found six basic types of monetary incentive programs around the country and four major types of non-monetary incentive programs. They were as follows:

Monetary Incentive Programs

1. *Merit Pay.* Programs that link teachers' salaries to periodic assessments of their performance. Financial bonuses are awarded to the teachers who receive the highest ratings.
2. *Payment by Results.* Merit pay programs that base individual teacher bonuses on their students' test scores gains.
3. *Merit Schools.* Plans that reward schools, not individual teachers, for improved performance. In some programs, schools compete against other schools for financial bonuses. In other programs, schools compete against their own past performance or against goals that have been established within the district.

4. *Career Ladders*. Programs that establish both a hierarchy of job classifications for teachers and a differentiated salary schedule. As teachers move up the career ladder, they receive additional pay for additional responsibilities, usually outside the classroom.

5. *Incentive Bonuses*. Some districts have offered special incentives for teachers willing to teach in high-turnover (especially inner-city) schools.

6. *Enhanced Professional Responsibilities (including Master Teacher Programs)*. Programs that provide increased professional opportunities and responsibilities for experienced teachers. These may include serving as "mentors" for beginning teachers, or working on special projects.

Non-Monetary Incentive Programs

1. *Teacher Recognition Programs*. Programs that provide public recognition of outstanding teachers. Teacher-of-the-Year programs are one well-known example.

2. *Non-monetary Performance by Objectives (PBO) Plans*. Programs that provide non-monetary rewards for teachers who achieve objectives that they have developed (usually in cooperation with principals) for the year. Rewards may include purchase of additional classroom equipment or attendance at a professional conference.

3. *Improved Working Conditions*. Programs to improve the physical and social conditions under which teachers work, in order to make teaching more professional and more enjoyable.

4. *Awards, Sabbaticals, and Training*. Some districts reward superior teachers with grants allowing them to pursue special projects. Other programs offer superior teachers sabbaticals or the opportunity to participate in special training programs (p. 31).

PRAISE AND RECOGNITION PROGRAMS

The National School Board Association (1987) concluded, "praise and recognition are among the most powerful motivators for changing behavior" (p. 40). Such recognition efforts are inexpensive, do not require complex negotiations with faculty organizations, and do not add to the complexity of salary schedules.

The Arlington County, Virginia, school district recognized outstanding performances of their teachers in a number of ways: (1) sabbatical leave; (2) special project grants; (3) tuition for recertification; (4) pay for summer curriculum development; (5) stipends for "contact" teachers, (6) mentoring positions; (7) paid attendance at in-service presentations; (8) pay for training other teachers in the district; (9) opportunities to attend professional meetings; and (10) department chair positions. The school board supported the program and liked the fact the available funds were spent directly on teachers.

A number of successful recognition program practices were submitted to Andrews and Erwin (2003). Four of them are summarized here:

I.A. *Johnson County Community College* has a Distinguished Service Award for full-time faculty. The criteria are based on percentages for various responsibilities: 65% for basic job responsibilities; 15% for divisional responsibilities; 10% for institutional/community work; and 10% for professional growth. The dollar amount is not less than $2,000 annually and awards are for a two-year period.

I. B. *Lieberman Teaching Excellence Award for Adjunct Faculty at Johnson County Community College* in Kansas presents six monetary awards for "outstanding performance" to adjunct faculty each year. One receives $750 and the other five receive $250 each. All nominees receive a plaque. The nominees must have worked for JCCC for a minimum of six semesters to qualify.

II. Foothill – De Anza Community College District in California offers Professional Achievement Awards. They are based upon rewarding excellence in the performance of the faculty employee's principal duties. In addition, the candidates must demonstrate continued professional growth and special service to the college or district. The award is $2,000.

III. Brevard Community College in Florida: A VIP Award is available to up to 10% of the assigned faculty for each of nine divisions. In addition, a college wide VIP determination process allows for up to thirty-five percent of the tenure-track faculty to receive awards

IV. Delaware Technical and Community College: An Excellence in Teaching Award is available for superior instructors selected by peers and is publicly acclaimed. Criteria involved a commitment to excellence in teaching and in the performance of other assigned instructional duties.

Andrews (1986a) identified a number of "recognition" systems in community colleges. They provided for recognition of performance with cash awards, plaques, and some form of public recognition. These systems varied in how such recognition was determined, some using administrative evaluation while others used student, peer, or self-evaluation, or a combination of them.

In a policy statement on the administrative evaluation system at the College of Southern Idaho, the college concluded that the dean of the college best determine merit recognition:

1. Merit is an administrative proclamation and should be determined by the administration.

2. Merit, by its nature, is very subjective and, therefore, cannot be quantified. We all realize how difficult it is to quantify a subjective test, like an essay, and be uniform.
3. It was the feeling of everyone on the committee that the philosophy of merit is commendable. If merit is inevitable, it was felt that the dean should be responsible for its determination. If he does his homework, he should be the most non-biased and best-informed person to do it. His system should be given full support of the faculty.
4. Merit should be based only on one year's performance.

At Walters State Community College in Morristown, Tennessee, one outstanding faculty member a year was recognized during the Annual Honors Day program. The president received the recommendation from an awards committee. The faculty member was recommended primarily on classroom teaching effectiveness.

The North County Community College of Saranac Lake, New York, recognized two to five faculty a year with awards ranging from $500 to $1,250. The awards were based on exceptional merit in the teacher's work for the college during the year, and performance above and beyond the call of duty. The college also awarded a George Hadson Merit Award to one or two persons yearly. This award was based upon criteria of: attitude toward work, consistency in job performance, versatility, personal responsibility, and cooperation with fellow employees (pp. 46-50).

In a second survey, conducted by Andrews (1993) in the 19-state North Central Association region, he found increasing numbers of merit recognition systems in place. Some examples of these systems follow.

Columbus State Community College in Ohio presented a Distinguished Teacher Award for excellence in teaching. A luncheon and presentation of a certificate was the form of recognition used.

The college president at Oklahoma City Community College has awarded the President's Award for Excellence in Teaching since 1991. This included a $1,000 cash award presented during the spring commencement. The four categories used in this selection are: (1) professional competence; (2) effective teaching that demonstrates quality, creativity and resourcefulness; (3) enthusiasm for teaching and commitment to students; and (4) contribution to the teaching profession.

An Outstanding Faculty Award program at Lake Michigan College was open to both full- and part-time faculty. The selection committee was comprised of the vice president for academic and student services, academic deans, and teaching faculty. One full-time and one part-time faculty member were selected annually as award recipients.

Four community college faculty winners were chosen from 56,000 full-and part-time community college faculty throughout the state of California to receive the 2003 Haywards Awards for Excellence in Education. These statewide awards help put the quality faculty members before the public and faculty within all colleges. The disappointing part of such awards is that there are so few for so many deserving faculty members.

A *U. S. News and World Report* (1996a, February 26) article stated that teachers' colleagues in their home school districts often frown upon teachers who work to "go the extra mile" in their work. It mentioned the case of Patricia Simonds, then a 26-year veteran of Truman Elementary School District in Vancouver, Washington. After earning the advanced license for teaching from the National Board for Professional Teaching Standards she was asked to attend a ceremony at the White House along with other winners. Little attention was given at her elementary school in celebration of this national recognition award (p. 69).

Sample nominations for recognition

Following are three examples of nominations for recognition that were written on behalf of a counselor and two faculty members:

Example 1: Merit Award Nomination (Counselor)

Excellence in performance of counseling duties

This counselor provides a comprehensive counseling experience for students. He is very knowledgeable, accurate, and exhibits concern for his students.

Assistance in program development

He has been especially instrumental in assisting with the program to provide academic and counseling services for special needs students. In addition, he attends seminars, workshops, and meetings with regional colleges and support service organizations in order to gain information and knowledge of the system. He has explored means of additional funding and has investigated sources by which to provide increased services to the students.

Initiative

This counselor has never been one who simply performs his duties and goes home. Rather, he appears to demonstrate an interest in new academic programs and new approaches; indeed, he has volunteered to become a part of new initiatives, such as college honors, tech prep, testing and remediation. Further, his participation extends to provide sound advice on how students can succeed in such programs—both on this campus and at institutions to which they will eventually transfer.

Example2: Merit Award Nomination (Faculty Member)

1. Excellence in teaching
    This instructor prepares and teaches a variety of courses in the areas of technical and business communications and journalism. She prepares her courses thoroughly and with care, updates syllabi regularly, and maintains high levels of student interest and enrollment. Her journalism students have performed well at the state universities, and at least twenty-five currently hold positions in the print and non-print media.

2. Excellence in the performance of academic assignments
    This instructor has taken the lead in the Tech Prep program. She has coordinated faculty workshops and worked with faculty in other disciplines and divisions to promote Tech Prep. Further, she has addressed faculty and administrators at other community colleges on the advantages of developing such a program.

3. Contributions to the college beyond assigned responsibilities and tasks
    One need only look to the stature and status of the college newspaper—the quality of its form and content. The paper has received numerous state and national awards. Further, and perhaps more important, the students whom she has trained have demonstrated abilities to secure positions with various newspapers and non-print media outlets.

SUMMARY

Research finds that many schools and colleges still have no recognition programs for their excellent teachers. A main objective in implementing faculty recognition programs should be to encourage and reward excellence in teaching. A recognition program that rewards excellence in teaching should produce increased motivation and improved instruction. A survey of elementary and secondary school superintendents and principals identified five desired outcomes: (1) improved quality of education, (2) promotion of positive atti-

Example 3: Merit Award Nomination (Faculty Member)

1. Excellence in teaching

    This instructor has been evaluated as an excellent instructor by several division chairs and the academic deans. Her major responsibility is in advanced chemistry and feedback from state universities show her students do extremely well academically in this area when they transfer.

2. Excellence in the performance of academic assignments

    This instructor is on three campus committees and willingly accepts new challenges. She has held several workshops in chemistry on campus for elementary and high school teachers.

3. Program development

    The instructor has developed several programs for elementary teachers to improve their knowledge of chemistry. She also works closely with the educational service regions in presenting these programs.

4. Contributions to the college/community beyond assigned responsibilities and tasks

    In community outreach efforts this instructor was instrumental in the development of the PADS program (Public Action to Deliver Shelter), and is an active leader in this program. In addition, through her efforts the college has been awarded two National Science Foundation (NSF) grants for the improvement of elementary science.

5. Initiative

    This instructor initiated each of the NSF grant proposals. She also obtained another grant that allowed for purchase of chemistry lab equipment. These initiatives involved a great deal of time beyond normal classroom and other job responsibilities.

tudes, (3) improved teaching environment, (4) improved public image of teaching and the school, and (5) a caring attitude projected by administration to faculty.

This chapter focused on the importance of improving student learning by clarifying the values upon which the program of recognition will be based. Recognition programs also need to be placed within the context of a quality faculty evaluation system.

The National School Board Association's study found four major types of non-monetary incentive programs in use: (1) teacher recognition programs; (2) non-monetary "performance by objectives" plans; (3) improved working conditions; and (4) rewards, sabbaticals, and training.

Praise and recognition programs being used successfully at several schools and colleges were described in this chapter. Samples of merit award nominations were also included.

A variety of recognition programs that were found to be acceptable to faculty have been outlined for consideration by schools and colleges. In order to improve student achievement results and motivate the faculty members of any institution, it is important to look for those incentives that work. Recognition has been presented as one of the intrinsic teacher reward programs that will make a difference in K-12 schools and community colleges.

SUGGESTED EXERCISES

1.   What outcomes should result from a teacher recognition program?
2.   Discuss the reasons merit pay and recognition programs create such different responses from faculty in most schools and community colleges.

Section III
IMPLEMENTING ACCOUNTABLE OUTCOMES

Accountable Teacher Evaluation

CHAPTER 10

PROGRESSIVE REMEDIATION: STANDING STRONG FOR QUALITY

> It is no big secret who the poor teachers are in our classrooms. Our administrators know, their fellow faculty members know, as do parents and students. In fact, the entire community knows.
>
> *Schwartz, (1997), p. 3*

Bennett (2002) states that "our task becomes putting principles in place—to set high standards for teachers, to develop strong accountability systems for measuring performance, and to reward those who perform and frown upon those who do not" (p. ix).

The process of identifying, evaluating, remediating, and, when it is necessary, discharging incompetent teachers is most critical in the process of improving instruction in schools according to Waintroob (1995). She also saw it as a process that school administrators often find personally unpleasant, frustrating, and anguishing.

Poor teachers demoralize good teachers. "Keeping poor teachers causes resentment among teachers who are working hard and shows those who aren't that there's no consequence to low performance," according to Kathy Christie who represents the Education Commission of the States (Glastris, 1997). Christie also reported that these poor teachers normally end up with those students who are poor and low performing and

---

who need the best teachers. Parents of these students simply do not complain.

Glastris (1997) showed that in Florida only .05 percent of the Florida teachers were dismissed and at an average cost of $60,000 per instructor. The American Federation of Teachers supported a bill that reduced the improvement time frame for remediation from two years to 90 days.

Glastris studied school reformers who were demanding that teacher evaluations be tougher and fairer. He noted that most evaluation systems are undemanding in terms of requiring change. He went on to say, "if the evaluation process is thorough and fair enough, even the most intransigent unions will have trouble defending bad teachers" (p. 32).

Faculty evaluation may be the most important means that administration and faculty have of assuring the public and the school's governing board that quality in the classroom is taken seriously. Non-tenured faculty, in elementary, middle or secondary schools and community colleges, have laws that vary in different states (from two years to seven years) to prove themselves as good classroom teachers prior to a decision to have tenure awarded. During this period administrators have a number of things they can do to help assure success for most of these teachers.

Bay de Noc Community College in Michigan formed a committee of faculty to develop a new evaluation process (Andrews et al. 1996). This action came on the heels of an unsuccessful attempt to dismiss a poorly performing tenured teacher. Working toward quality teaching as their goal, the committee developed a policy that included faculty development appraisal, determined performance appraisal procedures, and endorsed the board of trustees' right to manage the institution. Faculty responsibility was defined as the delivery of quality instruction. The committee also identified a list of observable and measurable characteristics of good teaching. Under this new system the faculty members who had performed poorly were to be re-evaluated and given time to remediate deficiencies. Remediation did not lead to improvement during the time frame established for the poorly performing instructor, and the instructor was subsequently dismissed.

FORMATIVE EVALUATION

Visitations to classes, written and verbal reviews of these visitations, in-service training, and professional meetings are the most significant components of formative evaluation. Each of these steps is taken to assist the faculty member in the *formative* evaluation process. In short, this is the process of assisting the teacher to become strengthened in the teaching pedagogy. Once an instructor has satisfactorily served the probationary period, tenure is usually awarded by official action of the governing board of the school or college.

Even after tenure is granted, faculty evaluation needs to continue, although not as frequently as during the probationary period. Formative evaluation should continue as a means of supporting the faculty member and encouraging changes that are deemed necessary for classroom or out-of-class job improvements.

The supervisors need to follow-up their suggestions and recommendations for teacher improvement during both probationary and tenured evaluation periods. Progress, or lack of progress, should be documented. Positive support should be forthcoming for those areas where improvements are observed. Further suggestions for improvement may be necessary for those faculty who are not making the desired progress. In such cases the faculty member may be neglecting or may be unable to perform the suggested improvements. Licata and Andrews (1990) identify this continuing assistance as being formative in nature (p. 48).

REMEDIATION

In his work as a school principal and superintendent, Kelleher (1985) used the term incompetent teacher to describe one "who has demonstrated his or her inability to meet minimum standards of performance over a number of years" (p. 362). He defined the remediation period necessary for such a person as being a year or more. In his plan for remediation there are four basic things that must occur:

1. The teacher must clearly understand what his or her teaching problems are.
2. The teacher must hear the same message about his or her problems from people at different levels and in different positions in the school system.
3. The teacher must receive a written evaluation plan.
4. The teacher must know that failure to improve will bring an escalating series of consequences (pp. 363-364).

Jentz et al. (1982) found administrators did not do a good job of telling teachers what their shortcomings or inadequacies were when discussing classroom observations with them. He found the administrators omitted key items, generalized rather than giving specifics, and threw in positive comments when they were not called for, thereby confusing the message that needed to be transmitted. Administrators apparently were trying to be kind by withholding negative information from the teacher. Kelleher strongly recommended that schools commit funds to in-service training for administrators to learn the interpersonal skills they need to handle these sensitive situations.

In Kelleher's plan (1985) an incompetent teacher hears about his or her work from several sources. Several administrators should be involved. He suggested that department chairpersons, assistant principals, and principals each participate in conducting the classroom observations. He also suggested that, if necessary, the district level administrators should be involved. The alternative, as he explained, is to allow incompetent teachers to continue year after year.

Conducting these evaluations is time-consuming. Handling student, parent, and board member complaints about a poor teacher is also very time consuming especially if nothing is done to address the problem and it continues to recur. Kelleher suggested that, if the teacher is not showing improvement in a reasonable length of time, the union should be informed. He said that union leaders had always been invited to take part in the in-service workshops that administrators received in his school district. He found the teacher union generally supportive: "The union is responsible for protecting the teacher's rights, but it is also in a position to support our efforts, if it perceives them as fair" (p. 363).

In reference to the written evaluation plan, the teacher should receive documentation of the specific problems, expectations for improvement, and the steps that will be followed by the administration to document improvement or lack of improvement. Kelleher also suggested that the teacher's union receive a copy of the notice. This notifies them what is expected of the teacher as well as showing them that the administration is giving the teacher the opportunity to improve, within certain time limits.

In Kelleher's experience, incompetent teachers tended to leave when they saw that their work was considered unsatisfactory by a number of administrators, fellow teachers, board members, and students. Confronting incompetence is necessary, and the school should "speak to an incompetent teacher with one voice about that teacher's problems, expressing the message compassionately and sensitively but, above all, clearly; then that teacher will either change dramatically or, more likely, resign" (p. 364). Kelleher concluded that everyone who participates in the process of improving instruction or in the removal of an incompetent teacher will gain pride in the fact that quality instruction is being sought within the school.

Rapp and Ortbal (1980) emphasize that it is important to allow time for poor performance to be remediated prior to moving toward termination. They state that, "if the reasons for dismissal are considered remediable, a board must give the teacher reasonable warning in writing stating the causes of the remediation notice which, if not removed, may result in charges and dismissal" (p. 39). The timeframe for remediation will vary by school or college. It is not unusual to give one semester to a year depending on the items outlined in the remediation document. The timeframe should be utilized by the supervisors to determine such remediation areas such as, how many times the teacher's classroom(s) will be visited, how soon course syllabi need to be updated and how much time will be given to each of the other remediation items.

Dismissal is part of the legal process that must be considered when a tenured faculty member is found to have 'deficiencies' or 'defects' in their teaching or other job responsibilities. The courts and laws in most states have made clear that due-process procedures must be granted to those faculty under tenure or with a continuing contract status. When due-process policies and procedures have not been followed, courts have consistently denied boards and administrators in schools and colleges support for their dismissal decisions. It is most important that colleges and school systems develop due-process procedures, which will provide for proper legal support in cases which may lead to dismissals.

Teacher evaluation *legislation* has been passed in a number of states. In Illinois, the law provides for a one-year "probation" period that leads to termination if sufficient progress is not forthcoming by the elementary or secondary school teacher involved.

REPRIMANDS: A REMEDIATION STEP

A reprimand to an employee is a means of letting a teacher know that certain behavior is not acceptable. The reprimand should be put in writing, read by the instructor involved, discussed with the supervisor, and placed in the personnel file of the instructor. Andrews (1987b) found that some faculty contracts ask that the person sign the form to be filed. This is to indicate that it has been read but not, necessarily, that there is agreement to the contents. The faculty member may wish to write a rebuttal and have it attached to the reprimand in the personnel file. Following are some sample reprimands (p. 4):

Dear Instructor:

Your absence from the December 2, 2003, meeting, whether from forgetfulness or not, is not excusable, especially following my verbal warning to you after you missed the November 4 department meeting. You are aware that important and essential business and not merely perfunctory tasks take place at these faculty meetings.

In short, this reprimand will be placed in your personnel file. You must plan to be at all future faculty meetings as part of your professional obligation. Please sign this letter of reprimand and return it to my attention within one week. I would like to discuss this matter further so please arrange an appointment with me this week.

Sincerely,
Dean of the Faculty

Dear Instructor:

On Thursday, September 12, 2002, at 11:30 a.m. you met in Dean Smith's office with Dr. Smith and myself to discuss your behavior leading to the need for such a meeting.

You had, earlier that morning, verbally and publicly abused a student who attempted to enter your classroom late. You spoke to that student in a loud voice and used profanity. The nature of your address to him was such that individuals in the classroom and in the halls outside of that room easily witnessed your anger and general loss of control.

Please know that such conduct cannot be tolerated. The profession that you serve and the discipline you represent do not tolerate such behavior; the institution in which you practice your profession cannot afford to (nor will it) tolerate such conduct.

In the future, please try to control your emotions. Students coming to your class late can be dealt with in other ways. You can begin by setting forth (at the onset of each term) clear, specific classroom policies concerning issues such as attendance. This practice will, in the end, allow students to know exactly what you expect of them. If any of them then come to class late you can refer the student to the dean of students' office before the student is allowed back to your class.

Sincerely,
Division Chairperson

There are situations where such reprimands are warranted. It is responsible behavior by the administration to address behaviors that are not in line with what is expected of professional teachers.

THE "NOTICE TO REMEDY"

A "notice to remedy" is a legal step available to governing boards and administrators to notify an instructor of the serious nature of his/her failure to change or improve teaching or other job behaviors. The "notice to remedy" is a strong statement from the board that provides a list of the precise defects and deficiencies that have been brought to them by the superintendent or college president. In addition, it spells out what changes are expected to remediate such problems. It gives a time frame and an expectation that the supervisor(s) will continue to evaluate for significant changes relating to the list of deficiencies given to the faculty member. It also makes clear that if these charges are not remediated, the board will be ready to consider termination from the institution. An example of a "notice to remedy" appears in Example 4.

EXAMPLE 4:
LIST OF DEFECTS AND DEFICIENCIES IN THE TEACHING AND OVERALL JOB PERFORMANCE OF

_____

1. *Lack of preparation in order to conduct an organized, logical, sequential classroom presentation.*

   Classroom observations have consistently documented that you do not properly prepare to conduct your classes. This lack of preparation keeps your students from learning the complex concepts and principles in your subject matter. You move from one concept to another without checking your students' understanding. Your preparation needs to provide assurance that you will present the *full syllabus* of required material in an organized, logical sequence. Allow students to ask questions, and use tests and quizzes regularly to check student understanding. You need to prepare daily outlines showing your objectives. Use technical support to illustrate your main points.

2. *Lack of organization in conducting your classroom presentation.*

   You must organize your classroom presentation in such a manner that your students can take notes and follow the material in a logical manner. Your method of presentation is so confusing and disorganized that it is difficult to determine what objectives or goals you wished to accomplish in any of the classes we have evaluated.

One minute you are on one concept and the next minute you have switched to a completely different topic, which has nothing to do with the course. You offer your students no closure from one topic to another. You do not check understanding or ask questions to assess understanding. On three occasions we observed you as you left your classroom to go get something in your office that you forgot to bring to the class. You have also been observed discussing topics at considerable length within your classes, such as recent basketball games and political biases that have nothing at all to do with the subject you are teaching. You must prepare in advance to be properly organized for teaching the required materials in your courses.

3. *Failure to communicate course expectations to your students.*

You need to communicate in writing the requirements and specific expectations of the students. Your policies and procedures for class attendance, tardiness, grading, as well as homework assignments, requirements for in-class participation, materials to be covered on tests, must all be covered in your student course outlines. The students in your courses are not receiving any report of their progress in your classes. Giving them their first exam in the fourteenth week of a sixteen-week semester is not an acceptable testing practice. Students need to have tests and quizzes paced throughout the semester to guide their understanding and progress. This failure to provide feedback of this type demonstrates a definite lack of preparation, organization, and consideration for the needs of your students.

4. *Failure to prepare specific objectives for your courses to be handed out to your students.*

You must prepare specific goals on a daily, weekly, monthly and semester basis for each of your courses. These goals must be given out to your students at the beginning of each of your courses. You need to have copies of these course outlines for the second semester to your principal in 45 days.

5. *Lack of preparation and planning in production of audio-visual materials to supplement lecture and discussion material.*

You must work closely with the audio-visual department in preparing this type of supplementary materials for use in your courses. The power-point materials you have used are outdated and the type size is too small for students in the back half of the room to read. The transparencies are also crowded with material and difficult to read. They need only the key concepts highlighted to help guide your lecture and do not need to have all of the lecture material.

6. *Failure to adequately prepare students to allow them to be meaningfully involved in the discussion.*

You ask such superficial questions to your students that there is no way of assessing whether they understand the basic principles of your lectures. "Any questions, okay, now let us discuss...." doesn't elicit student questions. Further, you do not have eye contact with students when you make that statement. Ask specific questions to individual students. They should know you will ask questions and be prepared to respond. Neither is happening. Your demeaning of students who do respond keeps most of the students from attempting to give answers. Give your students the facts and materials they need to maximize their participation in the discussion.

7. ***Insubordination.***

   On two separate occasions you were asked to meet with your supervisors to discuss the classroom evaluations they had made of you during the past month. You chose to ignore these requests. This is seen as an act of insubordination. Future actions of this type will not be tolerated. You are expected to attend all such meetings.

8. ***Conclusion.***

   This list of defects and deficiencies have been prepared by your supervisors after having observed these problems in your teaching and out-of-class job requirements. You should seriously evaluate how each one of these concerns can be addressed. Some of them will require a change in attitude. Others will require a great deal of preparation and planning. You will need to meet with your administrative supervisors within the next three weeks to outline a course of action for correcting these defects and deficiencies in your work. Close evaluation of your work will continue over the next several months with classroom visits continuing a minimum of once per month until further notice.

PROOF OF INCOMPETENCE

A legal definition of incompetence is not easy to find in the literature dealing with faculty remediation or dismissal. Rosenberger and Plimpton (1975) concluded: "There seems to have been no legal need to define incompetence. . . conventional wisdom and common sense, rather than precise standards, have been used in judging incompetence claims" (p. 469).

Wheeler et al. was cited in an earlier chapter describing incompetence as, "the intentional or unintentional failure to perform the duties and professional responsibilities of the teaching job in a minimally acceptable manner as specified by the employing district" (p. 15).

Strike and Bull (1981) found courts have accepted the following items as proof of incompetence:

1. Deficiencies of knowledge of subject matter;
2. Poor teaching methods;
3. Disorganized teaching or work habits;
4. Inability to maintain discipline or use of excessive force or other inappropriate methods;
5. Inability to motivate students;
6. Inflexibility or lack of adaptability;
7. Uncooperativeness;
8. Permitting or requiring vulgarities on the part of students;
9. Causing low morale;
10. Poor communication;
11. Poor attitude;
12. Violation of rules;
13. Mishandling of funds;
14. Low student achievement;
15. Unsatisfactory ratings;
16. Poor record keeping;
17. Arbitrary grading; and
18. Lack of self-control (p. 324).

While the discussion in this chapter does not spell out how each of these items can be identified in proving incompetence, the above list does show the type of charges that have been reported in court cases throughout the country. The circumstances surrounding each of them, that would lead an administrator to decide to move toward job termination of the faculty member, are different for each case. "Lack of self-control" or "mishandling of funds" are clearer charges to identify as areas of incompetence than that of "causing low morale" or "uncooperativeness."

Waintroob (1995) described what she has learned in many faculty incompetency cases in which she has provided counsel. She suggested that there are certain themes that continually emerge in this work:

1.   Incompetent teachers don't get it.

My mother once told me that the only person who is ever surprised when someone gets fired is the one who is fired. This bit of maternal wisdom certainly is true when it comes to teachers. Everyone connected with a school knows who the incompetent teachers are, including the other teachers, the parents, the kids, and the custodial staff. The only one who doesn't know it is the incompetent teacher (p. 1).

2.   You're your own worst enemy.

Most incompetent teachers have been 'enabled' by administrators to avoid facing their performance problems. Why are many poor employees rated 'satisfactory?' 'Grade inflation' is rampant in evaluations in all industries because honest, pointed evaluation is one of the most difficult tasks for any manager, whether in education or in private industry (p. 3).

3.   Forced confrontation.

Like alcoholics, incompetent teachers realize they must confront performance problems only when they have 'hit bottom' and been forced to confront those problems. As long as the failing teacher does not realize that his or her job is on the line, the teacher will continue to deny problems (p. 3).

ROLE OF ADMINISTRATOR IN EXPERT TESTIMONY

The role of "expert testimony and performance evaluations in making determinations about school employee competence are slowly winning approval in courts," according to Piele (1981, p. 69). In addition, he found that the courts had rejected most of the challenges by faculty regarding their dismissals for stated causes. This was in spite of what he described as the heightened attempts to have legal protection of tenure. This information becomes important as it gives boards and administrators a higher level of confidence that there will be sufficient support for their decisions to move toward remediation and/or dismissals of poor instructors. This is true if the case is sufficiently documented and due process requirements are properly followed.

Van Horn (1984) found that the most likely candidates to be called as witnesses were those administrators involved directly in the evaluation process. Such "expert witnesses" will have been involved in writing their observations, meeting with the faculty member, testifying during the notice to remedy and thus playing a major role in the dismissal process. More courts now view these persons as providing expert testimony.

Van Horn quoted an Ohio court that accepted this principle:

> Teaching is an art as well as a profession and requires a large amount of preparation in order to qualify one in that profession. The ordinary layman is not versed in that art; neither is he in a position to measure the necessary qualifications required for the teacher today. In our judgment this information can be properly imparted by one who is versed and alert in the profession and aware of the qualifications required.

For this reason, however, we think the principal... with the years of experience possessed by him can be classed properly as an expert in the teaching profession, and is in a similar position as a doctor in the medical profession. His testimony was not incompetent and certainly was an aid to the board and to the court in arriving at their respective conclusions (p. 22).

Strike and Bull (1981) formed several conclusions from their review of judicial decisions regarding incompetence:

1.   Courts are likely to rely on the professional judgment of administrators in the substantive aspects of evaluation.
2.   Judicial review of dismissal decisions is likely to be more restrictive when dealing with the procedural aspects of dismissal. Courts require that legislated or contractual procedures for evaluation or due process be rigorously followed. They may also insist, where the defect is remediable, that opportunity for improvement be given.
3.   Despite the lack of an authoritative legal definition and despite jurisdictional variations in interpretation, a general and widely accepted core of meaning for teaching incompetencies can be discerned in the case law. Moreover, incompetence is to be reflected in a pervasive pattern of teacher behavior that has proven to be irremediable (pp. 324-25).

Courts have indeed been supportive of the judgments of competent administrators. Boards should be willing to back competent administrators in their recommendations if they want improvements to achieve quality teaching.

KEY TESTS PRIOR TO ANY DISMISSAL DECISION

Van Horn (1984) suggested that there is a simple but most important test for determining if the unsatisfactory teaching or other job behaviors are at the point where dismissal is necessary. The question, "Can it be remediated?" must be answered first before any dismissal decision is considered. He pointed out that this test is required in a number of state statutes (p. 3).

When the time arrives to seek a formal "notice to remedy" from the governing board, the supervisors usually will have evaluated several classes of the instructor. They will have held post-evaluation conferences, clearly stated the weaknesses of the instructor and followed up on them in subsequent classroom visitations. When the recommended changes have not been made in a reasonable timeframe, it is necessary to seek the formal notice.

The administrator involved next needs to notify the elementary, middle, or secondary school superintendent or college president that the time has come to seek a *board notice to remediate* the problem.

The superintendent or president must review the materials presented, and if convinced that the case is well documented over a sufficient number of visits, have the school attorney review it for legal analysis. If concurrence is received from the attorney, than board action should be sought. A notice to remediate will be prepared. Boards will usually discuss the matter in an executive session before taking formal public action in those states having open-meeting laws for board actions.

It is important to note that supervisor ratings are the primary source of information in most cases leading to remediation or to termination of a teacher. The courts usually give greater weight to such supervisor ratings. Bonato (1987) added that having more than one supervisor involved in the evaluation of a teacher is even more persuasive than when only one supervisor has evaluated a teacher, as long as there is consistency in the findings. He cites from *Rosso v. Board of Education of School Directors* (1977) in which the court supports the use of more than one evaluator:

> The school district's evaluation procedures are a model of how a professional employee should be rated. The evaluations occurred at two levels. At the first level is the principal; if he rates a professional employee unsatisfactory, the matter is referred to the second level, the superintendent, for further evaluation. While a teacher might object to being rated so often in a short period of time by different persons, such a procedure clearly is in the employee's best interest since it brings into the evaluation different viewpoints, thereby lessening the influence personal bias and prejudice with respect to teaching methods can have (p. 25).

Bonato further endorses the need for multiple evaluators, if available, by citing that in almost all discharge cases involving a tenured teacher there have been bitter disputes regarding the quality of the instructor's performance of teaching. The teacher, as a defense, often alleges personality conflict with the evaluator and questions the evaluator's competency and expertise. Bonato recommends at least three different administrators or evaluators be used. The *Esther Fortson v. Detroit Board of Education* (1985) case was cited to support this recommendation. Fortson charged that the principal's evaluation reflected his personal animosity toward her. The Tenure Commission in Michigan rejected her argument:

> Finally, we address appellant's contention that her problem with appellee stemmed from an incident where her principal at Post Middle School, Mr. Shackelford, became angry with her after a run-in she had with him. Her initial unsatisfactory evaluation followed soon af-

ter this incident. Even if we were to completely discount Mr. Shackelford's observations, still we are left with similar observations of two other evaluators at Post—Ms. Hetes and Mr. Nash. In addition, we have the observations of two more evaluators at a different school—Mr. Kar and Mr. Tyler at Longfellow. There is no allegation that the evaluations of these four people were the result of personal bias or animosity against appellant. From these evaluations and from the testimony presented at both hearings, we find sufficient evidence to support the action taken against appellant (p. 32).

According to Andrews (1988) the stress related to remediation efforts and the possibility of teacher termination can affect department or division chairpersons, assistant principals, principals, superintendents, deans or vice presidents of instruction and others who are involved in the process at the supervisory level (p. 63).

At this point, the perception of the evaluation process as challenging, rather than stressful, can lead to a feeling of satisfaction that the goal of improvement has been worth pursuing. It is important that administrative personnel be able to recognize excellence in instruction, understand the due process policies and procedures of the college or school, be familiar with court cases in the areas of remediation and dismissal, and have a firm grasp on what is meant by "improvement of instruction." Improvement of instruction, if accomplished, will foster the learning environment for students in the future.

ARBITRATION TESTS

The American Arbitration Association in Washington, D.C., developed a common-law definition for "just cause" (Baer, 1974). All cases involved in arbitration are measured against this common-law definition. It provides a set of questions that can be applied in any case an arbitrator must decide:

1. Did the agency give the employee forewarning or foreknowledge of the possible or probable disciplinary consequences of the employee's conduct?

   Note A: Forewarning or foreknowledge may properly have been given orally by management or in writing through the medium of typed or printed sheets or books of shop rules and penalties for violation thereof.

   Note B: There must have been actual oral or written communication of the rules and penalties to the employee.

2. Did the agency, before administering discipline to an employee, make an effort to discover whether the employee did in fact violate or disobey a rule or order of management?

   Note A: The agency's investigation must normally be made before its disciplinary decision.

3. Was the agency's investigation conducted fairly and objectively?

4. Has the agency applied its rules, orders, and penalties evenhandedly and without discrimination to all employees?

   Note A: A "no" answer to this question requires a finding of discrimination and warrants negation or modification of the discipline imposed.

   Note B: If the agency has been lax in enforcing its rules and orders and decides henceforth to apply them rigorously, the agency may avoid a finding of discrimination by telling all employees in advance of its intent to enforce, hereafter, all rules as written.

5. Was the degree of discipline administered by the agency in a particular case reasonably related to: (a) the serious-

ness of the employee's proven offense, and (b) the record of the employee in his or her service with the agency (p. 88)?

These tests should put elementary, middle and secondary school and community college administrators on alert when they need to administer disciplinary or remedial evaluation action. These common-law questions point out the necessity of having written rules of evaluation. Such rules need to be applied evenhandedly to all persons involved.

The "notice to remedy" is a most important material item in the determination of whether the individual was given clear remediation directions. It also answers the first question above in regard to giving forewarning or probable disciplinary consequences.

SUMMARY

Remediation is a step in the process of classroom improvement for teachers who have been found and documented to having a pattern of poor teaching. It is a part of the evaluation process that many schools have avoided using. Developing a plan for remediation of teaching and other job responsibilities takes a special skill that must be developed by the administrators involved in the evaluation of teaching process. It provides an opportunity for the teacher to continue in the arena of formative evaluation. Remediation outlines very clearly the steps that a teacher can take to meet the established standards of the school.

A remediation plan needs to identify in detail those deficiencies that must be addressed before the teacher can be rated as doing satisfactory work. The plan clarifies the steps needed for improvement and the time frame in which changes must be made. Administrators involved will need to follow up all aspects of the notice to remediate. It provides both the teacher and the school or college a record of precisely what improvements must be made.

Remediation must be offered to those teachers who have been found incompetent in some aspects of their teaching job. In implementing a remediation plan, the administration must ensure that the teacher (1) clearly understands what his or her teaching problems are; (2) hears the same message about his or her performance from several different evaluators; (3) receives a written plan of remediation; and (4) knows that failure to improve may eventually lead to termination.

When improvements still are not forthcoming, the next step necessarily becomes a "notice to remedy." This is a serious step, taken through governing board action, providing for a notification to the teacher of the list of items that must be remediated. This remediation notice is a formal step that sets the stage for possible termination of the tenured teacher if the teacher continues to refuse or proves unable to make the required changes.

When all remediation efforts have been exhausted and the teacher's performance has still not reached an acceptable level, the administration must consider moving to the next step, which is termination. The decision needs to be legally defensible. Administrators at this point must answer "yes" to the following test questions: (1) Was the instructor evaluated several times after the notice to remediate? (2) Were post-evaluation sessions held with the instructor to discuss the teaching deficiencies? (3) Were both written and oral summaries of the weaknesses given to the instructor? (4) Were the discussions from these meetings documented? (5) Was the teaching behavior still found to be unsatisfactory in follow-up classroom visits? (6) Has the behavior proven to be irremediable?

While there are no authoritative legal definitions of incompetence, courts have regularly accepted as proof of incompetence certain types of charges, which have been listed in this chapter. Administrators are widely viewed by the courts as "expert witnesses" in providing the evidence necessary for defining a teacher's incompetence. The courts place importance on how well due process and the legislated or contractual procedures for evaluation have been followed. Satisfying the common-law definition of "just cause" in termination cases makes it vital to have written rules of evaluation and to apply them even-handedly to all teachers who are being evaluated.

SUGGESTED EXERCISES

1. Discuss how remediation provides accountability in the evaluation process.
2. Assuming the administration has provided a detailed and objective "remediation case" for the governing board, what happens if it is rejected by the board?

Accountable Teacher Evaluation

CHAPTER 11

RESEARCH ON POST-TENURE EVALUATION

> We must retain good teachers as well and ensure
> they perform at high levels, and when they do not, we
> must deal with incompetents.
>
> *Hickok (2002), p. 25*

A faculty leader bluntly described her feelings relative
to having continuing poor teaching in her school (Andrews,
1995):

> I would first fire all administrators who knew little
> or nothing or cared less about evaluation and quality
> education and replace [them] with competent people.
> Then I would create an evaluation system, which did
> the following: Distinguish those minimally competent
> from those below minimal competence. Provide
> remediation for the latter group with an outcome that
> would either (a) make them competent, or (b) permit
> their legal dismissal. Provide enrichment and improve-
> ment for all staff according to their needs and desires.
> Provide adequate funding and resources for this (p. 151).

This strong statement was one of many from faculty leaders around the country expressing their disgust with the state
of faculty evaluation in their community colleges. An earlier
19-state study conducted by Andrews and Licata (1988-1989)
addressed what both faculty and administrative instructional
leaders felt about the present role evaluation played in their
colleges. They were also asked what "should" be the role of
evaluation. A total of 357 instructional leaders responded. This
represented 58.5 percent of the population that received the

---

questionnaire. The findings of this study were quite different than the researchers had expected.

The large majority of the respondents were not negative in their response to having post-tenure faculty evaluation. They were supportive of the need for a competent evaluation system that has the main goal of improving teaching. They also emphasized a need to have competent evaluators involved in administering the faculty evaluation system. One of the unexpected responses from these faculty leaders was the call for remediation, enrichment and improvement efforts to change incompetent faculty. They wanted such action prior to having the administrators ask for a legal dismissal (p. 7).

Comments from faculty made it clear that some felt much more needed to be done in the area of recognition:

- I'd provide funds to give bonuses or other rewards to outstanding faculty without reducing funds to pay all other salaries.
- Reward the effective faculty member, not the sloucher; not enough distinction exists.
- There is a need for a significant reward system for effective educators.
- If you are planning to use these evaluations, tie them to excellence and pay for that excellence. You'd be surprised how quickly the 'sluggards' will come around without much being said.

Similar comments were offered by a number of the administrators:

- Fund a reward system for outstanding performance.
- More specific ratings with recognition for our outstanding faculty.
- Provide greater positive recognition of high achievers so as to encourage others to 'stretch' themselves.

- Add something to reward outstanding performance above and beyond a salary increase (pp. 24-25).

Schwartz (1997) asks that administrators get rid of their excuses for tolerating poor teachers. He noted, "we damage the credibility and reputation of the teaching profession in general by allowing poor teachers to taint the reputations of all teachers and make their challenging jobs more difficult" (p. 3). He found administrators not always honest in their evaluations of poor teachers. The result is that these *poor teachers remain in the classroom due to inaction by administrators* (emphasis added).

Licata (1984) found the majority of faculty and administrators in the seven community college campuses she surveyed to be supportive of post-tenure evaluation in their colleges. Post-tenure evaluation was, however, called into question regarding what *should be* its stated purpose. The respondents strongly supported the purpose to be development and improvement of instruction (p. 36).

EXISTING AND IDEAL POST-TENURE EVALUATION PRACTICES

Andrews et al. (2002c) conducted a 50-state survey of community college faculty leaders and chief academic administrators in what was the first national study of *post-tenure evaluation practices* in the community college system. Both of the respondent groups identified their present post-tenure evaluation systems emphasizing evaluation as a basis for individual faculty development and improvement. Forty-six percent of the faculty leaders and 31 percent of the administrators reported this finding. The responses included 530 faculty leaders and 664 instructional administrators. The total of 1,194 responses provided a solid base for these findings.

Having placed the focus of post-tenure evaluation on individual faculty development, the next two major reasons for post-tenure evaluation were "for making decisions on promotion, retention and dismissal," and "for making merit compensation or merit recognition decisions."

Both groups were also asked what the *ideal* purpose for evaluation should be. "Individual faculty development" was selected by 56 percent of the faculty leaders and by 59 percent of the administrators. In identifying what they felt should be other ideal reasons for evaluation, faculty leaders rated "making merit compensation or recognition decisions" as their second choice and administrators rated it as their third choice.

CRITERIA USED FOR POST-TENURE EVALUATION

Faculty and administrators were also asked to rank the criteria their colleges used to evaluate post-tenure faculty (Andrews and Licata, 1988-89). "Classroom effectiveness" was selected first by both faculty and administrators (p. 11). This was not unexpected since classroom teaching is the primary job of a faculty member in a community college. This differed significantly from four-year colleges and universities where the areas of research and publications have, in recent years, far outweighed teaching in the reward or merit systems (Sykes 1988, pp. 257-59).

PROBLEMS WITH POST-TENURE EVALUATION

Both faculty and administrators in the 2002c study (Andrews et al.) agreed that the following were major problems in their post-tenure evaluation systems:

1. Post-tenure review is not taken seriously because there is no significant follow-up action to the review;
2. There is little evidence of positive outcomes so far;
3. There are no sanctions for poor performance;
4. There is little done to promote faculty development;
5. There is a lack of any reward system (p. 6).

Faculty leaders and administrators were asked to identify the strengths of their post-tenure review systems. The items mentioned most often were:

1. Promotes focused growth and
   development   119
2. Improves quality of instruction   92
3. Provides a continuous process that
   promotes dialogue   86
4. Provides feedback to faculty on strengths
   and concerns   76 (p. 9).

DOUBTS ABOUT EFFECTIVENESS?

Both groups voiced concerns about the effectiveness of their evaluation systems:

1. Inconsistent and no follow-up   105
2. No real consequences or sanctions   91
3. Lack of objectivity   85
4. Inappropriate forms, processes, methods   69
5. Lack of seriousness given to process   44
6. Lack of training for evaluators   26(p. 11).

While this is not the full list, this sampling shows that there are serious concerns in a number of colleges that have evaluation systems in place.

THE QUESTION OF 'WEEDING OUT'

Andrews and Licata (1988-89) documented some concerns in comments received from faculty regarding post-tenure evaluations:

- Put some 'teeth' into the plan so incompetent staff can be dismissed.
- Give consequences to the results, both pro and con.

Administrative responses included:

- Develop a comprehensive plan . . .correlate results to merit pay, promotion, staff development and also demotion, termination, etc.
- I would implement a probation and dismissal system for those who do not perform adequately.

In the Andrews et al. study (2002a) 69 percent of administrators checked "disagree" or "strongly disagree" with the statement, "post-tenure evaluation *leads* to the weeding out of incompetent faculty." The percentage of faculty disagreeing with the statement was even higher, with a total of 72 percent checking "disagree" or "strongly disagree."

The next comment, "post-tenure evaluation *should* lead to the weeding out of incompetent faculty," produced very high percentages of 84 and 77 for administrators and faculty leaders, respectively, in the "strongly agree" and "agree" columns. These responses clearly tell college trustees and school boards and administrators that they need to make the "weeding out" of incompetent faculty a most important goal to be included in future evaluation practices.

A *USA Today* (2002, August 26) editorial/opinion article blamed administrators for teachers leaving the profession in large numbers. It stated that up to one-third of new teachers leave the profession in the first three years of their experience, and one-half within five years. The need for retraining was identified as a key problem. The administrators were faulted in the following ways:

- Failing to mentor new teachers. Too often these programs are poorly designed or non-existent.
- Assigning teachers unfamiliar subjects. Principals say they have no choice, but evidence seems to prove this not to be true. Where the assignment to courses outside of a teacher's field of preparation has been banned, the practice ends.
- Failing to ensure that the neediest schools have good teachers. Those schools with high enrollments of poor students have been found to have the least-qualified teachers. Seventy percent of middle-grade school math instructors, in these high-poverty schools, are being taught by those teachers who have neither a minor or major in mathematics (pp. 1-2).

The research summarized by Thomas in 1986 and 1991 shows that if administrators and governing boards move beyond "lip service" in taking action against incompetent teachers, there is support in the court system. In 1986 there were twelve incompetency cases reported across the country. Employees were not successful in defending themselves against the charges of incompetency in any of them. In 1991 all four incompetency cases reported across the country were upheld in the courts (p. 20).

SUMMARY

Three studies of faculty leaders and instructional administrators show both groups are supportive of the need for post-tenure evaluation. All three studies, conducted between 1984 and 2002, reported support for post-tenure evaluation, which had as a major goal individual faculty development. The same goal, *individual faculty development*, was given by both sets of these leaders when asked "what *should* be the main purpose of post-tenure evaluation."

Faculty leaders saw faculty recognition as an important outcome of post-tenure evaluation. Both faculty leaders and administrators in each of these studies were critical of the many evaluation systems that do little to support faculty development. Recognition for excellent instructors and consequences for poor instructors were both listed as areas needing to be addressed.

There is a high level of support for post-tenure evaluation among faculty leaders and instructional administrators. Governing boards and top administrators of K-12 schools and community colleges can use this support in strengthening their evaluation processes. The concerns about existing post-tenure evaluation systems need to be addressed.

Recommendations made in the studies included using evaluation more effectively for faculty development, dismissal, and rewards. It is important to move beyond "lip service" if evaluation practices are to produce results and gain the necessary respect from faculty, administrators and students.

SUGGESTED EXERCISES

1. Discuss the purposes of post-tenure faculty evaluation.
2. Explain why recognition and dismissal should both be considered in an evaluation system.

CHAPTER 12

GOVERNING BOARDS: RESPONSIBILITY FOR ASSURING HIGHLY QUALIFIED AND COMPETENT FACULTY

> The "product" of the community college is instruction. The quality of that instruction is one of the major concerns that administrators, faculty, and boards of trustees must keep as a priority focus.
>
> *Andrews (2000a)*

"**I**mproved student learning" is the outcome expected from instruction. Quality teaching is what it is all about! Governing boards have many concerns as they serve their K-12 schools or community colleges. Passing a balanced budget, paying the bills, keeping the school current in instructional supplies and technology are only a few of these responsibilities. Hiring new teachers, approving tenure, providing a teacher recognition program, moving on a 'notice to remediate' and approving a recommendation to terminate an incompetent teacher are the personnel decisions, which most influence the quality of education.

The demand of the *No Child Left Behind* legislation to provide *highly qualified teachers* in every classroom by 2005 is a signal to boards and administrators that much challenging work lies ahead. It is one thing to find teachers with a major or minor in the appropriate subject matter but it is another to assure that each of these *highly qualified teachers* are *competent* in their teaching.

How do governing boards fit into the process of faculty evaluation? Do they have rights in hiring and dismissal of faculty? What is the legal basis for such rights? These are a few of the questions that need to be addressed when setting up a faculty evaluation system. The governing boards must establish both a moral and a legal base for dealing with personnel policies, procedures, and decision-making.

Painter (2000) warned about the temptation to hire and grant tenure to poorly performing teachers at times when there appears to be a shortage of teachers in the field. She points out that: "A principal who believes little support is provided by the central office for remediation or dismissal of teachers is unlikely to expend much effort in addressing poor performers" (p. 1).

Painter further states that leaders and boards must communicate their values if they want the principals to hold teachers to high standards. The principals need to know their work to reform or remove poor teachers is going to be supported (p. 2).

Andrews (2000a) identified a number of values for boards to consider. They are repeated here to relate them to the policies of the governing boards:

Value 1:   Quality in every classroom;
Value 2:   Individual development needs of teachers;
Value 3:   A recognition plan for outstanding faculty; and
Value 4:   A strong stand on placing poor teachers into a remediation process and, if necessary, movement toward termination (p. 28).

It is important that superintendents, community college presidents and other high level administrators as well as governing boards make it clear that teacher evaluation is a *priority* so as to encourage principals, instructional deans and vice presidents to make it their priority as well.

MORAL BASE

Board members will achieve prestige from good policies that are properly administered. Solid personnel policies demanding quality in hiring, evaluation, and tenure and dismissal decisions will likely outweigh all other board responsibilities. Boards must learn the laws that govern educational institutions and avoid capricious action when making personnel decisions. Policies and procedures that remove all doubt about politically motivated appointments, nepotism, and patronage and allow for open searches for personnel must be established and honored as the boards seek personnel who will meet their quality standards.

Woodruff (1976) suggested seven basic rules that provide for board members to deal openly and honestly in personnel matters:

1. Avoid precipitous action. Do not lose your self-control.
2. Make sure you have all the facts. Do not rely on only one side's version of a disputed issue. Demand sufficient information before voting.
3. Remember your duty is to the institution you serve, not to any one member of the administration.
4. Follow the rules of the board or college policies and procedures that have been written down.
5. Make an effort to attend every board meeting. By being chronically absent, you may incur liability.
6. When in doubt, use your paid professionals. Consult your president, chancellor, and counsel.

7. Avoid conflicts of interest by disclosing potential ones up front. Refuse to debate, discuss, or vote on any matter in which you or your family have an interest (pp. 11-18).

Woodruff suggested that these "rules" should be part of the in-service training with governing boards.

LEGAL BASE AND AUTHORITY

A key responsibility of boards is to establish an evaluation system that leads to dismissal, when necessary, and the power of the boards lie in their enforcement of this system. Piele (1980) discussed board power saying:

> Boards of education have only those powers that are expressly granted or reasonably inferred to them by the legislature of the state or that have been granted to the board of education through the state board of education by rule or regulation.
>
> This power or authority cannot be delegated. Very often powers of boards are better known in the law and the courts. Many times individual board members do not understand or know them. Personnel matters are the ones that cause the greatest concern in college or K-12 schools (p. 8).

Boards have the power to establish policies for their own school districts. These policies have been found by the courts to carry the same authority as state laws when applied within the confines of the school district. However, courts may find some local policies and procedures unreasonable, arbitrary, or capricious.

Nason (1982) described board decisions as final in terms of legal authority as long as they are within their established policies. Courts or the legislature are the only ones who can legally challenge these board decisions (p. 15). Decisions by

---

boards are not always well-accepted or pleasing to faculty members or other personnel, but they will stand up legally unless challenged and later overturned through the court system.

A court decision, *Irby v. McGowan* (1974), stated that school authorities should have the right to make subjective evaluations of a work record of a teacher. The decision concluded it was not the court's job to judge every remark made concerning the employment or non-employment of non-tenured teachers. In addition, the court did not require that the teachers, who had not been re-employed, be entitled to a due-process hearing (p. 10).

Morris (1992) reported the South Dakota Supreme Court found *unlawful encroachment* upon boards' rights concerning dismissal of a tenured faculty member in *Worzella v. Board of Regents* (1958). The tenure policy that had been developed locally did not allow the board to dismiss a faculty member without first gaining approval of the college president and the faculty tenure committee. In this case the court ruled that:

> Such delegation of authority to subordinates is an unlawful encroachment upon the board of regents' constitutional and statutory power of control over the college (p. 7).

The sensitivity of board decisions in hiring and dismissal were described by Jasiek et al. (1985): "There is no greater responsibility of a board of trustees than personnel management. The board's role in hiring and firing is an issue that is so sensitive and misunderstood that no one wants to mention it" (p. 87). Jasiek et al. listed important elements of effective personnel management, dealing with hiring, retaining, or dismissal of college personnel:

- a strong governing board;
- a strong president and staff;

- mutual support, and;
- clearly defined personnel policies and procedures (p. 87).

Jasiek et al. further stated that the effectiveness of any college or school personnel system would be doomed if it lacked any one of these four ingredients.

Kauffman (1983) stated that the quality of the relationship between the board and the college president may determine how effectively board policies are enforced. He found the authority of the college president enhanced when the board assumed responsibility for approving major policy and fiscal matters, including tenure (p. 19).

Rebell (1990) found no explicit right to education in the Constitution. The Tenth Amendment to the Constitution placed rights for educational issues within individual states. Rebell's review of cases found courts specifically interested in how closely *procedural requirements* from state law, common-law, or due process requirements were followed. Most of the court cases he reviewed involved questions of interpretation of the specific requirements of the state statutes or state board regulations (p. 341).

TENURE

Tenure is one of the most misunderstood concepts by governing board members. It is very different than any concept in the private business sector. The way many administrators address tenure adds to the confusion and leads many board members, students, and lay people to believe that tenure is a guarantee of employment until retirement or death. Much of literature on tenure has perpetuated this belief. Ineffective faculty have seldom been removed from universities, which has greatly contributed to this idea. The literature and legal cases of community colleges and K-12 schools have documented that tenure is not a *sinecure* for faculty who are not performing competently. Appendix A presents a number of cases which will demonstrate to board members, administrators, faculty, and lay persons that incompetent faculty are dismissed.

Tenure is recognition that is granted after a specified number of years (usually three to seven) to those faculty who have met the standards of instructions and other job responsibilities required by the institutions that employ them. The governing board, by law, is the final authority on the rewarding or denial of tenure.

Olswang and Lee (1984) supported the protection of "academic freedom" that tenure has provided instructors. They do, however, point out that such a protection is not "unlimited." They indicated, "evaluating the continued competence of faculty does not infringe on faculty freedoms as *competence is a condition of tenure (emphasis added)*" (p. 3).

Olswang and Lee presented the court's view on individual professional freedom of faculty in the *Browzin v. Catholic University* (1975) case:

> Tenure's real concern is with arbitrary or retaliatory dismissals based on an administrator's or a trustee's distaste for the content of a professor's teaching or research, or even for positions taken completely outside the campus setting. It is designed to foster our society's interest in the unfettered progress of research and learning by protecting the profession's freedom of inquiry and instruction. . ." (p. 3).

The American Association of University Professors (AAUP) developed a statement on academic freedom in 1916 and tried to make special efforts to disassociate academic freedom from the protection of incompetence. Olswang and Lee stated:

> If the profession should prove itself unwilling to purge its ranks of the incompetent and the unworthy, or to prevent the freedom which it claims in the name of science from being used as a shelter for inefficiency,

for superficiality, or for uncritical and intemperate partisanship, it is certain that the task will be performed by others (p. 3).

The concern about neglect in dealing with incompetent and/or unworthy faculty was clearly stated. This statement from 1916 showed that there has been a longtime concern about the profession protecting incompetent personnel.

POLICIES ON TEACHER EVALUATION

With the legal right and authority to develop policies and practices that assure quality in instruction, it is most important that appropriate board policies be developed to improve instruction. Andrews (1995) provided samples of board policies that establish a framework for quality evaluation practices. Several changes have been made to address the *No Student Left Behind* legislation. Example 5 is a board policy relating to evaluation:

EXAMPLE 5:
Board Policy—Evaluation of Faculty
Tenured, Non-tenured, and Part-time

It is the policy of the governing board that supervisors shall evaluate all faculty of the college in order to assure that quality instruction and other professional conduct are achieved and maintained.

Persons to be covered by the above mentioned evaluation procedures will be: (1) tenured faculty; (2) non-tenured faculty; (3) part-time faculty; (4) counselors; and (5) assistants to instruction (p. 201).

Example 6 relates to boards' hiring of professional personnel:

EXAMPLE 6:
Board Policy—Hiring of Professional Staff

The Governing Board will hire a professional staff, educated and prepared in accordance with generally accepted standards and practices for teaching in the discipline and subject fields to which they are assigned. These standards include collegiate study and/or professional work experience. As a general rule, middle and secondary school teachers will have a major or minor in the subject areas they are assigned to teach. Community college faculty will have achieved a Master's Degree or beyond in the subjects taught, except in such subjects and fields in which college programs are not normally available or in which the work experience and related training is the principle teaching preparation necessary (p. 202).

Example 7 acknowledges the responsibility of the governing board in the dismissal of non-tenured faculty and/or other instructional support personnel:

EXAMPLE 7
Board Policy—Decision Not to Rehire
Non-tenured, Full-time and Instructional Support Personnel

A decision to dismiss a non-tenured faculty member or instructional support personnel for the ensuing school year or term will be made by the Governing Board reviewing the superintendent's or president's recommendation (p. 202).

These policies lay the foundation for governing boards' authorities and responsibilities related to teachers and instructional support staff.

IMPLEMENTING POLICIES

The ability to administer board policies on evaluation properly depends upon the quality of the administrative staff that is hired to implement them. The board needs to orient its administrators as to the importance of in-class evaluation procedures as well as laws related to evaluation, tenure, and dismissals. Administrative evaluators need to be well versed and experienced in quality classroom instructional methods. Although not necessary, the process of in-class evaluating is enhanced when evaluators were excellent classroom teachers themselves prior to becoming administrators.

A major question from faculty leaders has been, "Who is evaluating the evaluator?" This concern is legitimate in cases where administrators are given responsibilities for evaluation without knowing enough about the dynamic processes involved in teaching and learning.

WEAK IMPLEMENTATION

Weak implementation of board policies on evaluation by administrators may lead to costly litigation, public criticism, and court appearances. Brown (1977) found there was very little court involvement with instruction prior to the 1970s. Most of the disputes were decided within the school system. He describes the action since 1970 as an "explosion of litigation in the areas of tenure and employment contracts" (p. 279).

The Grand Rapids Board of Education, in Michigan, paid a heavy public relations price for the decision they made to quietly remove incompetent teachers and strike any evidence

---

of such incompetence from their records. *The Grand Rapids Press* (1988a, January 22) harshly criticized the board's action in preparing special agreements with the faculty members involved. One editorial pointed out clearly the inappropriateness of the board's action. The board replied defending its position. An angry taxpayer in the district wrote another response when the board attempted to justify their actions. Following is an edited version of each of these articles beginning with the editorial:

Expedite Over Principle

'The end doesn't justify the means' is an adage old enough to be stenciled on the consciences of all nine members of the Grand Rapids Board of Education. They ought to recall it the next time they dismiss a teacher for incompetence.

In each of three contested cases last year in which tenured teachers were permanently removed from city classrooms, the board agreed to cooperate with the teacher in hiding the whole matter from other employers. In one instance, the board went so far as to provide the ousted teacher with a letter of recommendation.

The arrangement is worked out in varying language in each settlement agreement. In all three cases, the board agrees to withdraw charges against the teacher and erase all mention of them from the teacher's personnel file. One settlement restricts the board from releasing evaluations of the teacher to any prospective employer; another requires that evaluations and 'all negative materials' be removed from the personnel file. The letter of recommendation given to one teacher noted 'she was a hard working and conscientious employee during her years of employment in Grand Rapids.'

Con men would take pride in such flim-flam. School trustees should be ashamed. The effect of sanitized files and misleading recommendations is to pass the Grand Rapids problem along to some other school district—and some other set of children . . . . No school

---

board, moreover, can define its moral responsibilities so narrowly as to include only children inside its own school buildings; a board is answerable for actions, which put children at risk, regardless of where they are.

The schools will be seeking removal of more teachers this spring. The cases might well go longer and cost more if the board refuses to set the teachers up for new jobs elsewhere.

There is at least an equal chance, however, that a policy of firmness and honesty over time will strengthen the board's hand in improving the faculty. At the least, such a commitment would assure that no child is made a victim of expedience.

The Board of Education response was printed on the editorial page (Grand Rapids Press, 1988b, February 2):

As trustees of public monies, were officials of the Grand Rapids Public Schools correct to negotiate a settlement with teachers who were being dismissed for alleged incompetence? During the proceedings, the teachers in question agreed to resign, but the district had to agree to remove any information pertaining to the tenure proceedings from their files.

After lengthy debate, the board made a very tough decision to accept those settlements in three out of four tenure cases that were heard in 1987, because we were concerned about the exorbitant legal cost to continue the hearings. As it was, this school district spent more than $100,000 to terminate three teachers who were allegedly incompetent. Continuing those cases could have cost an additional $100,000 to $300,000.

Even if we had fought these cases to the very end, and were upheld, would we have been able to tell potential employers that these people had been dismissed for incompetency? Without written notice to a former employee, a former employer cannot reveal the content of an employee's personnel file. If a district were to take this course, they would be subject to further financial liability.

You also severely criticized the district for agreeing to give one of the employees in question a letter of recommendation. The letter in question was agreed to only after long and intense negotiations with counsel representing the plaintiff. The letter does not recommend, but simply states that the individual was hard working and conscientious, which was true. We can't speak for your hiring practices, but that letter would certainly demand more scrutiny by personnel officials in receiving school districts.

What position would The Grand Rapids Press have taken editorially if this school district had to lay off up to a dozen highly qualified teachers to pay the legal cost to protect out-state and out-of-state school districts from incompetent teachers? After all, they too have highly qualified personnel departments to thoroughly examine and interview prospective new employees to measure their skills.

Board of Education,
Grand Rapids Public Schools

The third in this series of articles was a response by John Douglas, a local taxpayer, who was most upset with the attempted justification by the board. Douglas's response follows (Grand Rapids Press, 1988c, February 5):

Why pay so much, hide so much to fire teachers?

I was going to keep my mouth shut about the situation in which the Grand Rapids Board of Education spent more than $100,000 to fire three teachers because of their inability to teach. But when I read the letter sent to the Press by the members of the Board of Education which was printed in 'Dissent!' last Tuesday, I just had to leap into the fray.

In the first place, it is absolutely ridiculous for it to cost that much to do some weeding. Something is wrong. Perhaps we need to take a look at the tenure system and scrap it in favor of a less costly one. I've always felt that the combination of tenure and a union is a bit much, anyway.

I don't care what the school board said in its letter to the Press—giving an incompetent teacher a letter of recommendation is the pits. I'm willing to admit that a person can be a hard worker and a bad teacher. People often find themselves in the wrong field of endeavor. The least that could have been done was to see to it that the letter of recommendation not be used in obtaining another teaching position.

Our school system's personnel department was unable to spot problems with these people—why should other school systems be expected to do what we couldn't?

I also find it offensive that there seems to be some kind of extortion going on which forces the school board to give in lest it has to lay off teachers so it can afford to carry on the tenure hearings to their proper conclusions.

Is the world going mad? What is all this?

John Douglas

The above scenario only reinforces the public image that governing boards and administrators are afraid to challenge faculty members who are not performing. It clearly shows how incompetent teachers can be perpetuated through poor board procedures and poor execution. There is also the possibility of board and/or personal liability in the type of decision that resulted in letters of recommendation when the board had determined the teacher in question was indeed incompetent.

COLLECTIVE BARGAINING AND EVALUATION

Governing boards need to be knowledgeable concerning contract negotiations that relate to the evaluation process. A caution was given by Strike and Bull (1981) that boards be careful not to negotiate away their legislated prerogatives. Boards must be aware that contract language can end up violating a statute or a strong public policy. They concluded that "the substantial criteria of evaluation are usually not negotiable" (p. 328).

In the case of *Foleno v. Board of Education of the Township of Bedminster* (1978) the court found : "the board has the duty, in furnishing a thorough and efficient education, to evaluate the performances of its employees and to staff its classrooms with skillful and effective teachers" (Piele 1979, p. 11). Piele cites another court decision, *Teacneck Board of Education v. Teacneck Teachers Association* (1978), which ruled against bargaining teacher evaluation practices: "Nevertheless, negotiation of evaluation criteria is against public policy because retention or promotion of teachers is a management prerogative" (p. 147).

Orze (1977) did not find faculty power to be limitless when it comes to the faculty contractual negotiations. He saw reasonable boundaries being established as a result of legislative acts in some states. He stated that the "legal powers of the union extend only to the mandatory subjects for collective bargaining that the administration must negotiate with it" (pp. 507-508). He found that management sometimes goes beyond the board rights in negotiating away legal prerogatives:

> The union has no legal right to bargain for authority beyond those mandatory subjects. Whatever additional powers the union may gain at the bargaining table

can only be achieved if the administration is willing to share one or more of its managerial rights with the union. The administration controls the scope of negotiations, and, in so doing, it determines the actual limits of the legal powers of the union. Unions will attempt to expand the scope of bargaining as broadly as employers will allow them to, but the employer always has the right to say 'no' to any nonmandatory demand for negotiations (pp. 507-508).

In contrast to the cases above, the Supreme Courts in North Dakota and Indiana both allowed teacher evaluation policies to be permitted in negotiations. In the Indiana case of *Evansville-Vanderburgh School Corp. v. Roberts* (1979), the court upheld that the school board should have held discussions with the union before implementing its new teacher evaluation plan. In this case the term "discussible" was used to describe evaluation as a working condition between the board and union. Orze warned boards that once they negotiate a subject in the faculty contract it becomes almost impossible for the employer to negotiate it back out if the union wishes to retain it.

Piele (1979) pointed out that negotiated procedures on evaluation *do not* negate management's rights (p. 163). This includes the management's exclusive right to hire and to fire personnel. Negotiated procedures might include administrative, student, peer, or self-evaluation procedures. In 1978 the Michigan Supreme Court concluded, "adoption of student evaluations of faculty was within the mandatory scope of bargaining since it would affect reappointment, tenure, and promotion" (p. 146).

In Iowa the negotiated contract in one school was found to be contrary to public policy. The Iowa Supreme Court found the Davenport Community School District was in violation of what they could legally negotiate into the faculty contract in *Moravek v. Davenport Community School District* (1978).

In this case they had negotiated language that took away responsibility of the governing board of the school and allowed arbitrators to decide on the non-renewal issues of faculty members. The court ruled that this was not an item that could be negotiated away from the responsibility of the governing board of the school.

The faculty contract in the Rio Hondo Community College District in California clearly spelled out that *administrative evaluation* was the system that had been selected by the board of trustees. The administration did, however, allow for the procedures to be negotiated with the faculty.

Andrews (1991), in his study of community colleges in the North Central region of the country, found that 87 colleges out of the 283 responding had negotiated faculty evaluation systems. An additional 45 colleges reported that they had negotiated faculty contracts that contained no language about faculty evaluation. Eleven of the 19 states covered in the study reported they had no negotiated evaluation systems. Table 7 below shows that 42.5 percent of the administrators who responded that they had negotiated evaluation language were not satisfied with the contract language. Some 26 per-

Table 7: Instructional Leaders' Responses to Evaluation Systems Negotiated into Faculty Contracts
N = 87

Questions on Negotiated Language	Yes	No
1. Are you satisfied with the negotiated contract language	50(57.5%)	37(42.5%)
2. Has evaluation, in your opinion, been hindered for you as a supervisor since the language has been negotiated?	23(26%)	64 (74%)

cent indicated that they had been hindered as a supervisor by the restrictive language that had been negotiated (p. 4).

The areas that the administrative found to be of greatest concern were (1) poor language written into the contract; (2) the language imposed on the role as administrators who have responsibilities for evaluation; (3) deficiencies in procedures to develop criteria; and (4) use of student evaluation. Table 8 shows the number of responses received for each of these restrictions.

The specific restrictions on administrators were identified as follows:

1. Tenured teachers are no longer evaluated by administrators.
2. The system is now too confining; more avenues for evaluation are needed.
3. Department chairpersons are not allowed sufficient responsibility.
4. There is not enough language regarding supervisory evaluation.
5. It is now faculty controlled. Administrators are only used when a bona fide problem has been acknowledged.
6. The system does not include tenured faculty.
7. Evaluation needs to be more frequent.
8. Division chairs should be involved, as they are closest to faculty.
9. The language is too restrictive and not really formative.

The deficiencies in "criteria and procedures" were:

1. No provision is made for improvement of instruction.
2. They are not precise enough.
3. They don't focus on curriculum outcomes.
4. The system identifies strengths and concerns but does not provide for rewards or corrections.
5. No specifics and no consequences are given.

6.   It does not take into account the individual's goals.
7.   Plans of action are not clear enough (pp. 5-6).

One Wisconsin college response indicated that the contract requires student evaluation but does not make it a requirement to have supervisory evaluation. It was indicated, however, that movement was underway to change the condition. In another case, a large metropolitan college administrator submitted contract pages showing faculty evaluation to be restricted to student review. She pointed out that she was unable to visit a classroom *unless invited*. She stated that administrative evaluation should be a requirement.

In a Michigan College the contract was written to let the faculty member choose if he or she wished to have evaluation by a supervisor. A second respondent from Michigan

Table 8: Unsatisfactory or Incomplete Language Negotiated Into Faculty Contracts Categories of Written Responses by Instructional Leaders

Restrictions/Deficiencies in Contract Language	Number of Responses
1. Poor or incomplete language in content	11
2. Restrictions imposed on administrators	9
3. Deficiencies in criteria and procedures	8
4. Student evaluation concerns	4
Total written responses	32

mentioned that supervisory evaluation was almost non-existent except at a time the "department recognizes areas of deficiency" (p. 8). In an even more restrictive stipulation, the request for evaluation by the immediate supervisors must be made by no later than January 1 of any given year. The contract also stated that "such a request shall not become a part of the faculty member's personnel file, nor shall it serve as cause for dismissal." One other college contract made clear that any documents produced through supervisory review are "the property of the reviewed faculty member, and such documents or copies shall not be kept by the department members involved in the review, or become a permanent part of the faculty member's record without the faculty member's permission" (pp. 8-9).

It is little wonder that evaluation processes that produce substantial improvement in instruction is lacking in many elementary, middle and secondary schools and community colleges.

Licata (1986) questioned how a faculty union on campus might affect the viability of a post-tenure evaluation plan. Kleingartner (1984) found that all aspects of evaluation, including its implementation, came under the scope of negotiations, and that administrators must follow the negotiated collective bargaining agreement. Cohen and Brawer (1982) found that evaluation procedures became so elaborate and complex that they gained "labyrinthine complexity" (p. 75).

Arreola (1983) cited the importance of faculty evaluation: "Only when the administration realizes that well-constructed faculty evaluation and development programs do not diminish their ability to direct the course and quality of their institutions, but rather enhance and strengthen it, will a truly successful faculty evaluation and development program have been established" (p. 92).

Andrews (1985) described the steps in the total evaluation process that require involvement by governing boards.

He listed, "hiring, granting of tenure, dismissal of non-tenured staff, formal notices to remediate, establishing of supportive recognition programs, and firing of tenured faculty as both the prerogatives and/or legal responsibilities of governing boards" (p. 56).

STATUTES INTRODUCED

A number of statutes that have compromised the role previously given to governing boards of colleges, elementary, middle, and secondary schools have been introduced by legislative bodies in many states. Providing a statement of reason in the *non-renewal of non-tenured faculty* member's contract is one such change. The requirement of a predetermination hearing before an independent hearing officer has also been added.

Piele (1981) found a statute in Kentucky that requires, on request, a written statement of the grounds for dismissal of a non-tenured faculty member. He found similar requirements in Alaska and Vermont (p. 89). In a parallel case in Michigan, Piele, (1980), the question of whether a reason needed to be given for denial of tenure was addressed by the Supreme Court. After being evenly divided in a previous hearing of the case, one justice changed his mind, and the court concluded that it was not necessary to state reasons for such a dismissal. The decision cited the 1972 *Roth* case and concluded that the Michigan state tenure act did not give entitlement to such notice (p. 84). This case, while not succeeding in reversing the previously established practice, presents another in a line of court challenges and legislative attempts to challenge the power of governing boards in educational matters.

An Illinois case, *Board of Trustees of Community College District Number 513 v. Dale Krizek and the American Federation of Teachers, Local 1810* (1983), summarized the

---

power that is vested in the governing board. Citing several previous state cases, the Third District Appellate Court concluded:

> The Supreme Court has made it unmistakably clear that when a governing board is vested with the power to grant tenure, or to not renew, then the governing board cannot delegate, modify or condition its final authority to make such decisions. Although the statute here in question differs slightly from the one at issue in the prior cases, there is no variation from the essential factor relied on in those cases, i.e., the governing board's ultimate authority on tenure questions. There can be no dilution of the board's authority whether the evaluation of teachers is mandated by contract or by statute.

The court went on to describe the fine balance necessary to maintain quality in the schools and to address the issue of job security:

> We are mindful that the tenure laws represent an elaborate balance between the need to maintain the quality of schools and the opposing interest in job security in Board of Education of the *City of Chicago v. Chicago Teachers Union, Local 1* (1981). In attempting to strike that balance, the legislature has crafted a system where there appears to be unlimited power in boards to dismiss probationary teachers at the board's discretion while the power to dismiss tenured teachers is considerably restricted. (*Lockport Area Special Education Cooperative v. Lockport Area Special Education Cooperative Association* (1975).) We perceive Krizek's position as an attempt to erode the area of the board's discretion by injecting elements of cause into the board's decision to terminate. Inasmuch as this is repugnant to the policy embodied in the statute, we decline to adopt the statutory construction proffered by Krizek.
>
> Finally, in her brief Krizek raises a constitutional issue concerning infringement of her right to due pro-

cess. Although the Board seeks to have those portions of the brief stricken as representing theories not pursued in the court below, we hereby deny the motion to strike, but dismiss the substantive issue raised by Krizek as without merit, relying on the authority of *Board of Trustees v. Cook County College Teachers Union* (1987), which presented the same question for review in a factually indistinguishable setting.

We conclude, then, that the decision of the circuit court of LaSalle County was correct, and its judgment should be affirmed for the reasons we have set forth.

In this case Krizak was dismissed by the college prior to receiving tenure and the board of trustees decision was confirmed.

Lewis (1980), as a board member, discussed the duties of the board relative to delivering excellence in education. He directed his plea to college presidents when he said, "If you decide to help us, be expansive and generous, and give us a little more instruction. Tell us that our primary duty is to determine and, if necessary, redetermine the mission and purpose of our college, and that only in that context do we really involve ourselves with 'policy'—policy related to the delivery of excellent education services at the classroom (or equivalent) level, is above all, else, our *raison d'etre*" (p. 20).

RECOGNITION PROGRAMS BY BOARDS

It is important that boards also understand the positive impact that recognition can have on the improvement of instruction in the K-12 schools and community colleges. Andrews (2000C) reported from his survey of faculty leaders in community colleges across the country that recognition and merit compensation were the second most important reasons for having evaluation systems. They asked that administrators and boards consider the following:

- Utilize results (of evaluation) in a meaningful way to let faculty know when they are doing an excellent job and when they need help;
- Provide more feedback and awards from the system;
- Reward the effective faculty members, not the slouchers; not enough distinction now; and
- Give consequences to the results, both pro and con (p. 29).

The list of values discussed earlier in this chapter included "recognition" as a responsible and important value for boards and the institutions.

SUMMARY

Proper board policies arc paramount in guaranteeing students in every classroom quality instruction. Board members need to learn to develop and implement policies early in their work on boards.

The basis for quality instruction is carefully conceived in board policies that relate to board values. These are policies relating to hiring, granting of tenure, recognition programs, remediation and dismissal. Abilities and attitudes of administrative staff, from the college president or elementary, middle or secondary school superintendent through other key instructional leaders, determine how well board policies are carried out. These administrators should also provide assurance to the boards that quality instruction in every classroom can be guaranteed to all students.

The willingness of board members to make the difficult, as well as the easy decisions, helps to assure the students and parents of a school district or college that students will attend a quality institution.

SUGGESTED EXERCISES

1. Write two board policies that will assure a board that evaluation will be conducted for the purposes of improving instruction.
2. What happens within the institution if the board rejects the administration's recommendation for remediation or dismissal?

CHAPTER 13

THE LEGAL BASIS FOR TEACHER TERMINATIONS

> The system of how we protect mediocrity in teaching has gotten so calcified and thick it's no longer possible to see through it. At least not well enough to discern the look on the faces of students when they are told: "There's nothing we can do about so-so." That's a look no educator or policymaker should ever forget.
>
> *Chicago Tribune, Editorial (2001), December 23*

The *Chicago Tribune* (2001, December 23) editorial stated how appalled it was by a school principal bringing a group of bright high school journalists to the *Tribune* office. The editor stated that these students "spoke animatedly about how every student knows exactly who the lousy teachers are. They know who the mediocre ones are, too" (Section 1, p. 18). The principal, during this discussion, told the students that it takes up to two years to remove a poor teacher because there are so many intricate legal procedures involved. When one student asked, "What about the mediocre teachers?" the principal answered that she didn't even try to remove them because it is too complicated to do.

Schwartz (1997) stated that as public and legislated mandates for school improvement and accountability grow, we can no longer indulge poorly performing teachers while expecting to improve student achievement (p. 4). Lovain (1983-84) pointed to the difficulty that termination of a tenured faculty member creates within the institution:

One of the most difficult personnel actions that a college or university can take is to terminate the employment of a tenured faculty member for cause. The emotional repercussions of such actions often extend far beyond the terminated faculty member (p. 419).

In discussing the frustration in dealing with teachers with problems, Chapman (1998) reported on a case in Northern Virginia. The teacher, he pointed out, had a drinking problem and was caught drinking in her classroom. She could not, however, be fired! The tenure laws were made the villain. A board member in California, in discussing the need to have tenure changed, said, "I don't see it [change] forthcoming. I recognize that the power and muscle of the teacher organizations in California are so dominant over the state legislature that the legislators are not too inclined to mess with them" (p. 114).

Chapman reported other cases in which tenure made it difficult to fire incompetent teachers and felons:

A New York City teacher was convicted of selling cocaine. He had tenure and it took two years and $185,000 to fire him. In 1993 an Oakland high school teacher sat by as her students watched a pornographic video....twice. The state couldn't revoke her license. She still teaches.

In Illinois, a district spent about $700,000 to get rid of a high school math teacher who couldn't do basic algebra and let students sleep in class (p. 114).

There are 2.6 million school teachers in the United States public schools according to Chapman. He reported that Mary Jo McGrath of McGrath Systems Inc., in Santa Barbara, California, estimated that 18 percent, or 468,000 teachers, were considered incompetent. Her estimate came from her survey of 50,000 school administrators. She assists schools in removing "lousy teachers."

A 1994 study conducted by the New York State School Boards Association found that it takes an average of 455 days and $176,870 for a tenured teacher to be fired by a school board in that state. When the teacher makes appeals, the amount goes to approximately $317,000.

Those very persons who have the responsibility to execute proper evaluation techniques from which a decision for dismissal can be made often misunderstand the process involved in the dismissal of a tenured faculty member. Dismissals have strict legal requirements, create much emotional stress, and are seldom carried out without a significant financial burden on the elementary, middle, or secondary school or college.

Bridges (1990b) spoke about strong leadership being essential in dealing with the incompetent teachers. He felt the institution must hold the appraisers accountable in evaluating and carrying out the steps necessary in dealing with the incompetent faculty members.

Jenkins et al. (1979) addressed the concern of many persons in the educational reform movement:

> Guaranteed lifetime employment has more often come about because administrators and boards of education have been unsure of the process of discharging the unsatisfactory teachers. Or they have had an inadequate system of evaluating the teacher—particularly of recording such evaluations—and therefore have been hesitant to move against the teacher. *Boards and administrators frequently blame tenure for what in fact is their own failures in evaluating teachers and in securing qualified teaching staffs* (emphasis added). This is widely reflected in the small amounts of time and money allocated to the evaluation of personnel performance in our schools (p. 11).

'DANCE OF THE LEMONS'

School districts have been found to have done little to develop and utilize effective evaluation systems when there was a shortage of qualified teachers (Bridges, 1990b). A lack of clearly defined criteria, poor preparation of administrative personnel, and a lack of accountability for principals to do this task exacerbated the problem (p. 147).

The school districts reacted to what Bridges saw as a complaint-driven approach to teacher evaluation. In short, when a parent complained, principals would go into the classroom and come out with favorable ratings so as to avoid the difficult job of having to deal honestly with poor instruction. Bridges found that principals either overlooked such poor performances, inflated performance ratings hoping this would encourage the persons to improve through positive reinforcement, or would "send the person packing" to another school within the district (p. 148). Wheeler et al. (1993) defined this moving around of poor teachers, as the 'dance of the lemons' (p. 11). Some schools do not face the need to move toward dismissal of their incompetent teachers, but rather transfer them. Usually the poorer schools ended up with a disproportionate number of these incompetent teachers as the administrators found these schools to be the path of least resistance. In the poorer school there were likely to be fewer complaints from the parents. Middle class parents were known to be more vocal and were much more willing to come forth to express their displeasure and expect action when poor instruction was found.

Small schools did not have these "escape hatches," according to Bridges. These schools had to deal more directly with the teachers, and used two courses of action: (1) sought improvement of the teacher's performance and (2) found a way to get rid of the teacher if this failed. Encouragement to resign or retire early was also used. The record shows that remediation efforts did little to improve the poor teachers.

The reasons for ineffectiveness are usually a complex mix rather than one discreetly identifiable problem. These causes can be lack of ability, lack of motivation, health problems or alcoholism, etc. Remediation, if aimed at a single problem, may not be effective because a single teacher may have a combination of problems.

A teacher shortage was predicted for the 1990's and Bridges (1990a) warned that history might repeat itself and allow poor teachers to slip into tenured positions due to a lack of evaluation efforts by administrators. He cited the 1950s, 1960s, and 1970s as periods when large numbers of teachers were hired and had little supervision during their non-tenure probationary periods (pp. 147-50).

THE CRITICAL DECISION TO AWARD TENURE

The courts and hearing officers in arbitration assume that once a person has achieved tenure they are, indeed, competent teachers. Bridges (1990a) stated that "incompetence, not competence, becomes the standard by which the teacher's continued employment is judged" (pp. 150-151). The burden is placed upon the school district to prove incompetence; otherwise the instructor will be considered to have the right to continued employment within the school district. Bridges went on to clarify what incompetence is in terms of the law:

> Incompetence does not mean marginal or mediocre; rather, it means that the person is a blatant failure in the classroom—so poor that no reasonable person would doubt that the teacher is inept in the classroom (pp. 150-51).

With this in mind it is imperative that future tenure decisions be made with the utmost of care and agreement as to a

---

teacher's ability to teach at the standard of performance expected by the school or college. Valente (1987) reinforced the presumption that those teachers receiving tenure are, indeed, competent employees and that there is a need to establish strong justification for considering removal of such a teacher (pp. 210-216).

Nelson (1997) wrote of weak faculty in higher educational institutions who had been able to get tenured. He referred to these professors as those who are performing their jobs but very poorly. Their tenure decisions are considered mistakes. Nelson pointed out that the teachers showed weaknesses prior to tenure as shown in teacher records. He said that collegiality, friendship, or self-deception contributed to their receiving tenure. He suggested that administrators need to be very careful not to hire marginal or second-rate teachers at the time they are candidates.

BOARD: POWER AND RESPONSIBILITIES

The governing boards of K-12 schools and colleges are only as successful as those persons hired by them to perform at a quality level. An effective evaluation system gives the boards much better means of determining who is performing at the levels expected. It also offers them a means of removing those teachers who for reason of inability or for reason of refusal, are not, performing at the level expected by the school.

A review of board powers found that state laws usually grant such powers. Piele (1980) states, "It is a well settled rule of law that boards of education have only those powers that are expressly granted or reasonably inferred to them by the legislature of the state or that have been granted to the board of education through the state board of education by rule or regulation" (p.8). He suggested that boards should not, and cannot, delegate such powers. He concluded that, based upon case study, board members knew little about their powers as established by law or in courts.

Policies of boards, if properly conceived and judiciously applied, carry a great deal of power. Piele (1979) saw policies as "carrying the same weight of authority as state law within the confines of the school district. Policies that are unreasonable, arbitrary, or capricious must be found so by the courts" (p. 14).

While boards are given their authority by law, in practice there are many situations that usurp the board's authority in these matters (*U. S. News and World Report*, 1996b, February 26). An attorney in Chicago representing school boards, Mary Jo McGrath, discussed how tough it is to fight the tenure system and indicated that many administrators simply do not bother. She said that, "instead, they are willing to sometimes cut deals of giving satisfactory ratings to some poor teachers if the unions will assist them to move them to other schools. A professor of public administration at New York University counseled that "it says to hard-working teachers that there are no standards, that it doesn't matter" (p. 66). The Tenth Amendment to the Constitution places educational issues in the realm of state responsibility. Rebell (1990) determined that most questions on issues of faculty evaluation that come before the court system center on "questions of interpretation of the specific requirements of state statutes or state board regulations" (p. 341). The specific procedural requirements are most important when dealing with faculty dismissal cases. Procedural requirements are usually spelled out clearly and are required by state-law, common-law, or due process rules.

Nason (1982) found that, "only the courts or the legislature can legally challenge a board's decisions" (p.14). Such decisions are normally considered as final legal authority. If board policies on evaluation procedures and actions are reasonable and within the statutes, the decisions made are held as final unless challenged through the court process and found to violate the letter of the law. Piele (1980) stated that boards, in most states, are "the only bodies that can hire or fire employees" (p. 12).

NON-TENURE DISMISSALS: THE BOARD'S ULTIMATE AUTHORITY

Boards and administrators have an excellent opportunity to strengthen their teaching faculties over the coming years through (1) "open" faculty searches which are free from political and nepotism pressures, and (2) early evaluation and formative assistance for all new persons hired. There should be no pressure on the boards or administrators to tenure all faculty. The courts have, indeed, considered the wisdom of the probationary period, prior to a tenure decision being made, and have given boards almost unlimited power to decide whether tenure will be awarded.

In 1972 a major United States Supreme Court decision reaffirmed the power of local educational boards. In *Board of Regents v. Roth* (1972), it was determined by the court that *no property interest rights* exist for non-tenured teachers. In short, the court told boards, administrators, and teachers that there was no need to provide cause or to provide formal dismissal proceedings when they were involved in dismissing non-tenured teachers.

The Roth decision has been used by courts in any number of challenges to local governing boards by faculty members and local unions. Knowles and Wedlock (1973) presented the New Jersey case of *Katz v. Board of Trustees of Gloucester County College* (1972) in which a faculty member challenged his dismissal. The instructor claimed that his non-retention was based upon his exercise of lawful union activities and thus violated his First Amendment rights. The court, in holding against the instructor, felt that to decide otherwise would be tantamount to abolishing the tenure system. The court further stated that:

> Inherent in our legislatively enacted tenure policy is the existence of a probationary period during which the board will have a chance to evaluate a teacher with no commitments to re-employ him. We hold that it is the prerogative of the board of trustees to discontinue the employment of a non-tenured teacher at the end of his teaching contract with or without reason (p. 205).

Court cases through the 1990's and early into the 2000's have continued to support boards in their role in making tenure decisions. The board was upheld in *Rivera v. Community School District Nine* (2001) for terminating a probationary teacher for helping students to cheat on standardized tests. The federal trial court found the teacher not eligible for due process as no property right existed.

A New York board rescinded its decision to offer tenure to a teacher who admitted to having consumed alcohol at a school function in *Remus v. Board of Education for Tonwanda City School District* (2001). He admitted this act after the board had voted in the spring for tenure but before the start of the next school year when tenure would have gone into effect. The Court of Appeals of New York agreed that the tenure offer could be rescinded up to the start of the new school year.

A New York appellate court in *Williams v. Franklin Square Union Free School District* (1999) denied a teacher judicial review of her dismissal. The court pointed out that the teacher had received permissible reasons from the board that kept her from obtaining tenure.

A Louisiana appellate court, in *McKenzie v. Webster Parish School Board* (1995), upheld the dismissal of a non-tenured teacher. The appeal had been made to show the board had not complied with the requisite professional assistance form and had not set a deadline for the instructor to show improvement. The court found that the teacher had been given two years and nine months in which to show improvement in his classroom control and had been evaluated sixteen times over a three-year period. In addition, he had been provided with written recommendations and suggestions on the needed improvements by three well-qualified educators.

In *Conway v. Pacific University* (1994), an Oregon appeals court upheld a teacher's dismissal after the lower court had found in favor of the teacher. His suit claimed misrepresentation as he was told that the evaluations of his teaching were not to be used in the decision of his tenure. The court did not find a special relationship existing between the college and the faculty member. A misrepresentation claim against the university was not sustained.

In some cases boards have made procedural errors but have still been upheld in the decision not to allow automatic tenure for teachers due to these procedural mistakes. This was the case in *Stratton v. Austin Independent School District* (1999) where the appellate court found a teacher with a one-year contract having no protected property interest in having a contract renewal. During the teacher's hearing, the school board violated its own policy by having a time limit of one hour for the teacher to present her evidence. The court found, however, that even with this policy violation the non-tenured teacher had no protected property interest.

Aspects of notice and procedural due process

Russo (2002) describes *procedural due process* as "addressing how persons are treated when they have been charged with violations of statutes or rules" (p. 16). Such due process is not required in most states for non-tenured teachers.

Not all probationary teachers, however, have been terminated automatically through evaluation processes and procedures. Some states have legislated procedures and processes that must be followed before "termination" is allowed.

In *Clark County School District v. Riley* (2000) a Nevada school board was not upheld in its dismissal of a teacher because it did not properly follow the 15-day requirement of notice-to-dismiss. It gave only four days notice and, in addition, the board failed to notify the instructor that a hearing was possible. The importance of proper "notice" was highlighted in *Bentley v. School District No. 015 of Custer County* (1998) in Nebraska. The Supreme Court's decision to reinstate a probationary teacher was based on the fact that the school board failed in their responsibility to follow the state statutory requirements in terms of a proper notice to the teacher. The evaluation of the teacher by the principal was not enough.

A third case was decided in favor of the teacher when the administrators did not follow the Ohio state requirements for the number of classroom evaluations. The Supreme Court of Ohio reversed in favor of a teacher due to the administration not following state law requiring four classroom observations of at least thirty minutes each. The operative collective bargaining agreement required only two evaluations, which was the number the administration conducted. The court found the district in failure of the state law in *Snyder v. Mendon-Union Local School District Board of Education* (1996).

NON-TENURED: LACK OF A PROPERTY INTEREST

A property interest in a job deals with "expectations that employees allege they have, therefore entitling them to due process before those expectations can be adversely affected"

(Russo, 2002, p. 16). The majority of the court and arbitration cases from the *Board of Regents v. Roth* case (1972) to the present have supported the governing boards and administrators relative to probationary teachers having a *lack of a property interest* in their positions. A sampling of cases following the 1972 Supreme Court decision follows.

A Michigan case, *Lipka v. Brown City Community Schools* (1978), which raised the issue of reasons and cause for a non-tenured dismissal, was decided by the state supreme court. In this case the court stated, "There can be no dilution of the board's authority whether the evaluation of teachers is mandated by contract or by statute." This decision was supported by the Roth case and concluded that there was no entitlement for tenure under the state tenure act.

In *Irby v. McGowan* (1974) the federal district court found no proof of deprivation of liberty or attachment of stigma. The court made a major statement in terms of clarifying boards' rights in evaluation:

> School authorities should have some right to make subjective evaluations of a work record of a person. The court simply cannot, and should not, sit in judgment on, and supervise every remark made concerning the employment or non-employment of persons in a school system and require that every person not re-employed be entitled to a due process hearing.

The Third District Appellate Court of Illinois supported the power that is vested with governing boards in *Board of Trustees of Community College District Number 513 v. Krizek and the American Federation of Teachers, Local 1810* (1983). The court cited the U. S. Supreme Court's earlier decision:

> The Supreme Court has made unmistakably clear that when a governing board is vested with the power to grant tenure, or to not renew, then the governing board

cannot delegate, modify or condition its final authority to make such decisions.

The key element in this case, as in previous cases, was the clarifying of the governing board's ultimate authority on tenure questions: *"There can be no dilution of the board's authority whether the evaluation of teachers is mandated by contract or by statute"* (emphasis added). The Illinois court also stated:

> It follows then that the power to grant tenure cannot be conditioned upon the decision of an administrator to make a recommendation or hold a consultation, nor can the power be limited by the preponderance of opinion of evaluators, even though their evaluations may be conducted at the behest of the board. So long as a procedure for evaluation has been implemented, and the results of those evaluations are available to the board, we believe that compliance with the statute has been achieved, and any subsequent decisions to terminate ordered by the board are statutorily sound.

This statement clearly places the board as the decision-makers in the process for retention or dismissal of non-tenured teachers.

This case also presented a reminder that faculty members have little to no due-process rights as probationary faculty. It becomes important that as board policies and procedures are written, hints of property interest should be avoided, as such language may well mislead faculty and administrators into believing such interests may exist. The cases presented here of non-tenure dismissal cases make it clear that governing boards are, indeed, the final authority on tenure-granting decisions.

Additional non-tenured faculty terminations supported through both arbitration and the courts are summarized in Appendix A.

TENURED DISMISSALS: DUE-PROCESS AND PROCEDURAL REQUIREMENTS

Lovain (1984) reported that if a college or university follows proper procedures a *tenured* teacher can be dismissed for *cause*. He found that the courts dismissed most recent challenges of tenured teacher terminations. This finding appeared to go counter to the beliefs of many administrators and governing boards. Many of them believed that courts would support a reversal of such terminations and that tenured faculty "firings" would not be carried out successfully (p. 419). The dismissal of non-tenured faculty members by board action without the need for formal procedures or presentation of cause was described above and upheld in the 1972 landmark Supreme Court decision in *Board of Regents v. Roth* (1972).

A second landmark Supreme Court decision was made in *Perry v. Sinderman* (1972). Long-term and tenured faculty were found to have a *property interest* in their positions. This meant that these faculty had assurance of continuing in their teaching position and could not be dismissed at the whim of the board or administration. It also provided faculty with the right to have due-process proceedings if the administration and board moved toward dismissing them. These two landmark decisions have been cited repeatedly in dismissal cases since 1972. In *Perry v. Sinderman* the court found:

> The contract renewal practice in effect in the college system (Texas) implicitly conferred upon long-term employees a legitimate expectation of future employment, which constituted a property interest sufficient to require formal procedures.

This case was in no way meant to deter boards and administrators from dismissing faculty who were found to be incompetent or for *cause* for other legitimate legal reasons. It provided a framework for administrators to develop well-documented cases while strictly adhering to due-process policies and procedures. These policies and procedures are to be developed in state laws and through local governing board actions. Wise et al. (1984) stated that when a tenured faculty member is considered for possible dismissal it is imperative that the school district have exceptional evaluation procedures (p. 93).

Tenured terminations

A significantly large number of tenured faculty termination cases have been supported in both arbitration hearings and in the various levels of state and federal courts, including the state and federal supreme courts. A sampling of these cases since 1972 are presented here.

In the Pennsylvania University case of *Edwards v. California University of Pennsylvania* (1998) it was affirmed by the federal trial court that it was necessary for the teacher to teach the curriculum as outlined. Students had complained that they had enrolled in a course that was to teach them a variety of effective classroom teaching techniques. The instructor, of his own will, decided to teach issues of bias, censorship, religion and humanism. He had challenged the university's decision for suspension with pay as violating his First and Fourteenth Amendment speech rights. The decision stated that a faculty member does not, indeed, have a First Amendment right to decide what will be taught in his or her classroom.

Tenured faculty dismissals must follow due process and show cause. The following tenured dismissal case was found lacking in substance that led to the dismissal.

The Supreme Court of Ohio found in favor of a teacher, due to the school board not "providing the teacher with a clear and substantive basis as to why it did not renew her contract," in *Geib v. Triway Local Board of Education* (1999). The board's statement, which referred to past "deficiencies" from prior evaluations, was not considered acceptable to the court.

The appellate court in Massachusetts reversed an arbitrator's decision and a reinstatement decision was put aside in *School District of Beverly v. Geller* (2000). In this case a teacher with 25 years of experience had three charges of physical force situations with students. The court found reinstatement was not possible in those states that have "a clearly defined public policy protecting students against physical harm."

A tenured teacher admitted to his not following a remediation plan to meet the defined standard for student assessment, and he was unable to produce legible records of his students' performance. The Illinois appellate court, in *Davis v. Board of Education of Chicago* (1995), found that his teacher evaluations during the remediation period were very similar to those received earlier.

Cope v. Board of Education of the Town of West Hartford (1985), an elementary school case in Connecticut, found the board's decision to dismiss a tenured faculty member to be supported by the evidence: continual neglect of her overall teaching responsibilities (supported by repeated warning and reprimands); and a pattern of failure to supervise her first grade students to the extent that safety of the students became an issue.

The appellate court of North Carolina supported the board in its dismissal of a career teacher for not providing adequate discipline in her classroom. School authorities were found to have been thoughtful, patient, persistent, but unable to obtain sufficient change on the part of the teacher to properly control her classes (*Crump v. Durham County Board of Education* 1985).

A tenured teacher in Michigan was dismissed for using corporal punishment with four students. This was in violation of the school board policy. Once the teacher was found to have kicked and pushed a student to get her to return to his classroom. He struck another student in the face with his fist as a disciplinary measure, and he received a written reprimand for this incident. In a third incident, he placed a student in a headlock and slapped or punched the student, leading to a cut on the student's face. The fourth incident was the teacher's striking a female high school student in the face and knocking her down. The teacher sought to have these earlier incidents inadmissible in the present dismissal case but the Court of Appeals allowed them. The court upheld the decision in *Tomczik v. State Tenure Commission, Center Line Public Schools* (1989).

The Missouri Court of Appeals, in *Hanlon v. Board of Education of the Parkway School District* (1984), held that Hanlon (1) had adequate notice of her deficiencies and more than the statutory period to correct them; (2) there was no error in the board's refusal to grant the teacher discovery of certain documents and discovery of substance of testimony of the superintendent's witnesses; and (3) the board's finding of incompetence and inefficiency was supported by complete and substantial evidence. Deficiencies were listed in the areas of organization of instruction, assignments, instruction, team teaching, supervision and control, relationship with room mothers and volunteers, communication with parents, grading, and record keeping.

A tenured instructor with a history of unexcused absences was terminated in *Stasny v. Board of Trustees* (1982). He was denied permission to take a leave of absence by a supervisor and was warned of disciplinary action if he defied the decision. He, nevertheless, took the leave and was dismissed for *inter alia* insubordination. In court he asserted that (1) his defiance was merely a single respectful act of disobedience, not insubordination; and (2) his dismissal violated his right to academic freedom and freedom of expression. These arguments were rejected by the appellate court, which found his contention on academic freedom to be wrong. They stated "academic freedom is not a license for activity at variance with job related procedures and requirement, nor does it encompass activities which are internally destructive to the proper function of the university or disruptive to the 'educational process.'"

A number of other tenured faculty terminations, supported in arbitration and by the courts, are summarized in Appendix A.

TEACHERS CAN BE FIRED!

Tenure is often cited as the reason that school districts do not move to dismiss poor tenured faculty. In a study by Kvenvold (1989), a survey of the Minnesota school districts presented statistics to show incompetent tenured faculty are indeed terminated. Approximately 77 percent of the 433 school districts in the state responded to this survey. Out of 303 schools that responded, an average of two tenured teachers per school were removed for incompetence between 1983 and 1986.

The challenges of administrators were clearly presented by Kvenvold. Obstacles to the removal of faculty for incompetence were (1) difficult legal process involving lengthy documentation; (2) strict tenure laws; (3) powerful teacher unions; and (4) an inordinate amount of time needed to follow-up with even one identified incompetent teacher.

Kvenvold found 97.7 percent of the reporting districts in his study to have formal evaluation of both elementary and secondary teachers within their schools. The evaluation processes included formal letters of deficiency to inform faculty that their performance was substandard and warn of future action again them. Staff development and improvement programs were used. Dismissals took an average of 12 months in order to satisfy due-process requirements. The administrators in the study considered this a major commitment in time. The following are results of their efforts. Of the 602 tenured teachers removed between 1983 and 1986:

1. Seventy were fired for incompetence. Seventeen of these faculty pursued the grievance procedure as far as requesting the school board for a hearing. Five took legal action, and not one was successful in overturning the school board's dismissal decision.

2. Another 341 teachers were "counseled out" or asked to resign and did so. Mounting evidence of their incompetence greatly assisted in these cases.

3. In addition, 191 were induced to leave with severance pay, early retirement benefits, contract buy-offs, extended medical coverage, and encouragement to retire under the "Rule of 85."

In total, 602 incompetent tenured teachers left teaching and an additional 436 were salvaged through intensive formative evaluation efforts through the same period.

Vander Wheele's report (1992) on Chicago's public schools found that principals would fire approximately 2,000 of its over 26,000 teachers if it were not for the lengthy dismissal process that the law and the union contract requires. A total of 457 city principals participated in the study.

The Chicago Board of Education addressed the needs of six of its poorest performing high schools with a state law passed in 1995 (Martinez, 2000). The term used in the law is "intervention," which allows the school officials to remove tenured teachers for non-performance. Dismissal of individual teachers based on their evaluations is allowed. The law was passed after the school board made complaints that such dismissals were a burdensome process, lasts a year, and cost the board up to $100,000 each in legal fees and staff time. Martinez (2000) reported that only 24 tenured teachers had been fired for their poor teaching since 1995, and another 150 retired as an option to being terminated.

An *Editorial* in the *Chicago Tribune* (1998, May 15) spoke to the changes that were being made to remove poor tenured teachers at seven of the city's lowest performing high schools. School officials, under the new state law approved for the Chicago Public Schools had removed about one third of the teachers for incompetence. Ten months later it was found that over half of the teachers had found work as full-time teachers in another of the Chicago public schools. The editorial stated that this was partly due to principals who, in a number of those schools, were also undergoing reconstitution. The editorial went on to say:

> ...but the fact that so many of the teachers removed from the city's worst high schools are still in the system, teaching students who deserve better than another school's castoffs, indicates that far too often that good sense is sorely lacking (p. 12).

Tenured faculty dismissals: A community college case

Petty (1986) dedicated the front page of a trustee newsletter to a court decision that upheld a tenured faculty dismissal in a community college. In opposition to a strongly held opinion among Illinois community college trustees – that tenured teacher termination does not get support from the court system – Petty shows that often when cases fail, it is for other reasons:

> While administrators and boards may often have a substantive case against an incompetent faculty member, documentation sufficient for judicial review often

fails to meet established court standards. In addition, the procedural process used by the board may neglect important constitutional rights of notice, due process, a right to a hearing, etc. Frequently, the "good case" in fact turns out to be a weak one in law. Given this trend, many boards have been reluctant to move against the incompetent faculty member out of fear that the cost and perceived odds of success are not worth the risk (p. 1).

Petty went on to show that the Illinois community college case he was referring to had followed board policies and administrative procedures that had been established. In addition, an evaluation system was clearly defined and was being followed. He saw adherence to these practices as building "a credible case which passes judicial scrutiny" (p. 1). He discussed some of the details in the case:

> Previous records of staff evaluations revealed little detailed documentation on the strengths or weaknesses of many faculty members. By way of example, the file on the dismissed tenured teacher revealed this statement: 'Good teacher, recommend for continued tenure,' with no supporting evidence to document such a conclusion.
>
> In the course of the administration's evaluation of the teacher in question, a number of defects and deficiencies were uncovered. These were documented and discussed with the teacher. She was given the opportunity to address the problems with her own plan of remediation. She submitted a plan but apparently failed to follow it. The board allowed her two semesters to correct the problems. She again failed to take corrective action; indeed, it was disclosed that she had not taken a professional development course in her field in over 12 years. During the evaluation process, the administration even went so far as to allow a representative from the faculty union to sit in on some of the performance review sessions with the teacher. In short, the

board met and exceeded all legal requirements of notice, hearing, due process, etc. in establishing its case against the teacher (p. 1).

Petty showed how, when the college's decision was given an arbitrator's "trial," the arbitrator found in favor of the board. This was done in spite of strong pressures from the instructor and faculty who brought forth testimonial support for the instructor from fellow teachers and students. In the decision, both were given little weight. The circuit court upheld the College Board and administration upon appeal.

Petty went on to point out that "court backing of a tenured faculty member's dismissal is certainly not in itself the occasion for celebration," but he saw it as necessary if the nature of the case warranted no other decision except that of termination. He ended his editorial by stating that this case should be used as an "inspiration for boards willing, when necessary, to do the same" (p. 1).

Tenured faculty dismissal: a secondary school case

The Appellate Court, in *DeBernard v. State Board of Education* (1988), found a tenured high school teacher to be incompetent, and not complying with the official notices to remedy her deficiencies in teaching. Evidence showed that she had consistently negative evaluations on her classroom performances. The court cited the findings of the hearing officer, which were extensive:

1. In seventeen evaluations, plaintiff did not state objectives of the lesson at the beginning of the lesson.
2. In five observations she did not outline at the beginning of the lesson the activities of the lesson for the students.
3. In ten of the observations she did not properly, clearly

and accurately sequence and present the subject matter of the lesson.

4. In seven of the observations she did not properly, clearly and accurately respond to student questions and errors.

5. In eight of the observations she did not respond to and dispel student confusion over the subject matter of the lesson.

6. In eight of the observations she did not reinforce student learning through summary or reteaching at appropriate times during the lesson.

7. In thirteen observations she did not pace the lesson to maintain organized instruction, activity and student involvement for the full class period.

8. In nine of the observations she did not require broad student involvement during lessons.

9. In eight of the observations she did not provide sufficient time to do and actually give clear directions for homework.

10. In nine of the observations she did not require homework with appropriate frequency.

11. In eleven of the observations she did not assess student readiness to proceed with each major segment of the lesson.

In the area of creating an atmosphere that was conducive to student achievement in the class, the hearing officer found:

1. In ten of the observations her classroom was too noisy, too often, for lengthy periods.

2. In nine of the observations too many students, too frequently did not pay attention to the lesson.

3. In seven of the observations too many students, too frequently, did not bring to class and/or use appropriate instructional materials.

It should be noted that the teacher was evaluated by the principal, the assistant principal for instruction and by the department chair. Each observation was followed by a conference with the evaluator who discussed the observation and any deficiencies that were noted.

The number of observations make it clear that once a teacher has been placed on official notice evaluation continues. The areas of deficiency must be charted as either improving or continuing. This case documented the pattern of incompetence continuing in a number of key instructional areas needed for quality instruction.

SUMMARY

Administrators and governing boards have used tenure as the excuse for allowing their systems to be saddled with incompetent teachers. Boards have failed for years to take action against incompetent teachers. The following reasons have been cited: (1) Many board members are unsure of the process for discharging unsatisfactory teachers, or (2) the evaluation system is inadequate and does not provide the necessary documentation. The transferring of incompetent teachers, known as the "dance of the lemons" has continued into the present. It has been easier to move teachers from one school building to another within the school district than to complete remediation and dismissal processes.

It is imperative that future tenure decisions be made with the utmost care and that boards should not award tenure to teachers who provide the administrative evaluators with doubts about their performance during their non-tenure years. Awarding a teacher tenure should be done because of the teacher's evaluated competence. It becomes a time-consuming and costly burden on the school district to prove incompetence after a teacher has been awarded tenure.

Boards are given the authority and responsibility in most states for the hiring and termination of teachers in their schools or colleges. Courts have given boards the ultimate authority on decisions to grant tenure or to decide on termination of non-tenured teachers. One landmark Supreme Court decision in 1972 established non-tenured teachers having no property or due-process rights in their positions. A second landmark case by the Supreme Court in the same year found tenured faculty having a *property interest* right in their positions.

SUGGESTED EXERCISES

1. Define those areas you can identify as signs of incompetence in teachers that you have had or are familiar with from other experiences.
2. Discuss individual faculty cases that you feel were not handled properly by administrators and/or the governing board.

CHAPTER 14

PRACTICAL CONSIDERATIONS AND REASONS FOR TENURE TERMINATIONS

> Building administrators must become actively involved. They must go into the woods. It is their job, and if they don't who will? Sometimes principals will have to be forced to enter the woods.
>
> *White (2001), p. 3*

White (2001) discussed why many administrators fail to collect vital information documenting poor instruction in their schools. Litigation and the negative climate it can create on the school campus, along with publicity that evolves when moving toward the removal of a poor teacher, often leads to an avoidance of the problem.

White also mentioned the role of the building administrator, who may well be seen in a negative light when involved in this unpopular process. These same administrators may fear that they will be criticized for having hired the teachers who later prove to be ineffective. It is important, therefore, that a climate of support is presented, beginning with board of education policies and including central office support and encouragement for responsible supervision of instruction (p. 2). White went on to say, "building administra-

---

tors must become actively involved. They must go into the woods" (p. 3).

It has been this author's experience that teachers who meet the expected standards know when a colleague is not performing at a satisfactory level. Regardless of the role that the faculty union takes to support a faculty member being put on notice to improve or remediate deficiencies, other teachers usually understand the administrations' action. Allhouse (1974) and Carr (1972) found that historically the removal of tenured faculty for cause had been rare. They also found that the academic community would often tolerate removal for cause.

Hollander (1992) discussed poor teachers being asked to voluntarily retire when they become eligible. However, the Age Discrimination in Employment Act only allows removal of a tenured faculty member for just cause. Hollander called for colleges to plan to have both criteria and methodology in place to evaluate these faculty members. Realizing that peers will have little desire to evaluate their own colleagues, administrators are asked to learn how to become classroom evaluators. Hollander also asked that procedures be carefully developed so that poor teachers can first be encouraged to retire rather than be removed through board action and arbitration hearings.

Andrews and Wisgoski (1987) developed guidelines for administrators and boards to consider when they are in the process of determining whether to terminate a tenured faculty member:

1. *Do so reluctantly.* Keep in mind that a life and a career are at stake.
2. *Do so as a last resort.* From both a legal and moral standpoint, there is much to do before dismissal is considered. There is a need to have a division chairperson, associate dean of instruction, and the dean of instruction,

by independent evaluation, determine that the individual's classroom instruction is inadequate.

3. *Do so after the individual has been given a detailed explanation of the nature of his or her inadequacies.*

4. *Do so after the individual has been given adequate time*—typically one to two years—to enlist the expertise of peers, supervisors, and other resources of the college to improve instruction.

5. *Do so when, at the end of the period of remediation, the individual has still failed* to raise the level of his or her performance to acceptable college standards, in the opinion of the college supervisors.

6. *Do so after the president and the board of trustees have agreed* with the assessment.

7. *Do so when a law firm specializing in school law has reviewed the case* in detail and issued an opinion that dismissal of the instructor has a strong likelihood of being upheld in court.

8. *Do so when the instructor has declined to accept early retirement,* voluntary transfer to a college assignment that does not involve classroom teaching, or resignation.

9. *Then,* notify the person of his or her dismissal and the reasons for the action, being careful to observe the correct form and the deadlines imposed by the laws of your particular state (p. 164).

These guidelines offer both legally and morally responsible steps in a process that may lead to termination. They include significant efforts to try to remediate a teacher's performance defects prior to a termination decision, and they require a specific time frame which allows for changes to take place. They include keeping the governing board aware throughout the process so that they have advance knowledge prior to be given a recommendation to terminate from the administration and board attorney.

Bridges (1990b) suggested, "there is a presumption that teachers who have achieved tenure are competent employees and, therefore, school officials should not be permitted to dismiss them without establishing a strong justification for doing so" (p. 343). In his article about dismissing a tenured teacher only as a last resort, Spitalli (2003) wanted to make it clear that he was not promoting the dismissal of all marginal teachers:

> Like marginal students, marginal teachers who are willing to improve can and should be given the appropriate support, supervision, evaluation, and mentoring that will help them improve. It should not be an option, though, for a marginal teacher to remain marginal. Schools should be filled with the kinds of teachers you would want your own children to have, not the ones you would rather not have your children endure for whatever reason. Even one marginal teacher can have a devastating impact on children's educational progress and a demoralizing effect on the school culture (p. 18).

DEFENSIBLE CAUSES OF TENURED TEACHER DISMISSAL

Valente (1987) described the four major causes, which vary from state to state, for which a tenured teacher may be dismissed: (1) *incompetence*, encompassing lack of knowledge, failure to adapt to new teaching methods, failure to maintain discipline, and excessive absence; (2) *neglect of duty* or incapability including physical and emotional illness; (3) *insubordination and unprofessional conduct*, including use of offensive language, use of corporal punishment, or involvement in shoplifting or similar types of incidents; and (4) *immorality*, including dishonesty, sexual misconduct, or criminal action (pp. 210-216). Courts have been very supportive

---

of dismissals of tenured teachers whose behaviors meet these criteria. The following is a sampling of court-tested and board-supported cases for dismissal in the four areas listed.

Incompetence

A loss of class control led to the dismissal of a teacher in Florida in *Walker v. Highlands County School Board* (2000). The case was upheld by the appellate court which found the behavior severe enough to impair the effectiveness of the teacher.

An Alaskan teacher failed to implement an effective behavior management plan for her classroom and was dismissed. The Supreme Court of Alaska found in *Linstad v. Sitka School District* (1998) that the teacher's argument that the board was required to give her notice of every allegation of improper behavior management was unnecessary. The court upheld her dismissal and supported the board on its general statement.

In *Sekor v. Board of Education of Town of Ridgefield* (1997), in Connecticut, the state Supreme Court upheld the board on a dismissal of a teacher for incompetence. The teacher was found to be incompetent in her teaching in two of the three subject areas in which she had been certified to teach. The court found that the board could, indeed, review her overall competence in making their decision in this case.

The Supreme Court of Mississippi, in *Mississippi Employment Security Commission v. Harris* (1996), reversed an earlier decision and supported the board in termination of a teacher for misconduct. She had shown the film *Silence of the Lambs* to students under 17 years of age. The board supported the principal who had earlier warned the teacher to have films related to subject matter. In addition, the court found this teacher ineligible for unemployment compensation.

A court supported the school board in their dismissal of a tenured teacher for failure to maintain discipline in her home economics classes. The court ruled that the board did not need to transfer the teacher to a different teaching position in which she had taught satisfactorily for a number of years previously. It was also found in this case that a tenured teacher may be asked to resign before the governing board initiates dismissal proceedings. The hearing officer's decision to dismiss the teacher was upheld in *Stamper v. Board of Education of Elementary School District 143* (1986).

In *Mims v. West Baton Rouge* (1975) a number of factors were involved in the dismissal. Repeated violations of rules, lack of control of students and failure to follow administrators' instructions was held by the court to constitute incompetence.

Bridges (1990) found most dismissals for incompetency followed a pattern comprised of a number of factors rather than being caused by a single isolated incident (pp. 154-55). An exception was found, however, in *Mott v. Endicott* (1986). One incident was considered by the court as constituting reasonable cause without the need of any prior warning. In this case the teacher was dismissed for striking a student in the genitals.

Conversely, in *Aulwurm v. Board* (1977), the court overturned dismissal by the board because the teacher had not received adequate notice of what needed to be improved, as was required by state law. Courts expect boards to give notice and time to remediate if something can be reasonably remediated by a teacher.

Neglect of Duty

A Montana high school tenured teacher was dismissed for making jokes about testes and a student's menstrual periods, for "flipping his students off," and for making gender-based remarks with sexual innuendoes in his classroom. The Supreme Court in *Baldridge v. Board of Trustees, Rosebud*

School District #19 (1997) saw the teacher as unfit and upheld his dismissal.

In *Brahim v. Ohio College of Podiatric Medicine* (1994), a medical school professor failed to win his suit against the college's president and other administrators involved in his termination. Both the trial court and the appellate court in Ohio agreed that termination was supported by sufficient evidence. The professor was found persistently neglecting his duties as defined in the faculty handbook. It was further found that his claim did not rise to the level whereby the administrators' actions met his claim of tortuous interference with his contract. They were within the scope of the administrators' duties.

Two faculty were found to violate terms of their teaching contract in *Shaw v. Board of Trustees of Frederick Community College* (1976). One was tenured and the other worked under a continuing appointment. Both boycotted a faculty workshop and a commencement exercise in their protest of the college's plan to abolish tenure at the college.

Insubordination

Cases involving insubordination are often focused on teachers' beliefs that they have been discriminated against after they have exercised their rights of "academic freedom" or "free speech." Teachers may view this as a constitutionally guaranteed right which is being denied. The courts, however, have found such charges to be unfounded in a number of cases and dismissal has been upheld.

An eleventh grade honors teacher was dismissed in *Farris v. Burke County Board of Education* (2001). The teacher continued to use sexually explicit terms in describing literary works. Both the trial and appellate courts upheld the board's decision to terminate as prior warning had been given and had been ignored by the teacher.

In a Supreme Court case in Colorado the tapping of a third grade student on the head to get his attention was upheld as a case of insubordination. The case of *Board of Education of West Yuma School District RJ-1 v. Flaming* (1997) found that this was the teacher's fourth such incident involving inappropriate behavior of physical contacts with children. These incidents were documented over an eight year period.

The appellate court case of *Newman v. Sobol* (1996) in New York affirmed the dismissal of a teacher. The teacher had struck a student in the eye. This tenured teacher had been on notice prior to the incident through both written and oral warnings concerning use of excessive force with students.

In the case of *Stasny v. Board of Trustees* (1982), the court found that by taking an unapproved leave of absence, the faculty member was insubordinate. The court stated, "academic freedom is not a license for activity at variance with job related procedures and requirements."

A vocational instructor from a state school in Kentucky was dismissed for "friction" between her and her supervisor (*Wagner v. Department of Education State Personnel Board* 1977). The Supreme Court rejected the instructor's claim of statutory and constitutional violations. It also found that sufficient evidence was presented to find her uncooperative and insubordinate to her superiors.

Immorality

A female special education teacher was dismissed in Oklahoma for moral turpitude. In this case, *Andrews v. Independent School District No. 57* (2000), the teacher was having a romantic relationship with a 17-year-old boy. The behavior of the teacher included public hugging and kissing. In this case the court upheld the admission of testimony that had been given by a former student who fifteen years previously had had sexual relations with the same teacher. Allowing this testimony helped impeach her testimony that she had not had improper relations with minors.

A teacher had admitted using marijuana at home for a two-year period during his testimony at a criminal trial on the sale of a controlled substance. In *Woo v. Putnam County Board of Education* (1998), the Supreme Court of Appeals of West Virginia affirmed his dismissal. The court ruled his admission was enough to impair his effectiveness in the classroom.

The court found swearing at students as a means "to motivate them" was not protected under first amendment rights or freedom of speech. It led to the dismissal of a faculty member at Midland College. The court in *Martin v. Parrish* (1986), ruled the teacher's behavior as a "superfluous attack on a captive audience." In this case the students had paid to be in the instructor's subject area.

In *Korf v. Ball State University* (1984) a tenured male faculty member was removed on grounds of sexual harassment for making sexual advances and offering grades to male students for sexual favors. Using established institutional procedures, the charges were investigated, plaintiff was notified, a hearing was held, and the president decided to dismiss the plaintiff. The teacher admitted to a relationship with a male student, but he denied that grades were involved. The plaintiff challenged and argued that his constitutional rights of substantive and procedural due process, equal protection, free speech, freedom of association, and privacy had been violated. Most of his arguments hinged on the claim that the relationship being questioned was a private consensual sexual activity outside the institution's purview. The board was supported by the Seventh Circuit Court which found the plaintiff's arguments lacking in merit. They determined the facts supported the institution in dismissing the plaintiff for unethical behavior. They further found that he had, indeed, exploited students. The court made note that this teacher was not like any ordinary person on the street, but rather found him to have a special relationship with the students which he had violated.

In *Board of Education of Agro-Summit School District 104 v. Hunt* (1985), a tenured, male physical education teacher who pinched three second grade female students on the buttocks during class was found guilty of "irremediable" conduct. In this case the teacher was dismissed without first having been given a notice to remedy by the board of education. The court focused on the damage done to the students rather than on the traditional analysis of whether or not a warning might have prevented such conduct.

OUTSIDE INTERVENTION

Knight (1986), in his essay about the need to "clean up our act in tenure and evaluation," referred to the National Commission on Higher Education report (1982), which noted that "campus academic administrators, working closely with appropriate faculty committees, should develop a system of post-tenure evaluation" (p. 10). He reasoned that the commission report was needed because educators had failed to clean up their own houses. Knight went on to say, "refusing to support administrative and public measures to develop evaluation methods, to remediate unacceptable teaching performance, or, that failing, to remove such teachers from the profession, we have invited outside intervention, and we are now receiving it" (pp. 3-4). He quoted from the National Commission's report relating to incompetency, which stated, "incompetent faculty must not be protected at the expense of the student or the maintenance of quality" (p. 10). Knight's concern is that if educators do not take care of their own problems in providing quality education, they will find outside forces moving in to do it.

SUMMARY

To prove incompetence, it is important for administrators to develop well-documented cases as well as to strictly adhere to proper due-process policies and procedures of the local board and the state.

Although dismissing tenured teachers is still somewhat rare, it does happen. Administrators often hide behind obstacles to terminating incompetent teachers such as (1) the large amount of documentation needed, (2) strict tenure laws, (3) powerful teachers unions, and (4) the inordinate amount of time needed for the evaluation and remediation process.

Administrators need to follow both legal and moral guidelines in the termination process. Teachers need to hear clearly, in face-to-face meetings and in writing, what deficiencies have been identified and need to be remedied. They also need to be given adequate time to make the improvements. Termination needs to be sought if, at the end of the period of remediation, the individual has still failed to raise his or her performance to the level expected by the school or community college. A school superintendent or college president, governing board, and the school's attorney must all agree that the administrator's assessment is valid and that the case is legally defensible before an arbitrator and the courts.

Courts have proven to be supportive of dismissals of tenured teachers in the four main areas under cause: (1) incompetence, (2) neglect of duty, (3) insubordination, and (4) immorality. Examples of cases in each of these areas are presented in this chapter and in Appendix A.

SUGGESTED EXERCISES

1. Discuss what procedures will support your efforts to document incompetence in a faculty member.
2. What situations in your K-12 school or college experi-

ences may have placed a faculty member you had into one of the four categories for termination outlined in this chapter?

CHAPTER 15

TENURE DISMISSAL PROCESSES

> A bad one [teacher] can thwart a child's progress
> for at least four years, according to a University of Ten-
> nessee statistician.
>
> *Marks, (2002), p. 1*

Incompetence is defined in the Teacher Evaluation Glossary (2003) as, "the intentional or unintentional failure to perform the duties and professional responsibilities of the teaching job in a minimally acceptable manner as specified by the employing district. Incompetence usually results in remediation, reassignment, or dismissal" (p. 15).

In their national study of evaluation practices, Andrews, et al. (2002a) reported 50 percent of the administrative leaders in community colleges reported their evaluation systems as highly questionable or ineffective. Faculty leaders in this same study had only 34 percent rating evaluation practices in their community colleges as "effective" or "very effective" while 51 percent rated them as "uncertain about or ineffective." These are alarming numbers when you consider the amount of time put into developing and administering these evaluation processes.

It should be obvious to any serious observers of faculty evaluation that these reported low levels of effectiveness can provide sanctuaries for incompetent and lazy teachers. Both administrations and faculty leaders responses were very similar.

Administrators must keep in mind that they are writing the performance evaluation for problem faculty for two audiences, according to Waintroob (1995). These audiences are the teacher and the neutral fact-finder. The latter must pass judgment on whether the person has been properly terminated. Waintroob pointed out that the problems must be presented in a clear and pointed way:

> Problems should be so clearly described that an individual unfamiliar with education would understand what is wrong. Educational jargon should be avoided. Ratings must be honest. Unsatisfactory performance must be accurately labeled. Negative adjectives like "unsatisfactory," "poor," "unsuccessful," and "unacceptable" must be used if the administrator is to convey successfully the extent of a performance problem to the employee or to a fact-finder reviewing a later discharge.
>
> In summary, to successfully remediate or, if necessary, discharge incompetent teachers, administrators must overcome their personal predilections and training and act like bosses, not colleagues, friends, social workers or punching bags (p. 4).

A *Chicago Tribune* (2001, December 23) editorial voiced the opinion that, "If you're a lousy teacher, it shouldn't take a full year to get you fired. If you're a so-so teacher, you shouldn't continue getting your 3 percent annual raises simply because you show up for work. If your students aren't learning year after year, you shouldn't be in the classroom" (p. 10).

COMPONENTS FOR A FAIR HEARING

Bridges and Groves (1984) listed 12 components that they found necessary from state statutes in order to assure the faculty member's rights in a due-process termination hearing:

1. A statement of charges and the materials upon which they are based;
2. A hearing before the school board, a hearing panel, or a hearing officer if requested;
3. A timely written notice of the date, time, and place of the hearing;
4. A hearing in public or private;
5. An opportunity to be represented by counsel;
6. An opportunity to call witnesses on his own behalf;
7. An opportunity to subpoena a person who has made allegations that are used as a basis for the decision of the employer;
8. An opportunity to cross-examine witnesses;
9. Witness testimony under oath or affirmation;
10. A shorthand reporting or tape recording of the hearing upon request;
11. A written decision that contains the specific findings or grounds on which it is based;
12. A written statement of his or her rights to appeal (p. 63).

Bridges and Groves showed that if any of the due process rights mandated by state statutes are neglected, arbitrators or the courts have set aside the dismissal decision. When this occurs, the governing board and administrators find themselves in a difficult position. The laws are very specific relative to due process rights and dismissal processes in most states. It is important to consult legal counsel on the procedural rights of the teacher in order to avoid making a serious procedural mistake.

Morris (1992) summarized the case of *Cleveland Board of Education v. Loudermill* (1985). The Supreme Court ruled that three conditions have to be satisfied before a school district can consider they have had a complete hearing on the termination of a teacher:

The essential requirements of due process. . . are notice and an opportunity to respond. The opportunity to present reasons, either in person or in writing, why proposed action should not be taken is a fundamental due-process requirement. The tenured public employee is entitled to oral or written notice of the charges against him, an explanation of the employer's evidence, and an opportunity to present his side of the story. To require more than this prior to termination would intrude to an unwarranted extent on the government's interest in quickly removing an unsatisfactory employee. We conclude that all the process that is due is provided by a pre-termination opportunity to respond, coupled with post-termination administrative procedures as provided by the Ohio statute (p. 22).

A CASE STUDY

The following is a case study concerning the dismissal of a tenured teacher for incompetence. The instructor was evaluated for both his in-class and out-of-class professional teaching responsibilities. Some specifics in the case have been changed somewhat to protect confidentiality.

First meeting

The instructional dean advised the instructor of the college's concern over low enrollments in his classes and told him that the college was having trouble providing him with a full teaching load. Low enrollments, while a problem, were not cited as a charge against the instructor. They did, however, lead the instructional administrators to conduct in-classroom evaluations in the months that followed this face-to-face meeting.

The instructional dean followed up the original meeting with the instructor with a memorandum notifying him that he was, in part, accountable for lack of enrollments in his classes. The memorandum included the following points:

1. The instructor had not been engaging in professional activities for several years;
2. His appearance was unkempt and there was a personal hygiene concern;
3. His part-time work might be a problem (drawing time away from his professional duties);
4. Weekly outlines consistent with his course syllabus for each course were needed; and
5. He should prepare a plan for self-improvement in areas of personal hygiene, and respectful treatment of students. This plan was to be completed and provided to the division chairperson within 30 days of this memorandum.

In-class evaluation

In the months subsequent to the original meeting with the instructor, the division chairperson and dean of instruction conducted seven in-class evaluations to assess classroom techniques, organization, and effectiveness communicating with students. These evaluations led to significant concerns. After several evaluations and after discussing the improvements needed, the following letter was written to the teacher:

Dear Instructor:

We are sorry to learn through our in-class evaluations that your in-class preparation and performance is much below what we expect at this college. You have spent eight weeks of the spring semester teaching American Literature before 1865 in your Literature 201 course. That material should have been taught in the Literature 200 course. Not only are students not being taught what the course description says, but they will also lack knowledge of the necessary material when they transfer to four-year schools. These courses are articulated to four-year colleges throughout the state. Our agreement with these colleges is that we will teach the same course content as they do in terms of each course description and syllabus.

Handouts, tests, and other materials that we have reviewed from your classes confirm neglect and failure to update and revise these materials each semester, which is your professional responsibility. One example is your old copies of the course syllabus which has dates crossed out and new ones hand written over them. This is not acceptable.

We recommend that you immediately prepare and follow weekly outlines, which address the proper course material for Literature 201. Weekly outlines are also expected for each of your other courses. Further, you need to review handouts, tests and other materials and update them so they apply to current classes.

Your neglect of major aspects of your job which include preparation, audio-visual support, proper presentation of material (both content and proper placing of material in your course outlines), and testing throughout the semester, put you in a very critical position in terms of retaining your position at this college.

Your division chairperson and I will plan to discuss these concerns with you again during the next week. We will continue to evaluate your classes several times in the next four weeks.

Sincerely,
Dean of Instruction

Moving to a "notice to remedy"

A "notice to remedy" was determined to be necessary by the instructional administrators and the college president for this instructor. This is an official notification from the board of trustees of the need to remediate all of the deficiencies and

E X A M P L E 8:
NOTICE TO REMEDY

You are being notified of the Board of Trustees' action in passing a formal notice of remediation. The following is a list of deficiencies that you must address in the very near future.

1. *Lack of preparation for class lecture, use of poorly prepared course outlines and failure to present daily objectives to students.*

    The steps required in the resolution of this deficiency are to prepare daily, weekly, and semester outlines so you can adequately cover the material necessary for your courses; and to update and pass out course outlines that tell students what to expect for daily lectures, readings, administering and reviewing tests. Students must be told the daily objectives. You must plan in advance so lectures and activities meet these objectives.

2. *Disregard of the course syllabus in teaching of your courses.*

    You must teach the material that is outlined for the Literature 200 and 201 courses during the proper semester. These are transfer courses to other colleges, and you are under obligation to guarantee teaching of the courses as they are articulated for transfer to four-year colleges and universities.

3. *Poor, outdated audiovisual support relating to lectures.*

    Your use of audio-visuals material needs to be reviewed. Transparencies on the overhead projector are poorly organized, have far too much information included on each of them and are almost non-legible. These need to be revised immediately.

4. *Dated tests and handouts.*

    Tests used are old, updated by hand, and have markings on them by students who have previously used them. Some of your handouts are so old they are difficult to copy and are now most difficult to read. This is one more area in which lack of planning and effort is very evident. Future materials should show marked improvements.

5. *Lack of professional upgrading.*

    By your own admission in a recent communication to the administration, you have not applied for a professional conference in your field for over 12 years. This demonstrates lack of motivation and/or low priority given to improving your standard of teaching. You were unable to name any professional journal in your field of American literature to which you subscribe, read, or use. The last professional activity documented in your professional development

EXAMPLE 8 (continued)

file took place ten years ago. You must begin to address these deficiencies in your professional development now.

6. *Conclusion.*

In our judgment, the defects and deficiencies discussed above are both clearly stated and easy to understand, and it is reasonable to expect you to address and correct them. The defects and deficiencies cited can only be removed, however, with a much stronger commitment to your full-time job at this college than your performance suggests you have been giving for some time. There is no question that such a performance in your job is not conducive to students enrolling in your classes. Further, students who are enrolled are being "cheated" due to the poor quality of teaching.

---

defects that the administrators outlined in the attached document. A list of these deficiencies is outlined in Example 8.

Remediation efforts

The board of trustees voted 7 - 0 to support the administration in their efforts to remediate the deficiencies in teaching and other job responsibilities of the instructor.

A meeting was set up with the instructor the morning following board action. The division chairperson and dean of instruction reviewed the charges and allowed for any clarifications that were necessary. The dean, in the follow-up memorandum of the meeting, made clear that the instructor was continuing to deny the allegations in the letter of deficiencies from the board of trustees. The dean concluded that the meeting was less than productive based upon the instructor's negative attitude and denial of the charges in the remediation letter.

This meeting was followed by several more in-class evaluations over the next few weeks, along with verbal and written reports addressing both progress and lack of progress in overcoming the specific deficiencies cited in the "notice to remedy." The daily objectives and handouts prepared for the students were returned to the instructor who was told they were still "too general" and did not meet the specific board remediation demands.

The administration asked the instructor to spend time during the upcoming summer months to update his course materials and advised him not to teach during the summer. These requirements were to be completed and turned in one week prior to the start of classes in the fall. The course outlines were not received, and a letter was sent to the instructor as a reprimand for failing to follow-through with the basic requests in the remediation process. The deficiencies were monitored through more classroom visits during the fall semester. These were supplemented with written memos continuing to advise the instructor to provide the written materials that were now long overdue. Seven months following the board of trustees "notice to remedy," the administration had still not received the updated course outlines. These were finally produced after a face-to-face meeting with the instructor very late into the fall semester (10th week). They were unsatisfactory in content and were not weekly outlines as had been requested. The instructor was then given until the beginning of the winter semester (in January) to make these changes and have them conform to the required format asked for in previous correspondence.

The following deficiencies were documented as still existing during the fall semester classroom visitations:

1. Lack of planning and preparation for each class;
2. Failure to stay with relevant material, with lengthy diversions dealing with minute details;
3. Loss of direction in the presentation in the last half of each class visited;
4. Failure to present material in an organized, logical manner;

5.   Failure to arrive to class on time happening frequently enough to constitute a pattern of lateness.

The Dean's report also stated:

> You are once again directed to read and re-read these comments and start making effort to properly plan for these classes. The students suffer from your lack of effort to make the changes required. It has been noted that you still work many hours on another job away from the college while your work at the college continues to show much neglect.

In a late fall semester evaluation of the instructor's class in one of the college's off-campus centers, the dean and division chairperson once again noted in their report that the instructor's lecture was "well behind the course schedule outline, disorganized, hurried, and tantamount to useless." The division chairperson's written report further stated:

> My observations today follows a recent somewhat improved evaluation on campus. I can only conclude that the instructor is not willing to devote the consistent time and energy that it takes to be a professional. With our frequent visits to his classroom earlier this semester, he demonstrated some improvements in his presentation, but when the evaluation was unexpected, he demonstrated poor performance, with the same deficiencies (i.e. being behind schedule, disorganized, and lacking current weekly outlines) as noted earlier.

Efforts to remediate have been unsuccessful. The instructor was notified by the Board of Trustees Resolution to address the deficiencies nine months ago and still, his classroom performance does not meet the standards of this institution.

Recommendation for dismissal

At this point the question of termination became a critical issue with the dean of instruction and division chairperson. All of the evaluative evidence gathered since the official board of trustees "notice to remedy" was shared with the college president and the college attorney. The board of trustees, based upon recommendation of the president and board attorney, ordered the administration to prepare proper legal documents to present to the board at their next meeting.

The board of trustees, 10 months after their action to deliver the "notice to remedy", voted 7 - 0 to dismiss the instructor. They presented him with a "Notice of Charges and Bill of Particulars" listing the following six charges:

I.   You have disregarded the official college course syllabus in teaching your courses.
II. You have failed to prepare for and properly manage your lectures.
III. You have failed to use effective evaluation and testing procedures for student learning.
IV. You have refused to follow administrative and board directives to improve the quality of the audio-visual materials used in your classes.
V.   You have failed to engage in any significant attempts to upgrade your competence as a professional.
VI. You have been persistently negligent in carrying out your duties as a faculty member.

Proving just cause

In this case the state statute allowed for a hearing officer (arbitrator) to hear evidence from both the faculty member and representatives of the board of trustees if the instructor in

---

question decided to seek an appeal of the board's decision. Such a hearing helps to provide a forum for a final and binding decision based upon the evidence presented. The evidence must provide for substantial grounds in the dismissal decision before the hearing officer will rule in the board's favor. The state statute in this case says that the board must prove its charges by a *preponderance* of evidence. The faculty member did choose to appeal the board decision and to seek arbitration.

Outcomes on the formal charges

The two-day hearing with the arbitrator, which occurred three months later, resulted in the following findings:

1. Concerning Charge I, it would have been possible subsequent to the board's "notice to remedy" to reallocate the time allotted to each topic as requested by the administration. The instructor did not correct the situation in the following fall semester.

2. Concerning Charge II, the arbitrator saw the evaluations by administrators for the off-campus class as a significant indication that the instructor failed to properly prepare for and manage his lectures.

3. The arbitrator found the evidence for Charge III consisted of what was observed primarily during the class sessions the evaluators visited. He did not, therefore, believe that this charge had been proven, although this did not mean that he believed the instructor did prepare the students adequately and did cover tests properly. He just failed to find conclusive evidence in support of the Board's charge.

4. The arbitrator, upon close review of materials presented, concluded that he had not been supplied with sufficient evidence to support a finding to uphold Charge IV.

5. Concerning Charge V, the arbitrator was convinced from testimony from both the instructor and the board that the instructor had not made a significant effort to maintain his professional competence. He pointed out that despite the warning from the board in the previous spring, the instructor did not remedy the situation.

6. Charge VI centered on the failure of the instructor to meet board requests in a timely manner and the persistence of being late in holding office hours. The arbitrator referred to this last as a "catch all" charge and did not see it as adding much to the board's other charges.

The arbitrator's decision

In addition to reviewing the above six charges in light of the evidence provided, the arbitrator read favorable letters from five students and heard testimony on the instructor's behalf by three teachers and two students. While he indicated that he was impressed with this show of support on behalf of the instructor, he did not give as much weight to this evidence as he did to the findings in the administrative evaluations. He noted, "It seems normal for teachers to support another teacher with whom they have been associated for some time even though the teacher may be guilty of the charges made against him by the employer."

The arbitrator also noted that some student evaluation forms submitted by the faculty member in his support were given in small classes where the anonymity of students was not fully protected.

On the issue of holding a conference with the instructor after each evaluation, the board and administration was reprimanded. The administrators had omitted holding one such conference. The arbitrator, however, did not feel that this procedural error was of sufficient importance to serve as grounds to set aside the dismissal of the instructor.

In summary, the arbitrator concluded that the instructor did not remedy the deficiencies that he was advised to remedy 10 months earlier by the Board of Trustees. These were restated as Charges I, II, and V accompanying the dismissal resolution of the board that was sent to the instructor. The arbitrator further concluded that the board did, indeed, have just cause to dismiss the instructor. The decision of the board of trustees was upheld and the appeal of the instructor denied.

The circuit court also denied the appeal of the instructor at the next level and the case was not appealed further.

SUMMARY

There were several key points learned during the processing of this case:

1. Tenure does not guarantee a life-time position to a faculty member if competence in one's job becomes eroded.
2. Proving incompetence is a lengthy and tedious process. In-class evaluation by administrative supervisors carries a high degree of weight in such cases.
3. Student evaluations are unlikely to carry the same weight in arbitration and in the courts as are carefully conducted supervisory evaluations. In fact, student evaluations should be assigned much lower weight in board policies than that given to administrative evaluations.
4. The formal "notice to remedy" is a most important legal step to be taken in trying to improve an instructor. It also provides an excellent baseline by which to judge improvements and to conduct subsequent evaluations.
5. In-class observations, course syllabi, semester course outlines, grade books, copies of examinations, and records of individual faculty development efforts are all

documents important in determining a faculty member's competence to provide quality instruction.

6. An arbitrator may not find sufficient evidence to support all of the charges made by the governing board. The preponderance of the evidence did, however, provide enough evidence to obtain support for the termination of employment.

SUGGESTED EXERCISES

1. Discuss the key points made by the arbitrator that led to the dismissal in the above case.
2. List both strengths and weaknesses that were found by the arbitrator in the formal evaluation process and in how the process was administered.

CHAPTER 16

PART-TIME FACULTY: MAJOR GROWTH

> Results suggested that part-time faculty have lower
> levels of involvement in knowledge acquisition and other
> forms of scholarship, higher expectations of students,
> less autonomy from the institution, and make less effort
> to maintain educational integrity than full-time faculty.
> *Rifkin (1998)*

Sixty-four percent of the community college faculty is part-time according to Parsons (1998). This is an increase over Mangan's (1991) estimate of 40 percent of all higher education faculty being part-time employees. These numbers may not yet have peaked as the community colleges reach out to secondary schools with dual-credit program growth across the country in the early 2000s. Universities continue to expand their offerings to off-campus sites and through the Internet. Many new part-time faculty are continuing to be added to each of these growing programs.

How these community colleges integrate the new part-time faculty into their colleges to assure *quality classroom teaching* is a continuing concern. What guarantees are given the students that these are competent faculty? Who oversees their teaching preparation, testing and grading practices? What kind of evaluation of classroom instruction is used?

North Lake College in Irvine, Texas, was cited by Gomstyn (2003) as having to remove 145 part-time faculty from teaching. This action was a follow-up to their recent accreditation and a review by their internal auditor who found the teachers to be under-qualified to teach the courses they had been hired to teach. Some 215 part-time teachers did not have their credentials on file at the college. This action led to cutbacks in course sections offered and the need for over 400 students to take classes at other campuses in their community college district.

Freeland (1998) discussed a national survey of 1,500 part-time and full-time faculty from 127 community colleges. These subjects represented 41 states. Some of the findings included:

1. Part-time faculty showed lower levels of involvement in curriculum, instruction, and scholarship;
2. Part-time faculty expressed significantly higher expectations for their students;
3. There were no significant differences in the attitudes between the two groups in terms of commitment to teaching and to students (p. 1).

In an "on-campus trends" report by El-Khawas (1990) 56 percent of administrators surveyed expressed concerns about the impact of large numbers of part-time faculty upon their institutions. The increase in part-time faculty was viewed as causing additional strains upon the institutions' support systems.

Avakian (1995) states that part-time faculty have been given the title of *adjunct faculty* since the 1980s. She found the adjunct faculty members are, for the most part, professionals working in full time jobs elsewhere and are hired from one semester to the next at the college with little job security. She also noted that during the time of tight budgets, as exist in the early 2000s, increased enrollments have forced colleges to add more adjunct faculty.

Avakian proposed that great care be given to who is hired as adjunct teachers. Selection consideration should be similar to that given to hiring full-time faculty. Part-time faculty

---

should also be evaluated and receive honest and timely feedback. Further, she advocated *rewards for excellence* in their teaching. Rewards could be promotions in rank where rank exists, salary adjustments and/or recognizing their achievement in college publications, directories and catalogs. Career and professional development opportunities and tuition waivers for community college courses on space available basis were also suggested as rewards for excellence (p. 36).

PART-TIME AND SUBSTITUTE FACULTY EVALUATION NEEDS

The first experiences at faculty evaluation for this author were as dean of evening college working with part-time faculty at Kellogg Community College in the early 1970s. At the time there were over 75 part-time teachers, and *not one* of them had been evaluated in their classrooms. The evening program had been available to students for over 10 years and many part-time faculty taught these evening course sections. There were serious criticisms made by some of the evening students prior to the time that an evaluation plan was developed and executed. It became evident from the start of the evaluations that a few of these faculty were in need of much *help* and *support* to learn how to prepare for, organize, and teach their subject areas in meaningful ways. The majority of these teachers were teaching for the first time and had never had teacher preparation classes and related experiences under a supervisor.

Some of the part-time instructors were teaching so poorly that it was necessary to remove them following their first evaluation, before they returned to teach the next week. These teachers were given one or two additional weeks pay in order to compensate for their removal from the classes. It was a major challenge to find replacements for some of the more difficult areas. There were shortages of available and qualified people. A significant number of the other part-time teachers expressed appreciation for the in-class evaluations and for the positive comments and teaching improvement suggestions. Each of these instructors had follow-up meetings within a week, if not later the same evening of the evaluation, to discuss the outcomes.

Hiring of part-time teachers in the K-12 system, along with a core of substitute teachers, presents a constant challenge for the administrators and boards of education. It is important to hire persons for these positions who have strong qualifications for the subjects being taught. It is just as important to do in-class evaluations of these teachers to satisfy the administrators that use of part-time and substitute teachers has not lowered the standards and that competent instruction is being delivered.

PART-TIME FACULTY NEEDS

Norman (1984) made several recommendations for improving support systems for part-time faculty. He proposed changing titles to "adjunct" or "associate" instructors, and providing office space and clerical assistance. He also advocated parking privileges, names placed on mailboxes and telephone lists, invitations to social and departmental functions, mentoring with a full-time faculty member, and invitations to attend all faculty developmental programs offered on the campus.

Spinetta (1990) suggested part-time faculty be given pro-rata pay, that is, a proportion of the salary that is given to full-time faculty. He cites the Joint Committee for Review of the Master Plan for Higher Education, 1989, which recommended this as the long-term solution to the part-time faculty issue in the California community college system. Spinetta believes such a pay raise would increase part-time faculty's feeling of professionalism and job satisfaction, and possibly the college's effectiveness.

This is a proposal that has not been accepted and is highly unlikely to be put into effect in the future. With limited funds coming from the states and a reliance on significantly larger numbers of part-time faculty at the present part-time pay schedules, it appears nearly impossible to obtain sufficient funds to change the pay pattern at this time.

Pro-rata pay for part-time faculty would put an undue burden on an already financially strained system of education. Spinetta did not deal with the fact that economic savings is one of the main reasons that colleges have moved toward more part-time faculty. The K-12 systems also hire their substitute and part-time faculty at a much-lower rate than full-time faculty and usually offer no benefits to them.

The large Maricopa Community College system in Arizona made efforts to help part-time faculty with an improved orientation program. This included providing workshops and seminars taught by professionals in the subject matter areas being taught by the part-time instructors. They also established some mentoring programs for the part-time instructors.

ORIENTATION AND EVALUATION

Andrews (2001) surveyed all 50 states to determine what was being done to integrate the part-time faculty into the community college institutions. Questions were asked of both the faculty leaders and the chief instructional administrators. Andrews summarized data from the six states that have the largest community college systems: Michigan, Wisconsin, Illinois, Florida, North Carolina, and New York. These six states had a total of 220 community colleges. Eighty percent of the administrators responded, as did 68 percent of the faculty leaders.

An important finding was that administrators in 146 (83 percent) of the institutions responding indicated they were conducting some type of part-time faculty evaluation. Out of the 146 colleges, 32 indicated they used evaluation by a supervisor, while 39 indicated using only student evaluations. A larger group comprised of 94 institutions reported using a combination of supervisors, students and faculty peers in this process.

The most common services offered to part-time faculty to assist them in assimilating into the institutions were: (1) orientation by department; (2) assistance with course; (3) meetings with full-time staff; (4) assistance in teaching methodology; (5) review of materials by supervisor; (6) meetings during the semester; (7) assistance in test preparation; (8) attendance at professional meetings paid.

Thirty-four percent of the administrators and 41 percent of the faculty leaders reported having recognition programs for their part-time faculty. This was a significant improvement over the 13.2 percent Erwin and Andrews (1993) reported from an earlier 19-state North Central Association review of part-time services. This does, however, leave 66 percent of the institutions, reported by administrators, as not giving any formal recognition to their quality part-time teachers.

Services provided for part-time faculty

Erwin and Andrews (1993) conducted a study in 353 community, technical and junior colleges to find out how effective, comprehensive, and well-planned services were for part-time faculty. A return of 283 responses (80 percent) provided a significant overview of the services to part-time fac-

---

ulty in these colleges. The instructional vice president or dean was the person responding in each of these colleges.

The largest number of colleges (94) reported 50 or fewer part-time faculty. This was followed by 47 colleges having 51 to 100 part-time faculty and 44 colleges having between 101 and 150. Another 33 colleges had over 300, and 21 reported over 400. Six of the colleges reported having over 600 part-time faculty.

The services being offered most often were:

1. Course syllabi;
2. Meeting with full-time faculty;
3. Orientation by department;
4. Review of materials by supervisor; and
5. Meetings during the semester.

Evaluation

Investigating ways to improve services to part-time faculty in the future, several questions were asked. A total of 226 (88.6%) of the 283 respondent colleges indicated "yes," they did have a faculty evaluation program for their part-time faculty. Yet 103 (41.2%) indicated they were "not satisfied" with the faculty evaluation process. In replying to which type of evaluation components were utilized in the colleges of the respondents, answers were:

1. Evaluation by students   204
2. Evaluation by supervisor'   160
3. Evaluation by faculty   50
        Total   414

The 414 figure from the 226 respondent colleges with evaluation programs would indicate that a combination of these methods is utilized in a significant number of the colleges.

Recognition

Only 33 of the colleges in the Erwin and Andrews's study reported any type of recognition programs for their part-time faculty. This represented 13.2 percent. On the other hand, 166 (60%) reported they now had recognition programs for their full-time faculty.

The type of part-time recognition programs reported were "recognition and small stipend," "associate faculty member of the year award," "part-time teacher of the year award by the president," "extra mile award," and "similar (awards) to those for full-time faculty." This area of recognition was found to be very under-developed, reflecting the lack of or weakly developed evaluation programs.

There were several areas of concern regarding the implementation of part-time faculty evaluation. Thirty-six respondents in the study said that systematic improvements were needed to address the following problems:

1. Poor implementation;
2. No consistency;
3. Too cumbersome;
4. Inadequate follow-up;
5. Done too late in semester;
6. Done too sporadically;
7. Doesn't distinguish 'good' from 'bad' teachers.

Twenty-two colleges reported having no evaluation system in place or having one considered too weak or incomplete to be effective. Sixteen colleges were concerned that there were "too many part-time faculty and not enough administrative help" available to administer a system of evaluation effectively.

Andrews (1987c) listed four recommendations which would lead to an effective evaluation system for part-time faculty: (1) establishing minimum qualifications for instruction, (2) providing teaching orientation, (3) conducting in-class observation and evaluation, and (4) performing follow-up action as a result of evaluation. In-class observations are necessary to provide the faculty with feedback and suggestions for improving their teaching, as well as to assist in the retention or dismissal of these faculty members. Such assistance should enhance the image part-time faculty have of their work and also show that the college does care about the quality of their teaching. Evaluation is a way to provide the part-time faculty with suggestions for improvement and to share the teaching expectations of the college with them.

Problems inherent in hiring a large number of part-time faculty need to be anticipated. It is important for the administration to face these problems and to make plans to assist these faculty to be successful:

1. Deans, division chairpersons, and others may have to become the "teacher education" trainers for many of these faculty members, who have little or no orientation or training in teaching methodology.
2. The influx of part-time faculty presently and in the future means that more students will judge the colleges by the quality of work of the part-time teachers. Students will relate their positive or negative experiences to relatives and friends at home and in the workplace. Poor instruction, if left unchecked, can damage the colleges' reputations.

EVALUATING PART-TIME FACULTY

Colleges need to develop practical methods for supervisory personnel to evaluate their part-time faculty. In some colleges the numbers will be small enough for a dean or vice president of instruction and division chairpersons to conduct classroom visitations of all part-time faculty. In colleges with large part-time teaching staffs it will take more creative thinking to arrange and conduct effective evaluation practices.

Hiring of some of their full-time master teachers in the subject areas may assist the administration in evaluating all part-time faculty. This might be done as an overload pay assignment. In situations where the teaching is of high enough quality, further follow-up visitations may not be needed. After identifying those instructors having significant problems or concerns in their teaching, the administrative personnel would do the follow-up and conduct further evaluation of those teachers. If master teachers in a large college with 650 part-time faculty find 50 to 60 concerns, it would not be unreasonable for supervisory administrative personnel to be available to continue the evaluation of this number of part-time instructors.

Once a review of these part-time faculty has been made, it is not necessary to do in-class evaluations on a semester-to-semester or annual basis for those teachers meeting the college standards. A number of those teachers found to need assistance can be helped and will respond. They will need follow-up supervision. Some will simply not meet the expected standards or will be unable to make the adjustments necessary. These persons should be removed and replaced. This may cause some problems, especially when a poor instructor who was hired a number of years ago is now removed. It is during these decisions, however, that administrators must remember that students are their number one concern.

A second strategy for evaluating part-time faculty is to have in-class evaluation of 20 percent of the part-time faculty each year. All would be evaluated within a five-year period. Student complaints and in-class evaluations of part-time faculty will help to identify those teachers who need immediate assistance or need to be replaced early in the process.

Newly hired part-time faculty need to be a priority in the evaluation system. Early classroom observations and suggestions for improvement can be made before poor practices become ingrained in the faculty member's approach to teaching. Such observations should also lead to removal and replacement of incompetent part-time faculty during the semester.

Behrendt and Parsons (1983) recommended the following strategies to help improve the use of part-time faculty:

1. There must be a general institutional commitment to overall staff evaluation for adjunct faculty evaluations to be effective.
2. The institution must possess a base of expertise to conduct the evaluation system properly.
3. Adequate support services similar to those available to full-time faculty members must be provided to adjunct faculty.
4. While trying to integrate adjunct faculty into the college community through such techniques as evaluation, we must remember that the needs of these people are different from those of the full-time faculty members (p. 42).

K-12 Part-time and substitute teachers

Evaluation of part-time and substitute teachers in K-12 systems must also be addressed. With the *No Child Left Behind* legislation placing pressure on all school systems, it is critical that priority be given to assessing the credentials and performance of these teachers.

Some part-time faculty substitute for one day at a time, rotate through a number of disciplines, and sometimes fill in for a sick or absent teacher for weeks or months. While the legislation does not appear to address the part-time faculty, it behooves school administrators to conduct quality checks on these faculty in order to guarantee the school and students that they are also qualified and competent teachers.

SUMMARY

The number of part-time faculty members is increasing in both community colleges and K-12 school systems. As this population increases, it becomes more important that the appropriateness of their credentials be assessed prior to hiring and the quality of their teaching be evaluated.

The use of student evaluation is a weak method, at best, for determining whether quality teaching exists in the classrooms of part-time faculty. Yet many of the community colleges in Erwin and Andrews' study (204 out of 414) reported using evaluation by students. Less than half (160) reported using evaluation by supervisors. Only 58.5% of the colleges in the study felt satisfied with their part-time evaluation system.

The failure to recognize and reward good part-time faculty was one of the major weaknesses identified in several studies over the years. The total percentage of colleges reporting some form of recognition for their outstanding full-time faculty was 60%, but that dropped to 13.2% for their part-time faculty.

Overall, there are a number of gaps and a lack of systematic methods used to integrate part-time faculty into community, technical, and junior colleges. Many of the services offered to full-time faculty are neglected when considering part-time faculty.

Part-time teachers may teach from one to four courses in any given semester of work. They are accountable to their students who expect to receive quality instruction in each of their classes. Part-time faculty need orientation, mentoring, and administrative evaluators to discuss their strengths and weaknesses.

The K-12 systems will also have to consider the quality of their part-time and substitute teachers as they work to improve student outcomes and guarantee highly qualified teachers in all of their classrooms. As with college faculty, an effective evaluation system is necessary to achieve this.

SUGGESTED EXERCISES

1. What might you suggest that would help integrate part-time faculty and guarantee quality teaching by them at a secondary school or community college?

2. How might you provide competent supervisory evaluation of all part-time faculty in a K-12 school system or a community college?

Accountable Teacher Evaluation

CHAPTER 17

EPILOGUE: HIGHLY QUALIFIED AND COMPETENT TEACHERS IN EVERY CLASSROOM

The years ahead will see a continuation, and intensification, of the accountability movement in American education. The federal government has intervened to assure improvements in student learning that have failed to materialize through individual school and state reform efforts in many areas of the country.

This book supports the case that teachers are the major source for making these improvements. The *No Child Left Behind* legislation calls for *highly qualified teachers* in every K-12 classroom. Faculty evaluation of these highly qualified teachers is paramount in assuring students, parents and governing boards that their teachers can perform effectively in their classrooms. Teachers endorse efforts of evaluation in varying degrees but have expressed doubts about the quality of evaluators and evaluation processes. These doubts will not be founded if evaluation processes are jointly developed by boards, administrators, and faculty and are clear, comprehensive, fair, objective, and effective.

Faculty evaluation—quality control of instruction—is often relegated to students or peers at the community college level. Both faculty leaders and instructional administrators in these colleges report a high degree of frustration at what they view as ineffective evaluation with no significant outcomes. Both groups highlight the need for evaluation to provide developmental opportunities for all teachers. They also agree that the poor college teachers should be remediated or be dismissed. Most of them report that this is not presently happening in their colleges.

This author has argued that supervisory/administrative evaluation is crucial. Student and peer evaluation have proven ineffective, and both groups have been absent in legal cases involving dismissal for incompetent faculty. On the other hand, there are numerous cases in which administrative evaluation has been employed to document incompetence and provide evidence for faculty termination cases. Not one such case was found documented as I researched for this book in the areas of student or peer evaluation. Similarly, research indicates that input from students or peers rarely leads to improvement of teaching or to disciplinary measures. Administrative evaluators can recommend improvements, follow-up on these recommendations, and develop remediation plans. They can also take appropriate action if the teacher fails to remediate those concerns that have been outlined and discussed.

If excellence is to be achieved, it is necessary to dismiss teachers who have repeatedly failed to change their performance to conform to an acceptable standard. If dismissal is handled correctly, it will be legally defensible and will win quiet applause from conscientious and competent teachers. However, dismissal is a last resort. For maximum effectiveness, dismissal must be part of an ongoing process of evaluation and improvement. Further, replacing an incompetent teacher with a competent teacher will improve instruction immediately for the students involved.

Involvement of faculty in the design of a supervisory evaluation plan is most important. First, it offers one of the best means of gaining faculty support for evaluation. Faculty working together with administrators to define *quality teaching* is the first step in the process. Once quality teaching, methodologies, and techniques have been identified, they become the standard for all teachers in the system. The evaluation form needs to then reflect the quality standards that have been identified by the teachers and administrators. Faculty will usually give preference to an open-ended evaluation form that allows the evaluators to write responses and descriptions of what they have observed in classroom evaluations.

One-on-one meetings between teachers evaluated and their supervisor(s) to discuss the written evaluation report should follow a classroom visit as soon as possible, i. e., the same day, when possible, but usually no more than four or five days later. These conferences and written reports clearly identify strong teaching methods and organizational skills of those teachers who excel in teaching. The reports also clearly identify concerns and deficiencies in the teaching of those teachers needing to make improvements.

Faculty unions are not adverse to quality faculty evaluation if it is conceived as a means of improving instruction and results in increased efforts to meet the developmental needs of faculty members. Unions also have been found to support administrative movements to dismiss poor instructors. This support is provided as long as the poorly performing teachers are first given clear directions and support to improve within a reasonable time frame. Unions also expect tenured teachers to be given their due process rights if attempts at remediation have failed and dismissal is being considered.

Ineffective teachers put an additional burden on other teachers who depend on them to provide a strong foundation for subsequent grade levels and/or courses. Incompetence on the part of a teacher in an elementary or middle school makes for very difficult instruction at the next level. When one or more teachers are incompetent, all of the teachers within an elementary, middle or secondary school or community college department or division suffer.

The first question asked when discussing supervisory evaluation is, "Who will be doing the evaluation?" The second question normally is, "Who is evaluating the evaluators?"

These are important questions for governing boards and administrative leaders to consider when implementing quality evaluation processes.

The boards and administrators must make certain that evaluators have appropriate credentials and strong teaching backgrounds. Evaluators need to be flexible and well versed in learning theories, teaching methodologies and techniques.

Each teacher has his or her own unique personality; it is necessary to consider what works for the individual teacher during their delivery of instruction. Further, it is important to learn what "value added" or "improvement in learning" occurs in the classrooms. With the *No Child Left Behind* legislation, test scores are taking on more importance as accountability measures for both federal and state governments.

Whether a single evaluation system can accomplish both formative (assisting) and summative (decisions on tenure, remediation, promotion or dismissal) results is debated by a number of researchers. Licata and Andrews suggested that one system could, indeed, provide a *continuum* and achieve both formative and summative outcomes. The same evaluators visit classes and make formative suggestions. The evaluators look for positive movement toward improvement from individual teachers. They can move toward a remediation format when improvement is not made. Remediation continues to offer teachers improvement suggestions and clearly defined formative directions. Formative evaluation, in this analysis, continues up to the time that a decision on dismissal is made.

The large majority of teacher evaluations will show that the teachers are meeting or exceeding the expected standards. Yet, several research studies have documented a lack of recognition programs in schools and colleges throughout the United States. Recent research has found some increase in the number of community colleges offering such programs. Faculty are sometimes being rewarded for outstanding work through special recognition programs, small amounts of

---

money and plaques, and additional professional development opportunities. There are, however, far too many schools that continue to neglect this most important means of improving the school climate.

The majority of the community colleges reporting recognition for outstanding faculty offer *only* one or two such awards in any given year. These are not enough to make the impact necessary to reinforce quality teaching throughout a school or college. In these days of increased accountability, it behooves administrators and boards to develop means of reinforcing the best instructors within our elementary, middle, and secondary schools, and community colleges.

The number of part-time teachers, now comprising some 60 percent of the total teachers in community colleges, continues to increase. Although the part-time teachers do not teach nearly the number of classes as the full-time teachers, quality teaching must be expected of them. Yet, studies have found part-time teachers are often not provided with much classroom assistance, classroom evaluations, and other important support services necessary to guarantee quality instruction.

There is also a lack of recognition programs for part-time faculty. While recognition programs are expanding for full-time faculty, this has not occurred for part-time teachers. As K-12 schools and community colleges continue to rely heavily on part-time faculty, they must develop ways to reinforce quality teaching in their systems.

Governing boards can play major roles in the process of improving instruction by demanding an effective evaluation system in every school. Such evaluation systems must provide for honest assessment and support to assist teachers in their development. The laws and courts in most states support the role of boards in the granting of tenure, remediation, and, when necessary, dismissals for poor performance. Final decisions on personnel recommendations rest with governing boards.

The governing boards, administrators, and teachers must all work as a team to make quality improvements in the classroom. Governing boards need to support the superintendent or college president when decisions are made to improve faculty development and to develop recognition programs as well as when decisions are made for remediation and dismissal. With proper support, administrators will complete the steps and meet the challenges that are necessary to improve student learning. Boards need guidance from administrators and legal authority on how to make the tough personnel decisions that will move schools and colleges into a mode of continual improvements in student outcomes.

Faculty evaluation, when applied even handedly, can be a positive experience for the evaluator. It gives opportunities to highlight excellence in classroom instruction and to work with both experienced and new teachers in their further development. Teachers appreciate feedback if it is sincere and if the evaluator is respected. It is also rewarding to let a poor instructor know what changes need to be made and to see progress.

One can take pride in administrative work that does not allow poor instruction to continue in a school or college. The administrator must remember that decisions *must be made* on behalf of those students who are receiving poor instruction. Students may spend three or four years trying to "recover" from one poor elementary teacher.

Elementary, middle, and secondary schools and community colleges are focused on providing *highly qualified teachers* in every classroom in the next few years. Hiring teachers with the proper majors and minors provides one indication of proper preparation. Documenting *competence in classroom instruction* through faculty evaluation is the second major part of the equation. Both of these efforts will lead to improved teaching and learning outcomes at all levels of American education.

Appendix A

Legal Cases in Dismissals of Faculty

This appendix is designed to provide a variety of legal cases involving faculty terminations. These cases will give administrators, faculty and faculty unions, and governing boards a clearer sense of what is acceptable and unacceptable behavior in teaching and other professional job responsibilities. In a number of cases the instructors were reinstated due to inadequate administration and/or board action. Other cases clarify the need to properly follow legal procedural processes.

Free Speech Dismissal Challenges

The Texas Fifth Circuit Court in *Harris v. Victoria Ind. School District* (1999) reviewed a lower level decision and reversed a grant of summary judgment on behalf of a board that had transferred two teachers. The court "indicated that criticisms by two teachers on a site based management team voiced about their principal's failure to implement a school improvement plan constituted speech on a matter of public concern." The court further interpreted the transfers as being retaliatory due to the teachers' exercise of free speech. This case went further to find the superintendent and board of trustees not to be entitled to either qualified or absolute immunity for their act. By affirming the superintendent's decision to transfer the faculty members, the board acted as a policymaker and was opening itself up to liability.

In *Padilla v. South Harrison* (1999) the Missouri Eighth Circuit Court overturned a previous jury verdict in favor of a probationary teacher who had testified that he did not see anything wrong with having consensual sex between a teacher and a student. The court did not see this as a free speech retaliation claim when his contract was not renewed. The court saw his remarks did not involve a matter of public concern about a legitimate disagreement with the school board policies.

In *Madison v. Houston Independent School District* (1999) a former special education teacher was dismissed in Texas after hitting a student with a paddle while disciplining him. The teacher was unsuccessful in filing a retaliation claim under free speech. The teacher had previously released some videotapes about discipline problems in the school to the media. During the hearing the board only discussed the present discipline incident. The teacher claimed the board's action was a pretext but the court held that "[a] plaintiff's subjective belief of retaliation, however, is insufficient to prove First Amendment retaliation."

In *Stratton v. Austin Independent School District* (1999) the appellate court found a teacher with a one-year contract had no protected property interest in having a contract renewal. The school board, during the teacher's hearing, violated its own policy by having a limit of one hour for the teacher to present her evidence. The court found, however, that even with this policy violation the non-tenured teacher still had no protected property interest.

In the Pennsylvania University case of *Edwards v. California University of Pennsylvania* (1998) it was affirmed by the Federal trial court that it was necessary for the teacher to teach the curriculum as outlined. Students had complained that they had enrolled in a course that was outlined and promoted to teach various classroom tools. The instructor, on his own will, decided to teach issues of bias, censorship, religion and humanism. He had challenged the university's decision for suspension with pay as violating his First and Fourteenth Amendment speech rights. The decision stated that a faculty member does not, indeed, have a First Amendment right to decide what will be taught in his or her classroom.

A teacher's dismissal was supported in the Eighth Circuit Court in Minnesota. The teacher was uncooperative in discussing her classroom, which had been cited for disruptive classes and obstructive discipline. She refused to meet with the principal about these problem areas. In *Berg v. Bruce* (1997) the court supported the board and found the teacher to not have a free speech right when she refused discussion of her (1) classroom performance, (2) grading practices, and (3) attitude toward the principal.

The court found in favor of the school in *Landrum v. Eastern Kentucky University* (1984) when the faculty member in question alleged he had been denied his First Amendment rights. The plaintiff had made a number of critical statements to various groups about the dean and the vice president. The plaintiff alleged that these pronouncements were within the purview of free speech and could not be used as the reason to deny tenure. The district court ruled that when an employee speaks out, not on matters of public concern but rather on matters of personal interest as an employee, his pronouncements are outside the scope of the First Amendment. The court stated that, "the First Amendment does not require a public office to be run as a roundtable for employee complaints over internal office affairs." The court in this case characterized plaintiff's speech as that of "individual disputes and grievances" (Thomas, 1985, p. 309).

A Pennsylvania case, *Rossi v. Pennsylvania State University* (1985), was concerned with the dismissal of an employee who complained about supervisors on "non-public issues." The employee plaintiff complained about the way his supervisors managed the Instructional Services Division at a public institution. He defended himself by saying his pronouncements were matters of public policy and he was making recommendations on how to save the state taxpayers money.

The court found under common law that the employee could be dismissed at will and that the plaintiff's pronouncements did not concern public policy but rather were differences of opinion on how to manage this particular division of the university. It was ruled that the defendant college may dismiss an employee who becomes troublesome or hostile to his superiors.

Aspects of Notice

An appellate court in New York, in the case of *Burkes v. Enlarged City School District of Troy* (1999), reviewed the question raised by a teacher aide concerning not having sufficient time to prepare for a hearing. Numerous students had testified that the teacher aide had had physical contact with them. The court ruled that this testimony was sufficient to sustain the aide's dismissal from his job. The teacher aide claimed he was not aware that physical contact with students was not appropriate. Testimony proved that he had received warnings from three different witnesses.

In another case on hearing requirements, a trial court was hearing a faculty member, who was accused of teacher misconduct in *Elmore v. Plainview-Old Bethpage Central School District Board of Education* (1999). The decision to affirm the school board's decision to terminate was overturned because the hearing officer had not permitted the teacher to confer with his attorney on breaks during the hearing. The court saw this as interfering with the statutory right of the teacher to have meaningful representation.

The importance of proper "notice" was highlighted in *Bentley v. School District No. 015 of Custer County* (1998) in Nebraska. The Supreme Court's decision to reinstate a probationary teacher was based on the fact that the school board failed in their responsibility to follow the state statutory requirements in terms of a proper notice to the teacher. The results of the evaluation of the teacher by the principal was not enough to warrant dismissal.

The termination of a probationary teacher in New York was affirmed by the appellate court in *Perlin v. South Orangetown Central School District* (1997). The court found that the teacher should not have had an expectation of a review of the superintendent's decision after being given notice that he was not to be recommended for contract renewal.

In the case of *Clark v. Board of Directors of School District of Kansas City* (1996), a Missouri federal district court upheld the board in the termination of a tenured teacher. The teacher claimed he was not properly notified because the suspension letter that he had received didn't specifically state that he was allowed to have legal counsel. The federal court disagreed since he was notified orally that an attorney of his choosing could be present for the discussion before the board concerning his inappropriate disciplining of students.

A Texas teacher sued over the nonrenewal of her contract and claimed she was not given a hearing before the school board over her dismissal. The appellate court in *Gilder v. Meno* (1996) found that due process was given via the two hearings she had had on the issue of bias and on her deficiencies as a teacher. The court also noted that she had not offered to present any evidence herself, or through witnesses, at either one of the hearings in which she had been represented by counsel.

Two different tenured faculty cases were decided, in part, from procedural due process actions. The first one, in Alabama, involved a teacher who resigned prior to having a dismissal hearing. In *Swann v. Caylor* (1987) the instructor lost his right to procedural due process claims because when he resigned he lost "his property and tenure rights to that job."

The second case, (*Petrella v. Siegel*, 1988), found the teacher still had a protectable property interest and a procedural right to a due process hearing. The state law provided that such public officers can resign only in writing and the oral resignation given by the instructor did not negate this right.

Aspects of Hearing

A federal trial court case in Ohio looked at the school board's failure to allow a teacher to give her testimony on three of the five charges against her in the dismissal. The court determined in *McDaniel v. Princeton City School District Board of Education* (1999) that the teacher's due process rights were violated as they had been set forth in *Cleveland Board of Education v. Loudermill* (1972).

A middle school teacher accused of sexual misconduct was given a suspension with pay while his case was being investigated. Since the school board suspended the teacher with pay the federal trial court, in *Tweedall v. Fritz* (1997), granted a summary judgment for the board. The teacher had charged that his due process right to a pre-suspension hearing was violated. The court disagreed because of the higher private interest that was at stake. It saw the board having a significant interest to protect the school children from their teacher's alleged sexual charges.

In Connecticut a teacher filed a claim to be reinstated because the dismissal did not follow the process used in a court. The appellate panel in *Halpern v. Board of Education of City of Bristol* (1998) sustained the board in her dismissal for incompetence and insubordination. The panel stated unlimited time for oral arguments was not necessary.

In the case of *Kyle v. Morton High School* (1998) the Seventh District Court of Illinois supported the board in the dismissal of a probationary teacher. The board of education had failed to comply with the state's Open Meetings Act, but the court found the teacher did not have a right to procedural due process due to a lack of a property interest, and he was not reinstated.

Another case, in Mississippi, *Doty v. Tupelo Public School District* (1999), found in favor of the school board at the appellate court level. The dismissal of the teacher was upheld even though much of the testimony had been hearsay, which is not allowed for dismissals according to the state law. The principal, however, was supported for the testimony he had given based upon his observations of the teacher's behavior with children and of his conversations with parents of the students.

One case in Kansas, *Walker v. Board of Education, Unified School District No. 499* (1995), was reversed at the appellate court level in favor of a tenured teacher who had received a contract nonrenewal. The court found the teacher was denied an opportunity to question members of the board concerning discussions that took place in an executive session. She was awarded back pay.

When a teacher in New York resigned after he had been charged with sexual harassment against four students, the appellate court allowed a disciplinary hearing against him to proceed. In *Folta v. Sobol* (1994) the court further ruled that the resignation did not preclude such a proceeding for disciplinary reasons and penalty.

Due Process and Unfair Dismissal Claims

The United States Constitution mandates that procedural due process must be followed before adverse employment actions can be taken against personnel who have liberty and property interests in their jobs (*Cleveland Board of Education v. Loudermill,* 1985).

The following cases stem from allegations that school boards violated due process rights of teachers. In *Johanson v.*

Board of Education (1999) a teacher was dismissed by the board for unprofessional conduct against two students. The conduct included a fifth grade class being told to hide from a student and being allowed to tie him up with an extension cord. In addition, a student was physically and verbally abused by the teacher who referred to the student as an "idiot." The teacher had filed a claim that the board had failed to provide him with a summary of the nature of the testimony against him in advance of the termination. The Supreme Court of Nebraska found the testimony against him provided enough evidence to support the board in their termination for unprofessional conduct.

The Seventh Circuit Court in Illinois determined in *Strasburger v. Board of Education, Hardin County* (1998) that a temporary suspension of a teacher from his coaching and athletic director duties did not violate his liberty interests. The suspension was invoked while the board investigated the rumors about his past criminal charges. The court found that the charges were accurate and did not falsely malign him.

In *Stills v. Alabama State Tenure Commission* (1998) the teacher was reinstated by the appellate court because the plaintiff had not been notified, as required by state statute, that she was to have her contract cancelled.

Dismissal, Nonrenewal, Demotion, and Discipline

The Supreme Court of Ohio found in favor of a teacher, due to the school board not "providing the teacher with clear and substantive bases as to why it did not renew her contract," in *Geib v. Triway Local Board of Education* (1999). The board's statement, which referred to past "deficiencies" from prior evaluations, was not considered acceptable to the court.

That boards of education are vested with an exclusive

authority to dismiss teachers was demonstrated in *Chicago School Reform Board of Trustees v. Illinois Education Labor Relations Board* (1999) in an Illinois appellate court. This authority was interpreted from the state statutes and struck down an earlier order from the Illinois Education Labor Relations Board (IELRB) that had directed the board to reinstate one of their substitute teachers. The court made it clear that a negotiated contract agreement between the board and teachers cannot take away the authority of the board to employ, discharge, and lay off staff. This power was given as part of the changes in the school code that was written and enacted by the legislature of Illinois to help the Chicago School Reform Board of Trustees in reform efforts.

In another case, in which the appellate court in Massachusetts, *School District of Beverly v. Geller* (2000), reversed an arbitrator's decision, a reinstatement decision was put aside. In this case a teacher with 25 years of experience had charges of three physical force situations with students. The court found reinstatement was not possible in those states that have "a clearly defined public policy protecting students against physical harm," thus prohibiting corporal punishment.

A Michigan appeals court in *Widdoes v. Detroit Public School* (1996) reversed the termination of a teacher. He had been fired for allegedly using excessive force, but the board did not produce substantial and material evidence as was required to show violation of the corporal punishment statute.

Remediation is not required for willful neglect of duty, an appellate court in Louisiana ruled in *Williams v. Concordia Parish School Board* (1996). In supporting the termination of a tenured teacher, the court heard testimony that the teacher had read a narrative with sexually suggestive words to a seventh-grade class.

A tenured teacher admitted his failure to follow a remediation plan to meet the defined standard for student assessment, and he was unable to produce legible records of his students' performance. The Illinois appellate court in *Davis v. Board of Education of Chicago* (1995) found that his teacher evaluations during the remediation period were very similar to those received earlier. His deficiencies continued through the remediation period and confirmed his inability to carry out his job responsibilities.

The board's decision to dismiss a thirteen-year teacher for falsifying a sick leave statement was not upheld by the Ohio Court of Appeals. The faculty member had a good record otherwise, and a hearing referee had recommended suspension rather than termination. The court allowed that the board could reject a referee's recommendation but it had "failed to sufficiently articulate its reasons for rejecting the referee's recommendation of suspension." This was viewed by the court as an improper termination in *Katz v. Maple Heights City School District Board of Education* (1993).

A tenured teacher in Michigan was dismissed for using corporal punishment with four students in violation of the school board policy. Once he kicked and pushed a student to get her to return to his classroom. He struck another student in the face with his fist as a disciplinary measure and received a written reprimand for this incident. A third incident found him grabbing a student in a headlock and slapping or punching the student, leading to a cut on the student's face. In a fourth incident the teacher had struck a female high school student in the face and knocked her down. The teacher sought to have some of the earlier incidents deemed inadmissible in his present dismissal case, but the Court of Appeals allowed them. The court upheld the decision in *Tomczik v. State Tenure Commission, Center Line Public Schools* (1989).

A tenured teacher in New York was found to be terminated for just cause for her inability to control her class and for lack of planning and organization (*Mongitore vs. Regan*, 1987).

A home economics teacher can be fired for failing to

maintain discipline rather than being transferred to a previous position in which she had satisfactorily taught for a number of years, according to *Stamper v. Board of Education of Elementary School District 143* (1986). It was also found that a tenured teacher may be asked to resign before initiation of dismissal proceedings. The hearing officer's decision supporting the school in dismissing the teacher was upheld by the court.

An elementary school case in Connecticut, *Cope v. Board of Education of the Town of West Hartford* (1985), found the board's decision to dismiss a tenured faculty member to be supported by the evidence: continual neglect of her overall teaching responsibilities (supported by repeated warning and reprimands); and a pattern of failure to supervise her first grade students to the extent that safety of the students became an issue.

The appellate court of North Carolina supported the board in the dismissal of a career teacher for not providing adequate discipline in her classroom. School authorities were found to have been thoughtful, patient, persistent, but unable to obtain sufficient change on the part of the teacher to properly control her classes (*Crump v. Durham County Board of Education*, 1985).

In the Michigan case of *Board of Education of Benton Harbor Area Schools v. Wolff* (1985), the Court of Appeals supported the board in their dismissal of the teacher for failure to establish and maintain discipline. This lack of discipline was found to subvert the instructional process. Instances of students wandering freely about the room, talking out of turn, frequently fighting and leaving and entering the classroom without having to obtain permission were all documented. Efforts to remediate were not successful.

In *Hatta v. Board of Education, Union Endicott Central School District* (1977) in New York, the teacher dismissed was found to be incompetent for lack of control and discipline in the classroom. The decision was supported by the Supreme Court, Appellate Division, of the state.

Another elementary teacher, in *Rolando v. School Directors of District No. 125* (1976), was found dismissed properly by an appellate court in Illinois. He had used a cattle prod to discipline his pupils. His behavior was found to be irremediable, as the damage had already been done to the students, the faculty and the school. The court determined that none of the damage could have been corrected even if the board had served the plaintiff a written warning.

An Illinois appellate court upheld the dismissal of a tenured teacher for lack of discipline in classrooms, improper use of corporal punishment and poor teaching practices. The court conducted a full and independent review of the record of the school board and found that a fair hearing and proper evidence had been entered in the decision (*Hagerstrom v. Clay City Community Unit School*, 1976).

Incompetence

Incompetence necessarily relates to an employee's performance on the job (Russo, 1997, p. 23).

A school board's policy prohibiting strip searches led the Supreme Court of Connecticut to affirm the dismissal of the tenured teacher, who supervised such a search, in *Rogers v. Board of Education of the City of New Haven* (2000). This case is in the category of incompetence, and the teacher's behavior was determined to be below a requisite standard. The teacher was employed as an assistant principal at the time of the strip search of fifth and sixth grade female students.

In the case, *In re Termination of Kible* (1999), the Supreme Court of Mexico reversed a school board's dismissal of a teacher who had been arrested for driving while intoxicated and resisting arrest. The court found that the misdemeanors didn't involve moral turpitude and were not related

---

to his competence as a teacher. The court further found that this board action was representative of disparate treatment in comparison to the way they had previously handled some similar cases.

The appellate court in *Newcomb v. Humansville R-IV School District* (1995) upheld the firing of a tenured teacher in Missouri. The teacher had argued that the school district was to blame for the many disruptions in her classroom because of the class makeup of twenty-six boys and six girls.

In the Alabama appellate court case of *Dunson v. Alabama State Tenure Commission* (1994) a tenured teacher's dismissal was upheld. The grounds were incompetence and neglect of duty. The case was supported by evidence of (1) unsupervised second-graders who often disrupted nearby classrooms with noise; (2) teacher's loud outbursts and shouting at the classes; (3) her striking of a female student in the face with her fist; (4) her threatening to report students to law enforcement officers; (5) her threatening to beat them up; and (6) her failure to follow the state-mandated time allotments for time required on specific subjects.

Written charges for termination following a warning letter were enough to support a tenured teacher's termination for not having improved her competency and efficiency to a sufficient degree. In *Keesee v. Meadow Heights R-II School District* (1993) the Missouri court of appeals supported the board's decision.

Missouri court of appeals supported a tenured teacher's dismissal. In *Johnson v. Francis Howell R-3 Board of Education* (1994), the court found sufficient support for dismissal in the teacher's failure to maintain classroom discipline, provide adequate and individualized attention to students and do a proper job of evaluating the performance of her students.

A board's decision to terminate a special education teacher was upheld by a Louisiana court of appeals in *Muggivan v. Jefferson Parish School Board* (1994). The teacher had received eight charges from the board. Among the charges was a failure to construct adequate lessons plans and a failure to create a positive classroom climate. The court found this sufficient to rule incompetence and neglect of duty.

In *Nevels v. Board of Education of School District of Maplewood-Richmond Heights* (1991), a tenured teacher's dismissal was based upon errors in attendance reports and in the mid-quarter and quarterly progress reports turned into the administration. The Missouri "meet and confer" requirement was considered by the appellate court to have been met through meetings with the superintendent, school counselor and secretary. In addition, a teaching area specialist supported this requirement with a warning letter and observation over several weeks.

Dismissal of a tenured counselor was upheld in Alabama's appeal's court. The counselor was repeatedly negligent in preparing referral packets on students and reporting to work on time. He also had numerous unexplained work absences and failed to submit acceptable weekly and monthly plan books and yearly plans (*Alabama State Tenure Commission v. Birmingham Board of Education*, 1990).

In another elementary case a sixth grade teacher was ordered reinstated by the appellate court and charges of incompetency and insufficiency were determined to be unproven due to lack of specificity. In *Jefferson Consolidated School District C-123 v. Carden* (1989), the court found alleged deficiencies over a three month period were in the principal's and superintendent's notebooks but had not been presented in advance to Carden. The charges were determined not to be specific enough to comply with the applicable statute. The teacher was reinstated and to be paid her salary which was lost during the appeal process.

In *Bradshaw v. Alabama State Tenure Commission* (1988) the Alabama Court of Civil Appeals supported the board's decision to dismiss a long-time tenured teacher for behavioral reasons. His behavior included (1) smoking in front of students in the classroom; (2) using inappropriate language in the presence of students and fellow employees; (3) leaving his classroom unattended; (4) failing to submit proper lesson plans and class rolls; (5) using inappropriate materials in the classroom which created a danger to the health of the students; (6) making sexual remarks to female students and teachers; and (7) making harassing phone calls to the female assistant principal. The teacher tried to enter alcoholism as a cause in his case but the court found the behaviors in question did not occur while he was under the influence of alcohol.

The Missouri Court of Appeals held that a teacher, in *Hanlon v. Board of Education of the Parkway School District* (1985), (1) had been given adequate notice of her deficiencies and more than the statutory period to correct them; (2) there was no error in the board's refusal to grant teacher discovery of certain documents and discovery of substance of testimony of superintendent's witnesses or in its refusal to subpoena particular witness; and (3) that the board's finding of incompetence and inefficiency was supported by competent and substantial evidence. Deficiencies were listed in areas of organization of instruction, assignments, team teaching, supervision and control, relationship with room mothers and volunteers, communication with parents, grading, and record keeping.

The Supreme Court of Nebraska supported the school board's decision to dismiss a tenured teacher for incompetence. The seventh grade teacher was evaluated and had been told that improvement in controlling her classes in mathematics and English was needed. A second evaluation visit was made to her class and found marginal behavior in 13 areas and unsatisfactory behavior in two areas. Items listed included: (1) inability to control her classes; (2) changing the shrillness of her voice; (3) using improper English and grammar; (4) failure to control her emotions when correcting students, and

(5) lack of ability in using demonstrative instructional materials. The Supreme Court found that the teacher had been given adequate notice and that the teacher was found to be terminated properly by reason of incompetence (*Eshom v. Board of Education of School District No. 54,* 1985).

In *Hamburg v. North Penn School District* (1984), the second grade teacher was dismissed for incompetence based upon the following: continual failure to maintain poise and composure with her students as well as with other professional employees and parents.

The Supreme Court of Wyoming reversed the dismissal of a secondary school tenured teacher. It found the termination was based on charges that he had shown inability to establish rapport with students which was not considered a proper ground for dismissal (*Powell v. Board of Trustees of Crook County School District No. 1,* 1976).

Incompetence and Inefficiency

In *Jackson v. Sobol* (1991) the Appellate Division of the New York Supreme Court upheld dismissal of a tenured secondary school teacher. She had entered the principal's office without authorization, ignored established procedures for disciplining students despite prior warnings, refused to meet with a troubled student's parents, failed to send a student's parents progress reports, did not have her lesson plan book available on at least three occasions as required by school district policy, and inaccurately graded students.

A Missouri Court of Appeals, in *Beck v. James, Superintendent Palmyra R-1 School District* (1990), supported the school board's decision to terminate a long-term teacher due to her incompetence and inefficiency. Charges documented over a two-year period showed problems with spelling and grammar, failure to learn students' names and complaints from parents about the teaching.

The board was overturned in its effort to dismiss a tenured counselor in *Selby v. North Callaway Board of Education* (1989). The Missouri Court of Appeals found the board to be deficient in its documentation of whether the previous notice had led to a remediation of the behavior. In short, the board was found to have failed to meet this requirement. The court found the list of concerns in the warning statement could have led to termination of this long-term teacher's contract had the board followed all procedures faithfully.

Wiley was a tenured middle school teacher dismissed for willful neglect of duty over a three year period while serving two different parish school superintendents. In *Wiley v. Richland Parish School Board* (1985), the charges of repeated complaints from fellow teachers and parents, failure to follow directives, questions concerning grades, failure to comply with written directives of the superintendent, and being unreceptive to suggestions made to her for improvement were all well documented. The board decision to terminate was affirmed by a Louisiana Court of Appeals.

Insubordination

In the case of *Board of Education of City School District of New York v. Mills* (1998) the appellate court confirmed an administrative adjudication, which had supported the school board's dismissal of a teacher for refusing to answer questions during a pre-hearing investigation. This was a violation of state statute. The three years suspension was also upheld as a reasonable penalty for the teacher having become romantically involved with one of the students.

In a Supreme Court case in Colorado the tapping of a third grade student on the head to get his attention was upheld as a case of insubordination. The court, in *Board of Education of West Yuma School District RJ-1 v. Flaming* (1997), found that this was the teacher's fourth incident of inappro-

---

priate behavior with physical contacts with children. These incidents were documented over an eight-year period.

The appellate court case of *Newman v. Sobol* (1996) in New York affirmed the dismissal of a teacher for striking a student in the eye. The tenured teacher had been on notice prior to this incident with both written and oral warnings concerning using excessive force with students.

The New York appellate court did not find the dismissal of a tenured teacher so disproportionate to her offenses so as to be shocking to one's sense of fairness. The instructor was terminated in *Greenberg v. Cortines* (1995) for insubordination, incompetence, inefficiency, neglect and misconduct.

An Alabama teacher refused to report to new facilities and appeared at his former teaching location. The appellate court supported the teacher's dismissal by the board in *Stephens v. Alabama State Tenure Commission* (1994). The court did not see the teacher's concerns regarding the safety of the new facility as reason not to report as ordered.

A tenured teacher in Missouri was terminated when she was tardy two days and took a one-day unauthorized absence as part of her protest after the school had reassigned her from a kindergarten to a third-grade classroom. The appellate court, in Missouri, in the case of *Thomas v. Mahan* (1994), found dismissal for insubordination was justified.

In a case in which a tenured teacher was dismissed for conduct unbecoming a teacher, the board was upheld by a New York appellate court. The board in *Giles v. Schuyler-Chemung-Tioga Board of Cooperative Education Services* (1993) presented substantial evidence to show the teacher had struck a student with a book, had thrown a car jack through a window, and had struck another student with a telephone receiver. The evidence also supported a charge of insubordination on the part of the teacher. He had ignored a directive against bringing an automobile into the automotive program.

In *Meyer v. Board of Education of the Charlotte Valley*

Central School District (1992), a teacher's failure to prepare proper lesson plans led to a court assessed $8,000 fine payable in twenty-six biweekly payments. The appellate court upheld the fine as not being excessive and supported the need for "formal lesson plans" as being "indispensable to effective teaching."

In *Malverne Union Free School District v. Sobol* (1992) the charge of insubordination was upheld at the appellate level after a teacher was dismissed for refusing to submit her lesson plans and grade books to her supervisors.

A termination was reversed by the court in *Board of Education of Chicago v. Johnson* (1991) when it was decided the alleged misconduct on the part of the teacher was remediable under state statute. In addition, the teacher had not received the appropriate notice available under the law.

In the case of *Gaylord v. Board of Education, Unified School District No. 218* (1990), the Kansas court of appeals upheld the school district in the dismissal of a teacher for insubordination. The teacher had called in sick after being turned down in his request for a day off to be interviewed for a different job in another school district. His principal received a call from the principal in the district in which he had applied wanting a recommendation for Gaylord. The principal learned that Gaylord was, indeed, at an interview the morning he had called in sick. Teacher absences were not allowed during the first and last week of any semester according to the negotiated faculty contract.

The Court of Appeals in Louisiana supported the board in the dismissal of a preschool teacher. In *Ford v. Caldwell Parish School, et al.* (1989) Ford was dismissed for displaying an uncooperative attitude which caused problems between herself and her supervisors as well as problems managing her class following the policies set forth by supervisory personnel. The court found the plaintiff established a staggered attendance schedule for the students even after being told not to, left her class and the school without permission, and abruptly left a meeting between herself, the principal, and the school superintendent. This was sufficient evidence for dismissal in the case of the non-tenured teacher.

A New Mexico case involved dismissal of a tenured elementary teacher for insubordination, conduct unbecoming a teacher, unprofessional conduct, and open defiance of supervisory authority. Excessive tardiness, recurring absences from her classroom, inadequate supervision of her students, inadequate lesson plans and yelling or screaming at her direct supervisor within hearing distance or presence of students and parents were all cited as reasons leading to dismissal in *Kleinbert v. Board of Education of the Albuquerque Public Schools* (1988).

Caldwell, a continuing employment teacher, was found dismissed properly in *Caldwell v. The Blytheville, Arkansas School District, Number 5* (1988) by the Court of Appeals. He was dismissed based upon his conduct at a faculty meeting, his shouting at his supervisors, calling them "liars," and accusing them of conspiring to have him fired during a conference with the principal. He also walked out of the meeting. The case was sufficiently documented.

A tenured instructor with a history of unexcused absences was terminated in *Stasny v. Board of Trustees* (1982). He was denied permission to take a leave of absence by a supervisor and was warned of disciplinary action if he defied the decision. He, nevertheless, took the leave and was dismissed for *inter alia* insubordination. In court he asserted that (1) his defiance was merely a single respectful act of disobedience, not insubordination; and (2) his dismissal violated his right to academic freedom and freedom of expression. These arguments were rejected by the appellate court, which found his contention on academic freedom to be unsubstantiated. The court stated, "Academic freedom is not a license for activity at variance with job related procedures and requirements, nor does it encompass activities which are internally destructive to the proper function of the university or disruptive to the educational process."

A case of "inefficiency" was presented by Morris (1992). In the case of *Saunders v. Reorganized School District* (1975), the Missouri Supreme Court sustained the board decision for dismissal of a tenured community college faculty member. The court ruled that substantial evidence was presented to prove there was both "inefficiency" and "insubordination." Saunders had failed and refused to instruct the curriculum as requested; had refused to discuss the curriculum and its teaching with his superiors; had given one second-year class a choice as to whether he would teach the first year material again or teach the subject matter required; had refused to participate in the preparation of the course outline and to discuss teacher evaluations with his superiors; had been inefficient as shown by the evaluation reports; had refused and failed to use the required textbooks in his teaching; and had been guilty of excessive and unreasonable absence.

In an elementary school district a teacher refusing a classroom assignment was dismissed for behavior unbecoming a teacher. The Appellate Court of Illinois, First District, Third Division overturned an arbitrator and circuit court decision in *Board of Education of Chicago vs. Harris* (1991). The behavior was deemed to be irremediable. The teacher alleged to have notified the principal and superintendent of a medical problem, which was not found to be the case. The court found that her behavior was "irremediable and teacher could be discharged for insubordination and unbecoming conduct even without official warning from school board." They also found "the teacher's conduct was disruptive to faculty morale, parental relations, and orderly school administration, and the teacher did not actually show that failure to warn her, beyond oral and written warnings by the principal and district superintendent, was subterfuge to expedite dismissal or that she would have altered her conduct if officially warned by board."

In a Missouri case, *Nevels v. Board* (1991), a physical education instructor had been terminated for the following behaviors: (1) his teaching style was too remedial for the level of students he was teaching; (2) he used militaristic commands; (3) he made frequent errors in grading; (4) he used a pay phone outside his classroom after being instructed not to; (5) he inappropriately referred to the school secretary as the principal's "lap dog;" (6) and he told a seventh grade student "we are going to make love" when replying to a question regarding the lesson to be covered that day. Warnings had been given to this instructor on several previous occasions. The dismissal, upon being upheld by the circuit court, was appealed to the Missouri Court of Appeals.

A teacher, in the Florida case of *Johnson v. School Board* (1991), had been warned not to have physical contact with students. Despite this, the school board received numerous complaints of improper contact, and the teacher was dismissed. The court upheld the dismissal even though the hearing officer felt a one-year suspension would have been adequate. Insubordination was the cause cited by the board.

In a Missouri case, inefficiency, misconduct, and insubordination were all upheld as reasons for a teacher termination. The board found (1) use of profanity in front of students; (2) physically accosting students; (3) engaging in a physical confrontation with the parents of a student; and (4) refusal to accept duty schedules as cause for termination. The teacher's suit was not upheld by the circuit court. The Missouri Court of Appeals found for the board that they did have sufficient documentation to justify termination. The court found that the board has the discretion and authority to dismiss for a proven, one time violation of board regulations (*Catherine v. Board*, 1991).

The Missouri Court of Appeals found that the evidence of both inefficiency in teaching and insubordination supported a tenured schoolteacher's dismissal. Inefficiency was found in the following evidence: (1) poor rapport with students; (2) insufficient communication with parents; (3) many requests for transfer out of his classes; and (4) test scores indicating poor student progress. In the area of insubordination the teacher made no effort when asked to comply with directives to (1) improve his relationship and rapport with both students and parents; (2) provide worksheets containing assigned problems instead of having students copy them off the board, and (3) furnish each student with copies of tests and materials used to supplement textbook (*In re the Proposed Termination of James E. Johnson*, 1990).

The case of *Meckley v. The Kanawha County Board of Education* (1989) found the teacher to have a continuing course of infractions. These included failing to return a student's report card and a permanent record when directed to do so by the principal. The Supreme Court of Appeals of West Virginia found the teacher's conduct failing her obligations to the school authorities as well as to her duties as a teacher.

In *Roberts v. Santa Cruz Valley Unified School District No. 35* (1989), the elementary teacher was found to have exhibited "unprofessional conduct" by having her elementary students hit and kick other students as part of a "game" as well as when they noticed other students not following classroom rules.

The court of appeals supported the board's finding stating that the teacher's behavior did reach the level of incompetency and insubordination necessary for termination. The teacher was found not to have remedied the concerns from the earlier written warnings.

Other incompetency charges in Illinois and Missouri in *DeBernard v. State Board* (1988) and *Atherton v. Board* (1988) centered on failure to remedy teaching deficiencies in outlining objectives, sequencing subject matter, following lesson plans, and maintaining adequate and accurate grades for students.

In a Colorado case the instructor was terminated and the board upheld by the court when the instructor continued to use profanity in the presence of students after a prior directive to cease such behavior (*Ware v. Morgan County School District*, 1988).

In *Dunnigan v. Ambach* (1985), the Appellate Division of the New York Supreme Court found dismissal of a tenured teacher not to be arbitrary and capricious. Petitioner's alcoholism was viewed as not having sufficient enough weight to overturn the decision to terminate when viewed with other significant and uncontradicted evidence presented. Petitioner testified that she had deliberately chosen not to carry out the directives of her employer school. Reasons of incompetence and insubordination were supported for the dismissal.

Immorality

A female special education teacher was dismissed in Oklahoma for moral turpitude. In this case, *Andrews v. Independent School District No. 57* (2000), the teacher was engaged in a romantic relationship with a 17-year-old boy. Evidence of public hugging and kissing were presented. In this case the court upheld the admission of testimony that had been given by former students who fifteen years prior had had sexual relations with the same teacher. Allowing this testimony helped impeach the teacher's testimony that she had not had improper relations with minors.

In another immorality case, *Hierlmeier v. North Judson-San Pierre Bd. of School. Trustees* (2000), a female teacher was dismissed in Indiana for inappropriate sexual behavior with students. The teacher had been on a continuing contract but the appellate court supported the board's decision based upon the following objectionable conduct: (1) the teacher gave a cookie to one student without doing the same for other students; (2) the teacher kept a comment on the blackboard that another student had written which stated that the teacher loved the female student; and (3) several times the teacher had put comments on the students' quizzes that were unrelated to the school work.

The school case of *Parker-Bigback v. St. Labre School* (2000) involved the dismissal of a counselor from a Catholic school. The Supreme Court of Montana supported a summary judgment for the school in its termination of the counselor. The counselor was living with a man whom she was not married to, and the court found that her suit failed to present her with a marital status discrimination claim under the state law. It also found that the teacher's conduct violated Catholic teachings in the area of morality and found, therefore, that no discrimination was present, and her claim was meritless.

A teacher had admitted using marijuana at home for a two-year period during a testimony at a criminal trial on the sale of a controlled substance. Even though the teacher was acquitted in *Woo v. Putnam County Board of Education* (1998) the Supreme Court of Appeals of West Virginia affirmed his dismissal. The court ruled that his admission was enough to impair his effectiveness in the classroom.

The evidence was strong enough in *Hamm v. Poplar Bluff R-1 School District* (1997) to have the appellate court affirm the dismissal of a probationary teacher. A male teacher in Missouri had a fourteen-year-old girl in his apartment at 12:25 a.m. without parental permission, and the court saw him unfit as a teacher based upon immoral conduct.

A conviction of a tenured teacher who pled guilty in federal court for trafficking in counterfeit goods and services was supported by a Pennsylvania appellate court as reason to dismiss him in *Kinniry v. Abington School District* (1996).

A tenured California teacher, in the case of *Governing Board of ABC Unified School District v. Haar* (1994), was dismissed on grounds of immorality for hugging girls, holding a girl's hand, and calling a girl "cute" on several occasions. The appellate court found substantial evidence for his dismissal.

Unprofessional Conduct, Unfitness, Willful Neglect of Duty

The loss of classroom control led to the dismissal of a teacher in Florida in *Walker v. Highlands County School Board* (2000). The case was upheld at the appellate court level, which found the behavior severe enough to impair the effectiveness of the teacher. Within one day the teacher had two students in the office reporting an in-class theft; two others out of class being searched for stolen property, one highly intoxicated enough that two adults carried him from the classroom; and three other students trying to hide contraband. The statutory definition of "ineffectiveness" was considered to be met by the court in this case.

The Supreme Court of Appeals of West Virginia reversed an administrative law judge's order and supported the school board in the dismissal of a teacher for sexually harassing a student. The court felt the teacher's behavior did warrant dismissal in the case of *Harry v. Marion County Board of Education* (1998). In supporting the board it was noted by the court that the board did, indeed, have a policy that explicitly prohibited those behaviors that led to the dismissal of the teacher.

A Montana high school tenured teacher was dismissed for making jokes about testes, a student's menstrual periods, for "flipping" his students off, and for making gender-based remarks with sexual innuendoes in his classroom. The Supreme Court, in *Baldridge v. Board of Trustees, Rosebud*

School District #19 (1997), saw the teacher as unfit and upheld his dismissal.

In *Forte v. Mills* (1998) a New York appellate court backed the board on its dismissal of a male teacher who poked fourth and fifth grade female students and snapped their bra straps.

A teacher was given a two-semester suspension for showing an "R-rated" movie to five sections of his classes. He stopped after the principal had notified him of his dissatisfaction. The Louisiana court of appeals found in *Jones v. Rapides Parish School Board* (1993) that suspension rather than dismissal was an appropriate disciplinary action for this tenured teacher.

The power of the board of education to suspend a tenured teacher without pay on a short-term basis for verbally abusing students and using profanity was upheld by the Illinois Supreme Court. In *Kamrath v. Board of Education* (1987) the Supreme Court found the board had satisfied the teacher's constitutional due process rights. The board's suspension policy permitted suspension of up to 30 days for misconduct that would constitute legal cause for dismissal under the state school code. It also provided for written notice of the charges on which the suspension proceeding was based. The teacher was allowed a hearing before the board upon his request and was permitted representation by an attorney and the right to present and cross-examine witnesses at the hearing.

A sixth grade teacher was dismissed for being excessively absent from his duties. He was using more sick leave days than the most generous interpretation of the district policy allowed. A second charge was made that he failed to call the district to report his absences, which made it difficult to obtain a substitute in an orderly manner. The Commonwealth Court of Pennsylvania confirmed the board of education in their dismissal of the teacher in *Ward v. Board of Education of the School District of Philadelphia* (1985).

The courts have been found to be quite consistent in upholding tenured faculty dismissals if the documented evidence is produced to show "neglect of professional duties." In *McConnel v. Howard University* (1985) the teacher became embroiled in an argument with a student enrolled in his class. The instructor, working in a predominantly black institution, complained about the skills of students in his class and related a story about monkeys. This generated a verbal retort from a student in the class who called him a racist. The teacher refused to teach his class until this student apologized. The student refused and the administration refused to intercede to try to resolve the matter. Charges were brought against the faculty member when he remained adamant about not resuming teaching of the class.

The college grievance committee found him guilty of neglect of duty and he was subsequently removed. The dismissal was upheld by the federal district court in a summary judgment. It found no right had been violated in the institution's action again the teacher for neglect of professional duties.

School Board Policies and State Statutes

School Board policies, faculty contracts and state statutes create requirements that must be followed before employees can be disciplined.

In *Harjo v. Board of Education of Independent School District No. 7 of Seminole County* (1999), the dismissal of a probationary teacher was upheld by the appellate court that was reviewing the case based upon a state statute. While the state's Admonishment Statute called for an improvement plan, the court found that the teacher's behavior constituted misconduct, rather than inadequate teaching and, therefore, the statute did not apply.

The case of *Hughes v. Stanley County School Board* (1999) set a precedent that may be useful in other states. The ruling in the Supreme Court of South Dakota reinstated a counselor who had been found negligent in an earlier judgment because of a failure to report possible sexual abuse of a student by her father. The school board had dismissed the counselor and the dismissal had been supported at the first level of judgment. Because the counselor had had prior experience with this student in being untruthful about situations on many other occasions, the counselor believed the sexual abuse charge was a means for the student to gain attention. The court decided that in this case the student's reporting of improper touching by her father did not require the counselor to report these statements.

A teacher who had been reinstated by a lower court in Ohio had his case overturned at the appellate court level. The court found that the principal had, indeed, complied with the state statute on teacher evaluation. The two in-class observations and filed written reports had specific recommendations for improvements listed in them for this limited contract teacher in *McComb v. Gahanna-Jefferson City School District Board of Education* (1998).

An Arkansas teacher was reinstated by the state Supreme Court due to a school district's failure to notify the teacher about non-renewal prior to May 1 of that year. In *Hannon v. Armorel School District No. 9* (1997) the teacher was considered automatically rehired due to the failure of the board to follow the state statute. Any prior conduct that the school wished to add to the case was not allowed due to the untimely notice.

The Supreme Court of Ohio reversed in favor of a teacher due to the school's not following state law requiring four classroom observations of at least thirty minutes each. The operative collective bargaining agreement called for only two evaluation, which was the number the administration conducted. The court found the district failed to meet the requirements of the state law in *Snyder v. Mendon-Union Local School District Board of Education* (1996).

The appellate court reinstated a Texas teacher in *Wilmer-Hutchins Independent School District v. Brown* (1996). The Term Contract Nonrenewal Act was violated. The court found the board had failed to review any of the written evaluations of the teacher, and the board was found to have predetermined not to renew the contract prior to a hearing.

In *Bader v. Board of Education of Lansingburgh Central School District* (1995), a New York appellate court found a hearing panel violated state law when it did not make written findings of fact in placing a tenured faculty member on a one-year suspension without pay. The reasons of insubordination, incompetence, and conduct unbecoming a teacher were not strong enough to overcome the failure to follow state law.

In the Iowa Supreme Court case of *Sheldon Community School District Board of Directors v. Lundblad* (1995) a tenured teacher dismissal was upheld. The teacher's repeated use of sarcastic remarks to students led the court to support the administrator's assessment that this teacher no longer remained an effective role model. Further, he failed in helping build self-esteem, which was one of the district's goals.

In the case of a community college faculty member, the appellate tribunal required the instructor to process her complaint through the established grievance procedures of the college's collective bargaining agreement. *Quist v. Board of Trustees of Community College District No. 525* (1994) stated this requirement remained even if the faculty union was not in support of the teacher's grievance.

In *Jacobs v. Mundelein College* (1993) the appeals court affirmed in favor of Mundelein College in its dismissal of a non-tenured faculty member. The academic vice president was stated to be the sole decision maker in termination decisions according to the faculty handbook. He had sought counsel of

---

department members. They had unanimously voted to have the faculty member reappointed, but the academic vice president still recommended termination. The court did not see this as a breach of contract as the faculty person had no contractual right to evaluation or to grievance procedures other than those that he had been granted.

A faculty member was terminated in a legally supportable way according to the Supreme Court of Missouri in *Byrd v. Board of Curators of Lincoln University of Missouri* (1993). The faculty member did not file his suit within thirty days from the date of the final determination as required by the state's Administrative Procedures Act.

In an Indiana case, *Tishey v. Board of School Trustees,* (1991), a teacher who was not tenured was given notice and reasons for nonrenewal of contract. She was alleged to have been rude to personnel and parents. She also used profanity in the presence of students. The court found she received appropriate notice under the state law.

The collective bargaining agreement cannot assume delegated power of a board as shown in the dismissal of a nontenured teacher in Illinois (*Board of Trustees v. Cook County College Teachers Union*, 1987). The court ruled in favor of the state statutory authority of the board in the dismissal.

In Missouri, the state statute that governs termination of a probationary teacher does not prescribe a particular form for notice of termination. In *Lovan v. Dora R. Illinois School District* (1984), the court ruled that any language, written or spoken, that would reasonably be understood to mean that the teacher's employment would be terminated would suffice. In this case, the probationary kindergarten teacher admitted that she knew that the district had decided to terminate her employment after the superintendent talked to her. She was again told during the required statutory period, and the court found the statutory notice requirement was met.

In a Michigan case, *Sutherby v. Gobles Board. of Edu-*

cation (1984), it was established that a tenured faculty member can be dismissed even though the work in the classroom may be satisfactory. In this case Sutherby was dismissed for failure to meet standards of other job responsibilities: "Professional competence covers more than just classroom behavior and teaching skills." The Court of Appeals of Michigan upheld this teacher's dismissal for incompetence even though his classroom performance had been satisfactory. His failure to comply with reasonable administrative rules and regulations that are required for the effective operation of the school and the school system justified his dismissal for incompetence" (Thomas, p. 115).

Non-Tenure Dismissal

Boards need to be aware that non-renewal of contracts and denial of tenure will often give rise to litigation. Over the years courts have remained reluctant to address the merits of tenure, preferring to leave this responsibility to academic professionals (Russo, 1999, p.265). In the U. S. Supreme Court case of *Board of Regents v. Roth* (1972) it was determined that non-tenured teachers had no property interest rights in their positions.

A New York appellate court, in *Williams v. Franklin Square Union Free School District* (1999), denied a teacher judicial review of her dismissal. The court determined that the teacher had received permissible reasons from the board for not being tenured.

A non-tenured teacher in New York sued for breach of contract because the college had failed to give him a written evaluation of his teaching performance. The appellate court in *De Simone v. Siena College* (1997) found in favor of the board and showed that it was the teacher's inability to get along with his peers and staff that was the primary reason for his dismissal.

A Michigan appellate court gave affirmation to the summary judgment in favor of the school board in *VanGessel v. Lakewood Public Schools* (1997). It found that since the teaching was evaluated as unsatisfactory in his first year of teaching, he was not entitled to a remediation plan.

In the Idaho case of *Totman v. Eastern Idaho Technical College* (1997), a non-tenured teacher's dismissal was affirmed by an appellate court. The teacher was notified before his annual review that he would not be retained. He felt the college had breached his contract through this action. The summary judgment was given in favor of the college. The court further supported the college through its denial of the teacher's claim of protection under the First Amendment for his speaking out on the nonrenewal of his contract. The court interpreted this speech as "personal" rather than of public interest.

Teaching evaluations were consistently poor for the probationary faculty member involved in *Conway v. Pacific University* (1994). An Oregon appeals court upheld his dismissal after the lower court had found in favor of the teacher. The teacher's suit charged misrepresentation as he was told that the evaluations of his teaching were not to be used in the decision of his tenure. The court did not find a special relationship existing between the college and the faculty member. A misrepresentation claim against the university was not sustained.

A Pennsylvania appeals court, in *Riverview School District v. Riverview Education Association* (1994), supported the school district's role in choosing discipline in the dismissal of two faculty members. The teachers had used sick leave for a ski trip when they had previously been denied permission to do so under the school's personal leave policy. An arbitrator had earlier found in support of the teacher's action.

In the case of *Romer v. Board of Trustees of Hobart & William Smith Colleges* (1994) in New York, a male faculty member challenged his dismissal. The faculty member had a volatile and unpleasant public relationship with one of his female colleagues, which he blamed for leading to his dismissal. The court, however, found his dismissal was founded by the promotion and tenure review committee, which had based its decision on his record of inadequate teaching, research, and service.

In the Minnesota case of *Chronopoulos v. University of Minnesota* (1994), an appellate court supported the denial of tenure to a probationary assistant professor. This case again found support for the university, as the faculty member had no property interest or rights in the position.

The decision of an Alabama appellate court to affirm the decision of the board to dismiss a non-tenured teacher was based upon the board's policy. One favorable evaluation the teacher had received was not enough to create the right for re-employment in *King v. Jefferson County Board of Education* (1995).

A Louisiana appellate court, in *McKenzie v. Webster Parish School Board* (1995), upheld the dismissal of a non-tenured teacher. The appeal indicated the board had not complied with the requisite professional assistant form and had not set a deadline for the instructor to improve. The court found that the teacher had been given two years and nine months in which to show improvement in his classroom control and had been evaluated sixteen times over a three-year period. In addition, he had been provided with written recommendations and suggestions on the improvements he needed to make by three well-qualified educators.

Certification or Decertification or Suspension

In a New York appellate court decision, *Feldman v. Board of Education of City School District of City of New York*

(1999), the termination of two teachers' licenses was upheld. The teachers had failed to obtain passing grades on the National Teacher's Examination. Since passing was a basic requirement and the teachers had five years to achieve passing grades, the court found the board had not acted arbitrarily or capriciously.

In a case of suspension of a teacher's certificate, the appellate court in Illinois, in *Rush v. Board of Education of Crete-Monee Community Unit School District No. 201* (2000), found the teacher's behavior irremediable. The court declared the behavior of having students trade detention for electric shocks from a small engine warranted dismissal.

Title VII Discrimination

Title VII discrimination cases relate to gender and race discrimination.

A Tennessee university was sued, in *Dobbs-Weinstein v. Vanderbilt University* (1999), by the professor for gender and national origin discrimination in violation of Title VII. The Sixth Circuit Court, however, gave affirmation to a summary judgment in favor of Vanderbilt University. They found the dean's decision not to promote or award tenure was not action that constituted adverse employment action on behalf of the university.

In a contract dispute case at Kansas State University, *Babbar v. M. Ebadi* (1998), an assistant professor had been denied tenure. His suit asserted "tortuous contract interference and gender discrimination." The summary judgment granted the university's motion and did not find the administrators involved to have violated the plaintiff's due process rights, and there was no discrimination found on the charges of race and gender.

In an Illinois state university case, *Feldman v. Ho* (1999), the appellate court reversed a settlement that had been ruled in favor of a faculty member who was not given a contract renewal. The department chair was ruled to be protected under Eleventh Amendment sovereign immunity, and the nonrenewal of the contract for the faculty member was not considered retaliatory response to protected speech of the faculty member.

In the case of *Krystek v. University of S. Mississippi* (1999), an assistant professor sued for gender discrimination in violation of her title VII rights when she was denied tenure and promotion. The substantial evidence provided by the university did not support the teacher's discrimination claim that stated female faculty did not enjoy the same level of support for tenure and promotion as male faculty. The court further found that Krystek's failure to meet university publishing requirements for tenure gave the university sufficient reason to deny tenure and promotion.

In a case filed for age discrimination a fifty-eight-year-old female instructor in Illinois filed under the Age Discrimination Employment Act (ADEA). She had been denied tenure, and in her suit she charged that the university had retaliated because she had filed a complaint with the Equal Employment Opportunity Commission. In her case, *Vanasco v. National-Louis University* (1998), the Seventh Circuit court did not overrule the faculty tenure committee's decision on denial of tenure. It, instead, supported the decision that the instructor was unqualified.

Discrimination

The Eighth Circuit Court in Missouri upheld the denial of tenure for a non-tenure teacher for reasons other than gender discrimination. In *Lawrence v. Curators of the University of Missouri* (2002), the court found that the facts of the instructor's not publishing in highly rated professional journals and having all of her articles co-authored, as well as the results of an outside critique of her publication record, were solid reasons for denial of tenure on behalf of the university.

A federal district court in Virginia, in *Goodship v. University of Richmond* (1994), ruled in favor of the University of Richmond in its dismissal of a sixty-year-old faculty member who had filed an age discrimination suit. While there were some comments relative to her age in her file, the court found that she had been cautioned about a lack of scholarship and research in her work.

Denial of promotion to full professor was made on the basis of an evaluation process that found a teacher to have an accent in his speech that affected his teaching effectiveness. The faculty member, in *Hou v. Pennsylvania Department of Education* (1983), was found to be denied tenure on valid, educationally sound reasons. The teacher did have a distinct accent and a manner of speech that diminished communication skills in his teaching. Since communications were found to be a factor affecting teaching, the court did not find the decision to be discriminatory.

Dismissal for Cause

Contrary to public perception, tenure only grants an individual the right to due process in any action to terminate tenure and not the right to lifetime employment (Russo, 1999, p. 268).

Long-term and tenured faculty have been found by the U. S. Supreme Court to have a property interest in their positions (*Perry v. Sinderman*, 1972).

A New York professor, in *Klinge v. Ithaca College* (1997), charged that his college had breached his contract. He had been dismissed for malfeasance due to plagiarism in a published book. The appellate court found he was not treated arbitrarily and supported the college with a summary judgment.

A tenured medical school professor failed to win his suit against the college's president and other administrators involved in his termination. Both the trial court and the appellate court in *Brahim v. Ohio College of Podiatric Medicine* (1994) agreed that termination was supported by sufficient evidence. The professor was found persistently neglecting his duties as defined in the faculty handbook. It was further found that the administrators' actions did not satisfy his claim of tortuous interference with his contract. They were within the scope the administrators' duties.

In Ohio the appeals court upheld the dismissal of a thirty-year tenured faculty member. The instructor, in *Yackshaw v. John Carroll University Board of Trustees* (1993), had authored an anonymous letter that he had sent to the president. In the letter he alleged that faculty members in the English department had (1) committed sexual harassment; (2) were mentally ill; (3) engaged in improper sexual conduct with students and (4) were homosexuals. The slanderous letter was considered by the court to create a legitimate reason for termination. It gave the university cause that was based on moral turpitude.

Sexual misconduct

The Second Circuit Court in New York, in *DeMichele v. Greenburgh Central School District No. 5* (1999), reviewed a case in which the school board disciplined a teacher for conduct which occurred 24 years earlier. The summary judgment was awarded the school board and found that the three-year limitations statute did not apply to the state's tenure law. The faculty member claimed that he was being discharged for having had sexual contact with high school students 24 years prior to his being disciplined. The court rejected his due process rights claim since his conduct "had clearly been a crime."

The appellate court in Washington, in the case of *Wright v. Mead School District No. 355* (1997), upheld the dismissal of a teacher whose earlier sexual contact with two secondary school students had occurred some seven years earlier. The behavior was interpreted as irremediable "because it lacked a positive educational aspect or legitimate professional purpose."

In *Board of Education of City of Chicago v. Box* (1989), a tenured elementary school teacher was found by the appellate court to have had "unprofessional physical contact" with female students, which was considered as irremediable behavior. His discharge was considered warranted. In this case four students had testified that the teacher touched them on the buttocks, breasts, and in one case, had looked inside a student's blouse. He had denied the charges originally but later admitted to these behaviors on some occasions. Written warnings from the board were not necessary in this case as such warnings are not necessary in a case of irremediable action.

Sexual relations with a student led to termination of a teacher in Minnesota. In this case the student sued both the school and the teacher. The teacher asked the school to provide legal counsel on his behalf. When the school district refused, the teacher sued the district in *Queen v. Minneapolis Public Schools* (1992). The trial court found the school district did not owe the teacher legal support. The Minnesota Court of Appeals also found him ineligible for legal support because of being guilty of malfeasance in his office. Normally the school district would have been obligated.

The Supreme Court of South Dakota affirmed the dismissal of a tenured male teacher for sexual contact with a student in *Strain v. Rapid City School Board* (1989). The court affirmed that the school board was correct in allowing testimony of a former student who testified that the teacher had

---

sexual contact with her five or six years prior to the current complaint.

Providing controlled substances and having sexual activity with a juvenile teaching aide led to the discharge of a teacher on grounds of conduct unbecoming a teacher. The teacher's credibility, in *Hall v. Board of Education of City of Chicago* (1992), was held suspect by the hearing officer, and the students were not asked to testify.

In *Sauter v. Mount Vernon School District* (1990) a teacher was discharged for his several conversations with a student on whether they should engage in sexual intercourse. This behavior was determined to constitute sexual exploitation of a student, and the court of appeals in Washington supported the board on the basis of immoral conduct by the teacher.

In Pennsylvania, in *Manheim Central Education Association v. Manheim Central School District* (1990), a teacher's love letters and profession of love to students were found under state statute and the collective bargaining agreement to constitute "immorality" and "just cause" for dismissal.

Sexual harassment

In a Pennsylvania case, *Murphy v. Duquesne University of the Holy Ghost* (2000), a faculty member had been dismissed for sexually harassing students. The dismissal was upheld as a summary judgment on behalf of the board. The teacher had challenged the trial court's decision as having improperly deferred to the findings of the University. The appellate court affirmed that the record had substantial evidence of serious misconduct recorded and the decision to dismiss the instructor was warranted.

In *Holm v. Ithaca College* (1998) a professor claimed a breach of contract. The private college had dismissed him for recurrent sexual harassment in violation of the college policy.

The professor fought the dismissal with the argument that his due process rights were violated and the policy was not binding because there were procedural infractions that had been associated with its adoption. The appellate court in New York, in reviewing the case, affirmed a grant of summary judgment for the college. The court further agreed that the college acted within its rights in the dismissal.

In the dismissal of a non-tenure track teacher in *Hall v. Board of Trustees of State Institutions of Higher Learning* (1998), the Supreme Court of Mississippi supported an earlier finding that the due process rights of the teacher were not violated in his dismissal. It found university officials had not arbitrarily or capriciously investigated charges of sexual harassment. The teacher allegedly fondled a student's breast while he was explaining a mammogram procedure to her. The university had issued a letter of reprimand and did not choose to renew the teacher's contract. He argued that his due process rights were violated but, since he did not have tenure, the court found he did not have a property interest in the job.

In *Korf v. Ball State University* (1984) male students accused a tenured faculty member of making sexual advances and offering better grades for sexual favors. Following proper investigation of the charges, notification to the plaintiff, and a hearing, the plaintiff was dismissed by the president. While admitting to a relationship with a student (who testified at the hearing) the plaintiff denied that grades were involved. The plaintiff based his case on his constitutional rights of substantive and procedural due process, equal protection, free speech, freedom of association, and privacy having been violated. He claimed that the relationship being questioned was a private consensual sexual activity outside the institution's purview. The Seventh Circuit court found these arguments lacking in merit. They supported the teacher's dismissal for unethical behavior and found that he had exploited students for his own private advantage. He was found to be unlike any ordinary person on the street because he had a special relationship with the students, which he had violated.

In *Board of Education of Argo-Summit School District 104 v. Hunt* (1985), "irremediable" conduct was determined. This was the case of a male physical education teacher who pinched three second grade female students on the buttocks during class. The teacher was dismissed without having to receive notice to remedy from the governing board. The court, in determining that the conduct was irremediable, focused on the damage done to the students rather than on the traditional analysis of trying to determine whether a warning might have prevented the misconduct.

BIBLIOGRAPHY

Ackerman, A. (1996). Faculty performance review and evaluation: Principles, guidelines, and success. *In: The Olympics of Leadership: Overcoming Obstacles, Balancing Skills, Taking Risks.* Phoenix, AZ: Proceedings of the 5th Annual International Conference of the National Community College Chair Academy, Phoenix, AZ (ERIC Document Reproduction Service No. ED 394 566)

Allhouse, M. F. (1974). Tenure? A quest for truth and freedom. *Soundings, 57:* 471-81.

American Association of School Administrators. (2000, July 28). Sample of district, school plans for performance-based teacher pay. Arlington, VA: American Association of School Administrators. Retrieved February 23, 2003, from http://www.aasa.org/publications/In/07_00/07_27_00cintchpaybar2.htm

American Council on Education. (1999). *To touch the future: Transforming the way teachers are taught, Executive summary.* Washington, DC: American Council on Education.

Amundson, K. R. (1987). *Rewarding Excellence: Teacher Compensation and Incentive Plans.* Washington, DC: National School Board Association.

Anastasi, A. and Urbina, S. (1997). *Psychological Testing, 7th Edition.* Upper Saddle River, NJ: Prentice Hall.

Andrews, H. A. (2001). Mainstreaming part-time faculty. *Administrator, 17*(1):7-8.

Andrews, H. A. (2000a). Board Personnel Policies: Key to Quality. *Trustee Quarterly,* Summer: 28-29.

Andrews, H. A. (2000b). Mainstreaming Part-Time Faculty. *Academic Leader, 17*(1): 7-8.

Andrews, H. A. (2000c). Rewarding Quality Teaching. *Administrator, 19*(6): 2-3.

Andrews, H. A. (2000d). The Dean and the Faculty, *New Directions for Community Colleges,* 109, San Francisco: Jossey-Bass.

Andrews, H. A. (1995). *Teachers Can Be Fired: The Quest for Quality,* Chicago: Catfeet Press.

Andrews, H. A. (1993). Expanding merit recognition programs in community colleges. *Community College Review, 20*(5): 50-58.

Andrews, H. A. (1992). How to dismiss a tenured faculty member. *Administrative Action, 4*(6): 1-5.

Andrews, H. A. (1991). *Negative impact of faculty contract negotiations on community college faculty evaluation systems.* Oglesby: Illinois Valley Community College. (ERIC Document Reproduction Service No. ED 343 628)

Andrews, H. A. (1988a). Merit recognition: the acceptable alternative. *ACCT Quarterly, 12*(3): 24-27.

Andrews, H. A. (1988b). Objectives of a merit recognition system. *Administrative Action, 2*(3): 1.

Andrews, H. A. (1988c). The 'notice to remedy' in tenured faculty. *Journal of Personnel Evaluation in Education, 2:* 59-64.

Andrews, H. A. (1987a). Recognition in educational reversing neglect. *Administrative Action, 1*(5): 1-2.

Andrews, H. A. (1987b). Reprimands: Useful when necessary. *Administrative Action, 2*(1): 4.

Andrews, H. A. (1986a). *Awarding faculty merit based on higher level needs.* Oglesby: Illinois Valley Community College. (ERIC Document Reproduction Service No. ED 266 840)

Andrews, H. A. (1986b). Administrative vs. student evaluation in accountability and professionalism. *Administrative Action, 1*(1): 6.

Andrews, H. A. (1986c). A proposal: Faculty evaluation bill of rights. *Administrative Action, 1*(2): 2.

Andrews, H. A. (1986d). Merit pay and merit recognition plans in community and junior colleges. *Journal of Staff, Program, & Organization Development, 4*(2): 46-50.

Andrews, H. A. (1985). *Evaluating for excellence.* Stillwater, OK: New Forums Press.

Andrews, H., and Erwin, J. (2003). Recognition for outstanding teachers: A national Study. *Community College Journal, 74*(2): pp. 36-39.

Andrews, H.A., and Erwin, J. S., (1993). The State of Part-Time Faculty Services at Community Colleges in a Nineteen State Region. *Community/Junior College Quarterly of Research and Practice, 17*(6): 555-562.

Andrews, H.A., Erwin, J. S., and Barr, J. (1996). Faculty Evaluation: Number One Quality Control in TQM. *The Journal of Staff, Program, and Organization Development, 13*(4): 291-295.

Andrews, H. A., and Licata, C. M. (1991). Administrative perceptions of existing evaluation systems. *Journal of Personnel Evaluation in Education, 5:* 69-76.

Andrews, H. A., and Licata, C. M. (1990a). Faculty leaders' and administrators' perceptions on post-tenure faculty evaluation. *Journal of Staff, Program, & Organization Development, 8*(1): 17-21.

Andrews, H. A., and Licata, C. M. (1990b). The status of tenured faculty evaluation in the community college. *Community College Review, 18*(3): 42-50.

Andrews, H. A., and Licata, C. M. (1988-89). *The state of faculty evaluation in community, technical, and community colleges within the North Central region, 1988-1989.* Oglesby, IL: Illinois Valley Community College. (ERIC Document Reproduction Service No. ED 303 204).

Andrews, H. A., Licata, C., & Harris, J. (2002a). Faculty evaluation: Critical review by administrators, *The Journal of Faculty Development, 18*(2): 95-99.

Andrews, H. A., Licata, C. M., & Harris, J. (2002b). Faculty evaluation: Strengths and concerns, *The Community College Enterprise, 8*(1): 27-36.

Andrews, H. A., Licata, C. M., & Harris, J. (2002c). *The State of Post-Tenure and Long-Term Faculty Evaluation, Research Brief.* Washington, DC: American Association of Community Colleges.

Andrews, H. A., and Marzano, W. (1983). Faculty evaluation stimulates Expectations of excellence. *Community and Junior College Journal, 54*(4): 35-37.

Andrews, H. A., and Marzano, W. (1984). Awarding faculty merit based on higher level needs. *The Journal of Staff, Program, & Organization Development, 1:* 105-107.

Andrews, H. A., and Wisgoski, A. (1987). Assuring future quality: Systematic evaluation and reward of faculty. *The Journal of Staff, Program & Organization Development, 5*(2): 163-168.

Aper, J. P,. and Fry, J. E. (2003). Post-tenure review at graduate institutions in the United States. *The Journal of Higher Education, 74*(3): 241- 260.

Arreola, R. A (1995). *Developing a comprehensive faculty evaluation system.* Bolton, MA: Anker Publishing Company.

Arreola, R. A. (1983). Establishing successful faculty evaluation and development programs. In A. Smith (ed.), *Evaluating faculty and staff: New directions for community colleges* (pp. 83-93). San Francisco: Jossey-Bass.

Ascher, C., and Fruchter, N. (2001). Teacher quality and student performance in New York City's low-performing schools. *Journal of Education for Students Placed at Risk, 6*(3): 199-214.

Association of American Universities. (2001, April 10). Post-tenure review. Retrieved November 17, 2003, from http://www.aau.edu/reports/PostTenure4.01.pdf

Avakian, A. N. (1995). Conflicting demands for adjunct faculty. *Community College Journal, 65*(6): 34-37.

Baer, W. E. (1974). *Labor Arbitration Guide.* Homewood, IL: Dow Jones-Irwin, Inc.

Baker, G. A., Roueche, J. E., and Gillett-Karam, R. (1990). Teaching as leading. *ACJC Journal, 60*(5): 25-31.

Baker, G., and Prugh, S. (1988). Reward structures in unionized and nonunionized community colleges. *Community/Junior College Quarterly, 12:* 121-36.

Barber, L. W. (1990). Self-assessment. In J. Millman & L. Darling-Hammond (eds.), *The new handbook of teacher evaluation* (pp. 216-28). Newbury Park: Sage Publications, Inc.

Behrendt, R. L., and Parsons, M. H. (1983). Evaluating of part-time faculty. In A. Smith (ed.) *Evaluating faculty and staff: New directions for Community colleges*, (pp. 33-43). San Francisco: Jossey-Bass.

Bennett, W. J. (2002). Preface: What works in teaching. In L. T. Izumi and W. M. Evers (eds.), *Teacher quality* (pp. ix-xi). Stanford, CA: Hoover Institution Press.

Benton, J. (2003, September 21). Chattanooga entices its best teachers to the inner city. *Arkansas Democrat Gazette*, 3A.

Bonato, D. J. (1987). *Legal and Practical Aspects of Teacher Evaluation.* Lansing: Michigan Institute for Educational Management.

Bourne, B. (1988). Making ideas work: Ralph Bedell and the NDEA Institutes. *Journal of Counseling and Development, 67:* 136-142.

Boyer, E. (1983). *High School.* New York: Carnegie Foundation.

Bradley, A. (1999). Zeroing in on teachers. *Education Week on the Web*. Retrieved September 4, 2003, from http://www.edweek.org/sreports/qc99/ac/mc/mc6.htm, 1-10.

Brand, M. (1999, April 2). Why tenure is indispensable. Point of View, *The Chronicle of Higher Education*, A-64.

Bridges, E. M. (1990a). Evaluation for tenure and dismissal. In J. Millman and L. Darling-Hammond, (eds.), *The new handbook of teacher evaluation* (pp. 147-57). Newbury Park, CA: Sage Publications, Inc.

Bridges, E. M. (1990b). *Managing the incompetent teacher*, Second edition, Eugene, OR: University of Oregon. (ERIC Clearinghouse on Educational Management, EA021575)

Bridges, E. M. (1985, November 20). How do administrators cope with teacher incompetence? *Education Week* V, 24.

Bridges, E. M., and Groves, B. (1984). Managing the incompetent teacher. Eugene, OR: University of Oregon. (ERIC Clearinghouse on Educational Management, EA245296)

Brown, R. C. (1977). Tenure rights in contractual and constitutional contest. *Journal of Law and Education, 6:* 279-318.

Carr, R. K. (1972). The uneasy future of academic tenure. *Educational Record, 53:* 119-127.

Cashin, W. E. (1996). *Developing an effective faculty evaluation system.* Idea Paper No. 33. Manhattan, KS: Kansas State University, Center for Faculty Evaluation and Development.

Cashin, W. E. (1995). *Student ratings of teaching: The research revisited.* Manhattan, KS., Kansas State University Center for Evaluation & Development.

Cashin, W. E. (1988). *Student ratings of teaching: A summary of the research.* Manhattan, KS: Center for Faculty Evaluation and Development, Kansas State University.

Cashin, W. E. (1983). Concerns about using student ratings in community colleges. In A. Smith (ed.), *Evaluating faculty and staff: New directions for community colleges* (pp. 57-66). San Francisco: Jossey Bass.

Centra, J. A. (1979). *Determining faculty effectiveness.* San Francisco: Jossey-Bass.

Centra, J. A. (1977). How universities evaluate faculty performance: A survey of department heads. *GREB Research Report No. 75-5bR.* Princeton, NJ: Educational Testing Service.

Centra, J. A. (1973). Self-ratings of college teachers: A comparison with student ratings. *Journal of Educational Measurement, 10*(4): 287-295.

Centra, J. A. (1972). *Two studies on the utility of student ratings for instructional improvement.* Princeton, NJ: Educational Testing Service.

Chait, R. and Ford, A. T. (1982). *Beyond traditional tenure.* San Francisco: Jossey-Bass.

Chapman, M. (1998, September 25). Why bad teachers can't be fired: Unions defend tenure — at students' expense. *Investor's Business aily, 15*(114).

Cheshire, N., and Hagenmeyer, R. H. (1981-1982). Evaluating job performance. *Community and Junior College Journal, 52*(4): 34-37.

Chicago Tribune. (2001, December 23). Casting out bad teachers. Editorial.

Chicago Tribune. (2001, October 1). Great teaching, better pay. Editorial.

Chicago Tribune. (1998, May 15). Bad teachers out, bad teachers in. Section 1, Editorial, p. 12.

Chronicle of Higher Education. (1987) 'In box,' *33*(35): 16.

Cohen, A. M., and Brawer, F. B. (1982). *The American community college.* San Francisco, California: Jossey-Bass.

Conley, D. T. (1988). District performance standards: Missing link for effective teacher evaluation. *NASSP Bulletin, 72*(511): 78-83.

Conley, D. T., and Dixon, K. (1990). The evaluation report: A tool for teacher Growth. *NASSP Bulletin, 74*(527): 7-14. (ERIC Document Reproduction Service No. EJ 414 832)

Corbett, D., and Wilson, B. (2002). What urban students say about good teaching. *Educational Leadership, 60*(1): 18-22.

Deci, E. L. (1976). The hidden costs of rewards. *Organizational Dynamics, 4*(3), 61-72.

Duke, D. L., and Stiggins, R. J. (1990). Beyond minimum competence: Evaluation for professional development. In J. Millman & L. Darling-Hammond (eds.), *The new handbook of teacher evaluation: Assessing elementary and secondary school teachers* (pp. 116-32). Newbury Park: Sage Publications, Inc.

Duke, D. L., and Stiggins, R. J. (1986). Teacher evaluation: Five keys to growth. In *Reports on public education 1986: A summary of major recommendations* (p. 5). Washington, DC: National School Boards Association.

Dunwell, R. R. (1986). Merit, motivation, and mythology. *Teacher Education and Practice, 3*(1): 17-21.

East Richland Community Unit District #1. Evaluaton process. Olney, IL: Office of Superintendent of Schools, 1-19.

Education Commission of the States. (1983). *Action for excellence.* Report of the Task Force on Education for Economic Growth.

Education Week on the Web. (1999). Demanding results. Retrieved September 4, 2003, from http://www.edweek.org/sreports/qc99/exsum.htm.

Education Week. (2003, January 9). Quality counts 2003: If I can't learn from you…ensuring a highly qualified teacher for each classroom. Retrieved November 1, 2003, from http://www.edweek.org/

Education Week on the Web. (2003, August 6). No child left behind. Retrieved August 21, 2003, from http://www.edweek.org/context/topics/issuespage.cfm?id=59

Education Week on the Web. (2003, January 9). To close the gap, quality counts, executive summary. Retrieved September 24, 2003, from http://www.edweek.org/sreports/qc03/templates/article.cfm?slug=17exec.h22

Educational Research Service. (1983). *Merit pay plans for teachers: Status and descriptions.* ERS Report. Arlington, VA.

Educational Research Service. (1979). *Merit pay for teachers.* ERS Report. Arlington, VA.

Educational Research Service. (1978). *Evaluating teacher performance.* ERS Report. Arlington, VA.

El-Khawas, E. (1990). *Campus Trends, 1990.* Higher Education Panel Report No. 80. Washington, DC: American Council on Education.

Erwin, J. S. (1994). Student evaluations: Limits and prospects. *Journal of Applied Research in the Community College, 2*(1), 49-59.

Erwin, J., and Andrews, H. A. (1993). The state of part-time faculty services at community colleges in a 19-state region. *Community/Junior College Quarterly, 17*(6): 559-562.

Evertson, C. M. and Emmer, E. T. (1982). Effective management at the beginning of the school year in junior high classes. *Journal of Educational Psychology, 74*(4): 485-498.

Evertson, C. M., and Holley, F. M. (1981). Classroom observation. In J. Millman (ed.), *Handbook of teacher evaluation: National council on measurement in education* (pp. 90-109). Beverly Hills, CA: Sage Publications.

Filan, G. L. (1992). The trick to being a community college chair. *Leadership Abstracts* V (1): 1-2. Laguna Hills, CA: League of Innovation.

Filan, G., Okun, M., and Witter, R. (1986). Influence of ascribed and achieved social statuses, values, and rewards on job satisfaction among community college faculty. *Community/Junior College Quarterly, 10:* 113-122.

Frase, L. E., Hetzel, R. W., and Grant, R. T. (1982). Using Herzberg's Motivational-Hygiene Theory-Catalina Foothills School District…Reward system for excellent teaching. *Phi Delta Kappan, 64:* 266-269.

Frase, L. E., and Piland, W. E. (1989). Breaking the silence about faculty rewards. *Community College Review, 17*(1): 25-33.

Freeland, R. S. (1998). *Adjunct faculty in the community college.* Unpublished manuscript. (ERIC Clearinghouse for Community Colleges, ED 424 899)

Futrell, M. (1986). How principals, teachers can improve relationships. *NASSP Bulletin, 70*(489): 52-65.

Gaynes, C. (1990). Only the best. *Thrust for Educational Leadership, 20*(3): 30-32.

Gergen, D. (1997, December 8). Surprising but true: A union president serious about reform. *U. S. News and & World Report*, p. 100.

Gewertz, C. (2003, October 29). City schools report progress on hiring certified teachers. *Education Week on the Web.* Retrieved October 30, 2003 from http://www.edweek.org/ew/ewstory.cfm?slug=09Urbanteach.h23: 1-5.

Glastris, P. (1997, June 2). When teachers should be expelled from class: New hope for getting rid of the bad apples. *U. S. News & World Report*, p. 32.

Gomstyn, A. (2003). In bid to retain accreditation, community college in Texas drops 145 part-timer instructors. *The Chronicle of Higher Education, L(7):* A12.

Ghorpade, J., and Lackritz, J. R. (1991). Student evaluations: Equal opportunity concerns. *Thought & Action, 3*(1): 61-72.

Grand Rapids Press. (1988a, January 22). Expedite over principle. Editorial.

Grand Rapids Press. (1988b, February 2). Dissent! School personnel practices. Editorial reply by Board of Education.

Grand Rapids Press. (1988c, February 5). Why pay so much, hide so much to fire teachers? Editorial by J. Douglas.

Greenwald, A. G. (1997). Validity concerns and usefulness of student ratings of Instruction. *American Psychologist, 52*(11): 1182-1186.

Guskey, T. R., and Easton, J. Q. (1982). The characteristics of very effective community college teachers. *The Center for the Improvement of Teaching and Learning: City Colleges of Chicago Center Notebook, 1*(3): 36.

Hammons, J., and Wallace, H. (1977). Staff development needs of public community college department/division chairpersons. *Community Junior College Research Quarterly, 2*(1): 55-76.

Hanushek, E. A. (2002). Teacher quality. In L. T. Izumi and W. M. Evers (eds.), *Teacher Quality* (pp. 1-12). Stanford, CA: Hoover Institution Press.

Hart, P. D., and Teeter, R. M. (2002). A national priority: Americans speak on teacher quality, *Educational Testing Service* (p. 9). Princeton, NJ. Retrieved November 17, 2003, from http://222.ets.org/aboutets/americaspeaks/survey2002.html

Herzberg, F. (1966). *Work and the nature of man.* Cleveland and New York: The World Publishing Company.

Hickok, W. W. (2002). Teacher quality accountability systems: The view from Pennsylvania. In L. T. Izumi and W. M. Evers (eds.), *Teacher Quality*, (pp. 25-32). Stanford, CA: Hoover Institution Press.

Hocutt, M. O. (1987-88). De-grading student evaluations: What's wrong with student polls of teaching. *Academic Questions*, (Winter): 55-64.

Hollander, P.A. (1992). Evaluating tenured professors: Point of view. *The Chronicle of Higher Education, 38*(41): A44.

Honors and Awards (2003, September 29). Honors & Awards, *Community College Week, 16*(4): 1. Retrieved September 29, 2003, from http://www.ccweek.com/faclounge/honorsawarads.asp

Hunter, M. (1988a). Create rather than await your fate in teacher evaluation. In S. J. Stanley and W. J. Popham (eds.) *Teacher evaluation: Six prescriptions for success* (pp. 32-54). Alexandria, VA: Association for Supervision and Curriculum Development.

Hunter, M. (1988b). Reflecting a reconciliation between supervisor and evaluation—A reply to Popham. *Journal of Personnel Evaluation in Education, 1:* 275-280.

Isenberg, A. P. (1990). Evaluating teachers-Some questions and some considerations. *NASSP Bulletin, 74*(529): 16-18.

Jasiek, C. R., Wisgoski, A., and Andrews, H. A. (1985). The trustee role in college personnel management. In G. F. Petty (ed), *Active trusteeship for a changing era* (pp. 87-97). New Directions for Community Colleges, No. 51. San Francisco: Jossey-Bass.

Jenkins, N. N., Barnicle, T. M., Dempsey, G. E., Faulkner, J. T., and Kasson, C. D. (1979). *Formal dismissal procedures under Illinois tenure laws.* Springfield, IL: Illinois Association of School Boards.

Jentz, B., Cheever, D. S., Fisher, S. B., Jones, M. H., Kelleher, P., and Wofford, J. W. (1982). Entry: *The hiring, start-up, and supervision of administrators.* New York: McGraw-Hill.

Johnson, S. M. (1990). *Teachers at work: Achieving success in our schools.* New York: Basic Books.

Johnson, G. S., et al. (1985). The relationship between elementary school climate and teachers' attitudes toward evaluation. *Educational and Psychological Measurement, 5*(2): 89-112. (ERIC Document Reproduction Service No. EJ 320 577)

Kaplan, L. S., and Owings, W. A. (2003). No child left behind: The politics of teacher quality. *Phi Delta Kappan, 84*(9): 687-692.

Kauffman, J. F. (1983). Strengthening chair, CEO relationships. *AGB Reports, 25*(2).

Kelleher, P. (1985). Inducing incompetent teachers to resign. *Phi Delta Kappan, 66*(5): 362-364.

Keller, B. (2003, October 29). States claim teachers are 'qualified.' *Education Week on the Web.* Retrieved October 30, 2003, from http://www.edweek.org/ew/ewstory.cfm?slug=09Qualified.h23 : 1-4.

Keller, J. W., Mattie, N., Vodanovich, S. J., and Piotrowski, C. (1991). Teaching effectiveness: Comparisons between traditional and nontraditional college students. *Innovative Higher Education, 15*(2): 177-184.

Kleingartner, A. (1984). Post-tenure evaluation and collective bargaining. Paper presented at the American Council on Education Conference, Periodic Review of Tenured Faculty, November, Miami, Florida.

Knight, J. (1986). Tenure & evaluation: Cleaning up our act. *Administrative Action, 1*(2): 3-4.

Knowles, L. W., and Wedlock, E. D., Jr., (eds.). (1973). *The yearbook of school law,* 1973. Topeka, KS: National Organization on Legal Problems of Education.

Kvenvold, J. C. (1989). Incompetence and tenured teachers: A survey of teacher evaluation and follow-up. *NASSP Bulletin, 73*(516): 99-102.

Lashway, L. (1999). Holding schools accountable for achievement. *ERIC Digest* Retrieved November 3, 2003, from http://eric.uoregon.edu/publications/digests/digest130.html, pp. 1-5.

Leas, D. E. and Rodriguez, R. C. (1987). Identifying the ineffective university dean. *Thought and Action, 3*(1): 97-102.

Levin, J., and Quinn, M. (2003). Missed opportunities: How we keep high quality teachers out of urban Schools. New York, NY: The New Teacher Project. Retrieved November 11, 2003, http://www.tntp.org/ , 1-8.

Lewis, A. (2000, March 5). Douglas County shows off its performance-based pay plan. American Association of School Administrators,The Conference Daily. Retrieved February 24, 2003, from http://www.aasa.org/publications/conference/2000/sun_pay.htm

---

Lewis, R. L. (1980). Building effective trustee leadership or how to exploit your trustees. *Educational Record*, 61: 18-21.

Licata, C. M. (1998). Post-tenure review: At the crossroads of accountability and opportunity. *AAHE Bulletin, 50*(10), 3-6.

Licata, C. M. (1986). *Post-tenure faculty evaluation: Threat or opportunity?* ASHE-ERIC Higher Education Report No. 1. Washington, DC.

Licata, C. M. (1984). An investigation of the status of post-tenure evaluation in elected community colleges in the United States. Unpublished doctoral dissertation. The George Washington University.

Licata, C. M., and Andrews, H. A. (1990). The status of tenured faculty evaluation in the community college. *Community College Review, 18*(3): 42-50.

Lieberman, M. (1985). Educational specialty boards: A way out of the merit pay morass? *Phi Delta Kappan, 67*(2): 103-107.

Littler, S. (1914). Causes of failure among elementary school teachers. *School and Home Education* (March): pp. 255-256.

Lovain, T. B. (1983-84). Grounds for dismissing tenured post-secondary for cause. *The Journal of College and University Law, 10*(3): 419-433.

Mangan, K. S. (1991). Many colleges fill vacancies with part-time professors, citing economy and uncertainty about enrollments. *The Chronicle of Higher Education, 37*(47): A9.

Marks, M. (2000, January 9). The teacher factor. *New York Times, Q & A*, pp. 1-2.

Marshall, K. (2003). Recovering from HSPS (Hyperactive superficial principal syndrome): A progress report. *Phi Delta Kappan,* Bloomington, IN, *84*(9): 701-709.

Martinez, M. (2000, June 29). City schools put hammer down on 6 of its worst. *Chicago Tribune*: Section 1, pp. 1 and 8.

Maslow, A. H. (1954). *Motivation and personality.* New York: Harper & Row.

Mason, B. (1993). Trained teachers and high expectations help children learn to think! *The Phelps-Stokes Fund Dialogue* 2(May): 1-4.

Mathis, W. J. (2003). No child left behind: Costs and benefits. *Phi Delta Kappan, 84*(9): 679-686.

Mayer, D. P., Mullens, J. E. and Moore, M. T. (2000, Dec.). Monitoring school quality: An indicators report. Statistical analysis report. Washington, DC: National Center for Education Statistics. (ED450473)

McCormick, V. (1986). When teaching excellence doesn't pay off. *Education Week, 6*(24).

McDaniel, S. H. and McDaniel T. R. (1980). How to weed out incompetent teachers without getting hauled into court. *The National Elementary Principal.* (March): 31-36.

McLaughlin, M. W. (1990). Embracing contraries: implementing and sustaining teacher evaluation. In J. Millman and L. Darling-Hammond (eds.), *The new handbook of teacher evaluation: Assessing elementary and secondary school teachers* (pp. 403-15). Newbury Park, CA.: Sage Publications.

McMillen, L. (1984). A handful of 2-year colleges awarding 'merit' raises to outstanding teachers. *Chronicle of Higher Education, 29*(28).

Miller, R. I., Finley, C. and Vancko, C. S. (2000). *Evaluating, Improving, and Judging Faculty Performance in Two-Year Colleges.* Westport, CT: Bergin & Garvey.

Morris, A. A. (1992). *Dismissal of tenured higher education faculty: Legal implications of the elimination of mandatory retirement.* Topeka, KS: National Organization of Legal Problems of Education.

Nash, L. L. (1982). The rhythm of the semester. In M. Gullette (ed), *The Art and craft of teaching* (pp. 70-87). Cambridge: Harvard-Danforth Center for Teaching and Learning.

Nason, J. W. (1982). A sampler from John Nason's the nature of trusteeship. *AGB Reports, 24*(5): 14-15.

NASSP Bulletin. (1986). A Bulletin special: NEA's president describes issues in American education, how principals, teachers can improve relationships, *70*(489): 52-65.

National Commission on Higher Education Issues. (1982). *To strengthen in higher education.* Washington, DC: American Council on Education. (ERIC Document Reproduction Services No. ED 226 646)

National School Board Association. (1987). *Rewarding excellence: Teacher compensation and incentive plans.* Alexandria, VA: National School Board Association.

Nelson, C. (1997, November 14). The real problem with tenure is incompetent faculty hiring. *The Chronicle of Higher Education,* B4-5.

Nisbet, R. (1973). The future of tenure. *In Change: On learning and change.* (pp. 46-64). New Rochelle, NY: Change Magazine.

Nolin, M. J. (1994). Public elementary teacher's views on teacher performance evaluations. Ask ERIC, Retrieved August 20, 2003, from http://

www.askeric.org/plwebcgi/fastweb?getdoc+ericdb2+ericdb+1078350+1
+wAAA+%28

Norman, M. (1984). Advice and recommendations: Improving the work environment for Part-Timers. *AAHE Bulletin* (October): 13-14.

Olson, L. (1999). Shining a spotlight on results. *Education Week on the Web.* Quality Counts '99. Retrieved September 4, 2003, from http://www.edweek.com/sreports/qc99/ac/mc/mc-intro.htm

Olson, L. (1989). Fairfax County, VA, Merit pay loses teachers' union support. *Education Week, 8*(26): 7.

Olswang, S. G. and Lee, B. A. (1984). Faculty freedom and institutional accountability: Interactions and conflict. Washington, DC: *ASHE-ERIC Higher Education Research Report No. 5.*

Ory, J. C. (1990). Student ratings of instruction: Ethics and practice. *New Directions for teaching and learning,* 43: 63-74.

Ory, J., and Parker, S. (1989). A survey of assessment activities at large Research universities. *Research in Higher Education, 30:* 373-383.

Orze, J. J. (1977). Working with the faculty senate in a bargaining context. In G. Angell, E. Kelley, Jr. and Associates (ed.), *Handbook of faculty bargaining,* (504-519). San Francisco: Jossey-Bass.

Parsons, M. H. (1998, April). *How the other 2/3rds live: Institutional initiatives for part-time faculty assimilation in America's two-year colleges.* Hagerstown, MD: Hagerstown Junior College. Paper presented at Forum 8 of the Annual Convention of the American Association of Community Colleges, Miami, FL . (ED 417 793)

Painter, S. R. (2001). Barriers to evaluation: Beliefs of elementary and middle school principals. *Planning and Changing, 32*(1-2): 58-70.

Painter, S. R. (2000, October). Easing dismissals and non-renewals. *The School Administrator Web Edition,* Alexandria, VA. Retrieved February 24, 2003 from http://www.aasa.org/publications/sa/2000_10/Painter.htm

Peterson, K. D. (1995). *Teacher Evaluation: A Comprehensive Guide to New Directions and Practices.* Thousand Oaks, CA: Corwin Press, Inc., A Sage Publications Co.

Petty, G. F. (1986). Editorial: Courts uphold dismissal. (Editorial). *Illinois Trustee.* (January)1.

Piele, P. K. ed. (1981). *The yearbook of school law, 1981.* Topeka, KS: National Organization on Legal Problems of Education.

Piele, P. K. ed. (1980). *The yearbook of school law, 1980.* Topeka, KS: National Organization on Legal Problems of Education.

Piele, P. K. ed. (1979). *The yearbook of school law, 1979.* Topeka, KS: National Organization on Legal Problems of Education.

Piele, P. K. ed. (1975). *The Yearbook of School Law, 1975.* Topeka, KS: National Organization on Legal Problems of Education.

Poole, L. H., and Dellow, D. A. (1983). Evaluation of full-time Faculty. In A. Smith (ed.), *Evaluating faculty and staff: New directions for community colleges* (pp. 19-31). San Francisco: Jossey-Bass.

Popham, W. J. (1988). The dysfunctional marriage of formative and summative teacher evaluation, *Journal of Personnel Evaluation in Education, 1:* 269-274.

Rapp, J. A. and Ortbal, T. J. (1980). *Illinois public community college act: Tenure policies and procedures.* Springfield, IL: Illinois Community College Trustees Association.

Rebell, M. (1990). Legal issues concerning teacher evaluation. In J. Millman and L. Darling-Hammond (eds.), *The new handbook of teacher evaluation: Assessing elementary and secondary school teachers:* (pp. 337-55). Newbury Park, CA: Sage Publications.

Rice, J. K. (2003). Teacher quality: Understanding the effectiveness of teacher attributes: Executive summary Economic Policy Institute. Retrieved November 3, 2003, from http://www.epinet.org/cgi-bin/

Rifkin, T. (1998, April). Differences between the professional attitudes of full- and part-time faculty. Los Angeles, CA: ERIC Clearinghouse for Community Colleges. Paper presented at the American Association of Community Colleges Convention, Miami, FL (ED 417 783)

Rivers, J. C. and Sanders, W. L. (2002). Teacher quality and equity in educational Opportunity: Findings and Policy Implications. In L. T. Izumi and W. M. Evers (eds.), *Teacher Quality* (pp. 13-24), Stanford, CA: Hoover Institution Press.

Rosenberger, D. S. and Plimpton, R. A. (1975). Teacher incompetence and the courts. *Journal of Law and Education, 4:* 469-486.

Rosenholtz, S. (1985). Effective schools: Interpreting the evidence, *American Journal of Education, 93*(3): 368-369.

Rosenthal, L. (2003). What makes a great teacher. *Great schools.net.* Retrieved October 15, 2003, from http://www.greatschools.net/cgi-bin/showarticle/CA/259/improve

---

Roueche, J. E. (1983). Excellence for students. In *Celebrating Teaching Excellence: Proceedings, National Conference on Teaching Excellence and Conference of Presidents* (pp. 29-34). Austin: University of Texas at Austin.

Russo, C. J. (2002). *The yearbook of school law 2002*. Dayton, OH: Education Law Associates.

Russo, C. J. (2001). *The yearbook of school law 2001*. Topeka, KS: National Organization on Legal Problems of Education.

Russo, C. J. (2000). *The yearbook of school law 2000*. Topeka, KS: National Organization on Legal Problems of Education.

Russo, C. J. (1999). *The yearbook of school law 1999*. Topeka, KS: National Organization on Legal Problems of Education.

Russo, C. J. (1998). *The yearbook of school law 1998*. Topeka, KS: National Organization on Legal Problems of Education.

Russo, C. J. (1997). *The yearbook of school law 1997*. Topeka, KS: National Organization on Legal Problems of Education.

Russo, C. J. (1996). *The yearbook of school law 1996*. Topeka, KS: National Organization on Legal Problems of Education.

Russo, C. J. (1995). *The yearbook of school law, 1995*. Topeka, KS: National Organization on Legal Problems of Education.

Saint. Louis Post-Dispatch. (1999, November 21). Post-tenure review is coming. B2.

Sanders, W. L, and Rivers, J. C. (1996). *Cumulative and residual effects of teachers on future student academic achievement*. Knoxville, TN: University of Tennessee.

Savage, D. G. (1983). Teacher evaluation: The need for effective measures. *Learning, 12:* 54-56.

Sbaratta, P. (1983). Academic deans: Keep the heart pumping. *Community and Junior College Journal, 54*(3): 21-27.

Scherer, M. (1983). Merit pay—the great debate. *Instructor, 93*(3): 22-25.

Schwartz, R. A. (1997, March). Demystifying performance documentation: How to get rid of the excuses and tell it like it is. *School Administrator*, Alexandria, VA: American Association of School Administrators. Retrieved November 18, 2002, from http://www.aasa.org/publications/sa/1997_03/schwartz.htm

Selden, P., ed. (1994). *Changing practices in faculty evaluation: A critical assessment and recommendations for improvement.* San Francisco: Jossey-Bass.

Seldin, P., ed. (1984). *Changing practices in faculty evaluation: A critical assessment and recommendations for improvement.* San Francisco: Jossey-Bass.

Seldin, P. (1982). Improving faculty evaluation systems. *Peabody Journal of Education, 59*(2): 93-99.

Shanker, A. (1985). Collective bargaining with educational standards. *Education on trial: Strategies for the future.* (pp. 224-225). San Francisco: Institute for Contemporary Studies.

Shinkfield, A. (1995, July 9). Create - after five years: Keynote address. 1995 National Evaluation Institute, Kalamazoo, MI: Western Michigan University 1-24.

Spencer, P. A. and Flyr, M. L. (1992). *The formal evaluation as an impetus to classroom change: Myth or reality?* Unpublished paper, 30 pages. (ED 349 053)

Spinetta, K. I. (1990). Part-time instructors in the California community colleges: A need to revise current policies. *Community College Review, 18*(1): 43-49.

Spitalli, S. J. (2003). How do you dismiss a tenured teacher? Very carefully and only if you absolutely must: Last resort. *American School Board Journal,* June: 18-21.

Steinmetz, L. L. (1979). *Human relations: People and work.* New York: Harper & Row Publishers.

Stiggins, R. J., and Duke, D. L. (1988). *The case for commitment to teacher growth: Research on teacher evaluation.* Albany, NY: State University of New York Press.

Stodolsky, S. S. (1990). Classroom observation. In J. Millman and L. Darling-Hammond (eds.), *The new handbook of teacher evaluation: Assessing elementary and secondary school teachers* (pp. 175-190). Newbury Park, CA: Sage Publications.

Strike, K. A. (1990). The ethics of educational evaluation. In J. Millman and L. Darling-Hammond (eds.), *The new handbook of teacher evaluation: Assessing elementary and secondary school teachers* (pp. 356-373). Newbury Park, CA: Sage Publications.

Strike, K. A., and Bull, B. (1981). Fairness and the legal context of teacher evaluation. In J. Millman (ed.). *Handbook of teacher evaluation: Na-*

tional council on measurement in education (pp. 310-343). Beverly Hills, CA: Sage Publications.

Stufflebeam, D. L. (2003). Evaluation plans and operations checklist. Kalamazoo, MI: Western Michigan University, The Evaluation Center. Retrieved February 25, 2003 from http://www.wmich.edu/evalctr/checklists/plans_operations.htm

Stufflebeam, D. L. (1993). Toward an adaptable new model for guiding Evaluations of educational administrators. Western Michigan University: *The Evaluation Center, 3*(3): 1-6.

Stufflebeam, D., and Shinkfield, A. (1995). *Teacher evaluation: A guide to effective practice*. New York, NY: Kluwer Academic Publishers.

Sykes, C. J. (1988). *Profscam: Professors and the demise of higher education*. Washington, DC: Regnery Gateway

Teacher Evaluation Kit Glossary. (2003). *Teacher evaluation kit: Complete glossary*, Kalamazoo, MI: The Evaluation Center. Retrieved February 23, 2003, from http://www.wmich.edu/evalctr/ess/glossary/glossary.htm: 1-35.

Thomas, S. B. (1992). *The yearbook of school law 1992.* Topeka, KS: National Organization on Legal Problems of Education.

Thomas, S. B. (1991). *The yearbook of school law 1991.* Topeka, KS: National Organization on Legal Problems of Education.

Thomas, S. B. (1990). *The yearbook of school law 1990.* Topeka, KS: National Organization on Legal Problems of Education.

Thomas, S. B. (1989). *The yearbook of school law 1989.* Topeka, KS: National Organization on Legal Problems of Education.

Thomas, S. B. (1988). *The yearbook of school law 1988.* Topeka, KS: National Organization on Legal Problems of Education.

Thomas, S. B. (1987). *The yearbook of school law 1987.* Topeka, KS: National Organization on Legal Problems of Education.

Thomas, S. B. (1986). *The yearbook of school law 1986.* Topeka, KS: National Organization on Legal Problems of Education.

Thomas, S. B. (1985). *The yearbook of school law 1985.* Topeka, KS: National Organization on Legal Problems of Education.

Tirozzi, G. N. (2002). Principals hands are tied. Editorial Opinion, *USA Today*. Retrieved September 2, 2002 from http://www.usatoday.com/news/opinion/editorials/2002-08-26-oppose_x.htm

Turner, R. R. (1986). What teachers think about their evaluations. *Learning 86, 15*(9): 58-67.

U.S.A. Today. (2002, August 26). Principals too quick to use 'teacher shortage' as excuse. Retrieved September 2, 2002, from http://www.usatoday.com/news/opinion/editorials/2002- 08-26-edit_x.htm

U. S. Department of Education.My ED.gov (2003a). No Child Left Behind: A Desktop Reference. Retrieved September 3, 2003, from http://www.ed.gov/offices/OESE/reference/2a.html

U. S. Department of Education, My.ED.gov. (2003b). Paige marks 18-month anniversary of no child left behind act with update to congress. Retrieved August 12, 2003 from http://www.ed.gov/PressReleases/p7-2003/07082003a.html, 1-7.

US News and World Report. (1996a, February 26). Union contrarian: America's most militant teacher calls for reform, pp. 70-71.

US News and World Report. (1996b, February 26). Why teachers don't teach: How teacher unions are wrecking our schools, pp. 62-71.

US News and World Report. (1996, March 18). Letters.

Valente, W. (1987). *Law in the schools*, 2d ed. Columbus, OH: Merrill Publishing Company.

Van Horn, Jr., B. (1984). *Teacher incompetence. A legal memorandum.* Reston, VA: National Association of Secondary School Principals.

Van Sciver, J. H. (1990a). A few tips on teacher dismissals. *The School Administrator, 10*(47): 41.

Van Sciver, J. H. (1990b). Teacher dismissal. *Phi Delta Kappan, 72*(4): 318-319.

Vander Wheel, M. (1992, December 2). Principals report teachers lacking. *Chicago Sun-Times,* 3.

Van Sciver, J. H. (1990). A few tips on teacher dismissals. Reprint from *The School Administrator, 10*(47), 41.

Waintroob, A. R. (1995, May). Remediating and dismissing the incompetent teacher. *The School Administrator*: 1-4.

Walberg, H. J. (2002). Teaching methods. In L. T. Izumi and W. M. Evers (eds.), *Teacher quality,* (pp. 55-72). Stanford, CA: Hoover Institution Press.

Weld, J. (1999, April). The good, bad and empty of cash incentives. *Guest column: The School Administrator Web Edition*: 1-5. Retrieved July 15, 2003 from http://www.aasa.org/publivcations/sa/1999_04/col_weld.htm

Wheeler, P. W., Haertel, G. D., and Scriven, M. (1993). *Teacher evaluation glossary.* Kalamazoo, MI: Center for Research on Educational Accountability and Teacher Evaluation.

White, Sr., W. E. (2001, Jan.). The fear of entering the woods. Guest Column, *The School Administrator Web Edition*. Retrieved February 24, 2003 from http://www.aasa.org/publications/sa/2001_01/colwhite.htm

Williams, W. M. (1997). How'm I doing? *Change, 29*(5): 12.

Wilson, R. (1998, January 16). New research casts doubt on value of student evaluations of professors. *The Chronicle of Higher Education,* A12-A14.

Wise, A. E., and Gendler, T. (1990). Governance Issues in the evaluation of elementary and secondary schoolteachers. In J. Millman and L. Darling-Hammond (eds.), *The new handbook of teacher evaluation: Assessing elementary and secondary school teachers* (pp. 116-32). Newbury Park, CA: Sage Publications, Inc.

Wise, A. E., Darling-Hammond, L., McLaughlin, M. W., and Bernstein, H. T. (1985). Teacher evaluation: A study of effective practices. *The Elementary School Journal, 86*(1): 76-77.

Wise, A. E., Darling-Hammond, L., McLaughlin, M. W., and Bernstein, H. T. (1984). *Teacher evaluation: A study of effective practices.* Santa Monica, CA: The RAND Corporation.

Wolcowitz, J. (1982). The first day of class. In M. Gullette (ed.), *The art and craft of teaching* (pp. 10-24). Cambridge: Harvard-Danforth Center for Teaching and Learning.

Woodruff, B. E. (1976). Trustees must know the law. *AGB Reports, 18*(6): 11-18.

COURT CASES

Alabama State Tenure Commission v. Birmingham Bd. of Educ., 564 So.2d 980 (Ala. Ct. Civ. App. 1990).

Andrews v. Independent Sch. Dist. No. 57, 12 P.3d 491 [148 Educ. L. Rep. 1061] (Okla. Civ. App. 2000).

Atherton v. Board of Educ. of School Dist. of St. Joseph, 744 S.W.2d 518 (Mo. Ct. App. 1988).

Aulwurm v. Board of Education of Murphysboro Community Unit School Dist., 367 N.E.2d 1337 (Ill. 1977).

Babbar v. M. Ebadi, 36 F. Supp.2d 473 [133 Educ. L. Rep. 1269] (D.Kan. 1998).

Bader v. Board of Educ. of Lansingburgh Cent. Sch. Dist., 627 N.Y.S.2d 858 [101 EDUC. L. REP. 387] (N.Y. App. Div. 1995).

Baldridge v. Board of Trustees, Rosebud Sch. Dist. Nr. 19, Colstrip, Mont., 951 P.2d 1343 [124 Educ. L. Rep. 424] (Mont. 1997).

Bates v. Sponberg, 547 F.2d 325 (6th Cir. 1976).

Beck v. James, Superintendent Palmyra R-I School Dist., 793 S.W.2d 416 (Mo. Ct. App. 1990).

Bentley v. School Dist. No. 025 of Custer County, 586 N.W.2d 306 [130 Educ. L. Rep. 900] (Neb. 1998).

Berg v. Bruce, 112 F.3d 322 [117 Educ. L. Rep. 895] (8th Cir. 1997).

Board of Educ. of Argo-Summit School District 104 v. Hunt, 487 N.E. 2d 24 (1st Dist. 1985).

Board of Educ. of City of Chicago v. Box, 547 N.E.3d 627 (Ill. App. Ct. 1989).

Board of Educ. of Chicago v. Chicago Teachers Union, Local 1, 88 Ill. 2d 63, 430 N.E.2d 1111 (1981).

Board of Educ. of Chicago v. Harris, 578 N.E.2d 1244 (Ill. App. Ct. 1991).

Board of Educ. of Chicago v. Johnson, 570 N.E.2d 382 (Ill. App. Ct. 1991).

Board of Educ. of City Sch. Dist. of City of N.Y. v. Mills, 680 N.Y.S.2d 683 [131 Educ. L. Rep. 248] (N.Y. App. Div. 1998).

Board of Education v. Ingels, 394 N.E.2d 69, (1979).

Board of Educ. of Benton Harbor Area Schools v. Wolff, 361 N.W.2d 750 (Mich. Ct. App. 1985).

Board of Educ. of West Yuma Sch. Dist. RJ-1 v. Flaming, 938 P.2d 151 [118 Educ. L.Rep. 1202] (Colo. 1997).

Board of Regents v. Roth, 408 U.S. 564 (1972).

Board of Trustees of Comm. College Dist. No. 508 v. Cook County College Teachers Union, Local 1600, 522 N.E.2d 93 (Ill. App. Ct., 1987).

Board of Trustees of Community College District No. 513 v. Krizek and the American Federation of Teachers, Local 1810, N.E.2d 770 (Ill. 1983).

Bradshaw v. Alabama State Tenure Commission, 520 So.2d 541 (Ala. Civ. App. 1988).

Brahim v. Ohio College of Podiatric Medicine, 651 N.E.2d 30 [100 EDUC. L. REP. 1131] (Ohio Ct. App. 1994).

Brewerton v. Dalrymple, 997 S.W.2d 212 [137 Educ. L. Rep. 393] (Tex. 1999).

Browzin v. Catholic Univ. of America, 527 F.2d 843 (D.C. Cir. 1975).

Burkes v. Enlarged City Sch. Dist. of Troy, 684 N.Y.S.2d 57 [132 Educ. L. Rep. 527] (N.Y. App. Div. 1999).

Byrd v. Board of Curators of Lincoln Univ. of Mo., 863 S.W.2d 873 [86 Educ. L. Rep. 1105] (Mo. 1993).

Caldwell v. Blytheville Arkansas School Dist. No. 5, 746 S.W.2d 381 (Ark. Ct. App. 1988).

Catherine v. Bd. of Educ. of the City of St. Louis, 822 S.W.2d 881 (Mo. Ct. App. 1991).

Chicago Sch. Reform Bd. of Trustees v. Illinois Educ. Labor Relations Bd., 721 N.E.2d 676 (Ill. App. Ct. 1999).

Chronopoulos v. University of Minn., 520 N.W.2d 437 [93 Educ. L. Rep. 892] (Minn. Ct. App. 1994).

Chung v. Park, 377 F. Supp. 218 (M.D. Pa. 1974).

Clark v. Board of Dirs. of Sch. Dist. of Kansas City, 915 S.W.2d 766 [107 EDUC. L. REP. 368] (Mo. Ct. App. 1996).

Clark County Sch. Dist. v. Riley, 14P.3d22 [149 Educ. L., Rep. 615] (Nev. 2000).

Cleveland Bd. of Educ. v. Loudermill, 470 U.S. 532, 542 and 545-46 (1985).

Conley v. Board of Educ. of the City of New Britain, 123 A.2d 747 (Conn. 1956).

Conway v. Pacific Univ., 879 P.2d 201 [94 Educ. L. Rep. 531] (Or. Ct. App. 1994).

Cope v. Board of Educ. of the Town of West Hartford, 495 A.2d 718 (Conn. App. Ct. 1985).

Crump v. Durham County Board of Educ., 327 S.E.2d 599 (N.C. Ct. App. 1985).

Davis v. Board of Educ. of Chicago, 649 N.E.2d 86 [105 EDUC. L. REP. 1175] (Ill. App. Ct. 1995).

DeBernard v. State Board of Educ., 527 N.E.2d 616 (Ill. App. Ct. 1988).

DeMichele v. Greenburgh Cent. Sch. Dist. No. 5, 167 F.3d 784 [132 Educ. L. Rep. 632] (2d Cir. 1999).

DeSimone v. Siena College, 663 N.Y.S.2d 701 [121 Educ. L. Rep. 1126] (App. Div. 1997).

Dobbs-Weinstein v. Vanderbilt Univ., 185 F.3d 542 [137 Educ. L. Rep. 208] (6thCir. 1999).

Doty v. Tupelo Pub. Sch. Dist., 751 So. 2d 1212 [142 Educ. L. Rep. 1109] (Miss. Ct. App. 1999).

Dunnigan v. Ambach, 484 N.Y.S.2d 373 (N.Y. App. Div. 1985).

Dunson v. Alabama State Tenure Commission 653 So. 2d 995 [100 EDUC. L. REP. 450] (Ala. Civ. App. 1994).

Edwards v. California Univ. of Penn., 156 F.3d 488 [129 Ed. Law Rep. 622] (3rd Cir. 1998).

Elmore v. Plainview-Old Bethpage Cent. Sch. Dist. Bd. of Educ., 690 N.Y.S.2d 842 [135 Educ. L. Rep. 1040] (N.Y. Sup. Ct. 1999).

Eshom v. Board of Educ. of School Dist. No. 54, 364 N.W.2d 7 (Neb. 1985).

Esther Fortson v Detroit Board of Education (83-47).

Evansville-Vanderburgh School Corp. v. Roberts, 395 N.E.2d 291 (Ind. Ct. App. 1979), reconsidering, 392 N.E. 2d 810 (Ind. Ct. App. 1979).

Farris v. Burke County Bd. of Educ., 544 S.E.2d 578 [152 Educ. L. Rep. 824] (N.C. Ct. App. 2001).

Feldman v. Board of Educ. of City Sch. Dist. of City of N.Y., 686 N.Y.S.2d 842 [134 Educ. L. Rep. 262] (N.Y. App. Div. 1999).

Feldman v. Ho, 171 F.3d 494 [133 Educ. L. Rep. 413] (7th Cir. 1999).

Florida Educ. Code, sec 231.29(2) (1989).

Foleno v. Board of Education of the Twp. of Bedminster, Decision of N.J. Comm'r of Educ. (1978).

Folta v. Sobol, 621 N.Y.S.2d 136 [96 EDUC. L. REP. 1084] (N.Y. App. Div. 1994).

Ford v. Caldwell Parish School Bd., 541 So.2d 955 (La. Ct. App. 1989).

Forte v. Mills, 672 N.Y.S.2d 497 [126 Educ. L. Rep. 362] (App. Div. 1998).

Gaylord v. Board of Educ., Unified School Dist. No. 218, Morton County, 794 P.2d 307 (Kan. Ct. App. 1990).

Geib v. Triway Local Bd. of Educ., 705 N.E.2d 326 [131 Educ. L. Rep. 1102] (Ohio 1999).

Gilder v. Meno, 916 S.W.2d 357 [111 EDUC. L. REP. 1031] (Tex. Ct. App. 1996).

Giles v. Schuyler-Chemung-Tioga Bd. of Coop. Educ. Serv., 604 N.Y.S.2d 345 [87 Educ. L. Rep. 559] (N.Y. App. Div. 1993).

Goodship v. University of Richmond, 860 F. Supp. 1110 [94 Educ. L. Rep. 243] (E.D. Va. 1994).

Governing Bd. of ABC Unified Sch. Dist. v. Haar, 33 Cal. Rptr. 2d 744 [94 Educ. L. Rep. 384] (Cal. Ct. App. 1994).

Greenberg v. Cortines, 626 N.YY.S.2d 233 [100 EDUC. L. REP. 261] (N.Y. App. Div 1995).

Hagerstrom v. Clay City Comm. Unit High School Dist. 356 N.E.2d 438 (Ill. pp. 1976).

Hall v. Board of Educ. of City of Chicago, 592 N.E.2d 245 (Ill. App. Ct. 1992).

Hall v. Board of Trustees of State Insts. of Higher Learning, 712 So. 2d 312 [127 Educ. L. Rep. 494] (Miss. 1998).

Halpern v. Board of Educ. of City of Bristol, 706 A.2d 1001 [124 Educ. L. Rep. 649] (Conn. Super. Ct. 1998).

Hamburg v. North Penn School Dist., 484 A.2d 867 (Pa. Commw. Ct. 1984).

Hamm v. Poplar Bluff R-1 Sch. Dist., 955 S.W.2d 27 [122 Educ. L. Rep. 340] (Mo. Ct. App. 1997).

Hanlon v. Board of Educ. of the Parkway School Dist., 695 S.W.2d 930 (Mo. Ct. App. 1985).

Hannon v. Armorel Sch. Dist. No. 9, 946 S.W.2d 950 [119 Educ. L. Rep. 731] (Ark. (1997).

Harjo v. Board of Educ. of Indep. Sch. Dist. No. 7 of Seminole County, 976 P.2d 1096 [134 Educ. L. Rep. 616] (Okla. Ct. Civ. App. 1999).

Harris v. Victoria Indep. Sch. Dist., 168 F. 3d 216 [132 Educ. L. Rep. 662] 5th Cir. 1999).

Harry v. Marion County Bd. of Educ., 506 S.E.2d 319 [130 Educ. L. Rep. 918] (W. Va. 1998).

Hatta v. Board of Educ., Union Endicott Central School Dist., 394 N.Y.S.2d 301 (App. Div. 1977).

Hierlmeier v. North Judson-San Pierre Bd. of Sch. Trustees, 730 N.E.2d 821 [144 Educ. L. Rep. 1024] (Ind. Ct. App. 2000).

Holm v. Ithaca College, 682 N.Y.S.2d 295 [131 Educ. L. Rep. 823] (App. Div. 1998).

Hou v. Pennsylvania Depart. of Educ., 573 F. Supp. 1539 (W.D. Pa 1983).

Hughes v. Stanley County Sch. Bd., 594 N.W.2d 346 [134 Educ. L. Rep. 1024] (S.D. 1999).

Ianello v. The Univ. of Bridgeport, (see Carnegie Council on Policy Studies in Higher Education,1979).

Illinois Education Association v. Board of Education, 62 Ill. 2d 127, 340 N.E.2d 7 (1975).

In re Dismissal Proceedings Against Huang, 441 S.E.2d 696 [90 Educ. L. Rep. 468] (N.C. 1994).

In re Fugere, 592 A.2d 518 (N.H. 1991).

In re Termination of Kible, 996 P.2d 419 [143 Educ. L. Rep. 382] (N.M. 1999).

Irby v. McGowan, 380 F. Supp. 1024 (S.E. Ala. 1974).

Jackson v. Sobol as Commissioner of Educ. of the State of New York, et al., Respondents, 565 N.Y.S.2d 612 (App. Div., 1991).

Jacobs v. Mundelein College, 628 N.E.2d 201 [89 Educ. L. Rep. 549] (Ill. App. Ct. 1993).

Jawa v. Fayetteville Univ., 426 F. Supp. 218 (E.D. N.C. 1976.

Jefferson Cons. School Dist. C-123 v. Carden, 772 S.W.2d 753, 759 (Mo. Ct. App. 1989).

Johanson v. Board of Educ., 589 N.W.2d 815 [132 Educ. L. Rep. 916] (Neb. 1999).

Johnson v. Francis Howell R-3 Bd. of Educ., 868 S.W.2d 191 [88 Educ. L. Rep. 1253] (Mo. Ct. App. 1994).

Johnson v. School Board of Dade County, 578 So.2d 387 (Fla. Dist. Ct. App. 1991).

Johanson v. Board of Educ. of Lincoln County Sch. Dist., 589 N.W.2d 815 [132 Educ. L. Rep. 916] (Neb. 1999).

Jones v. Rapides Parish Sch. Bd., 634 So. 2d 1197 [90 Educ. L. Rep. 973] (La. Ct. App. 1993).

Kamrath v. Board of Educ. Ill. 2d N.E.2d (1987).

Katz v. Board of Trustees of Gloucester County College, 118 N.J. Sup. Ct. 398, 288 A.2d 43 (1972).

Katz v. Maple Heights City Sch. Dist. Bd. of Educ., 622 N.E.2d 1 [86 Educ. L. Rep. 944] (Ohio Ct. App. 1993).

Keesee v. Meadow Heights R-II Sch. Dist., 865 S.W.2d 818 [87 Educ. L. Rep. 661] (Mo. Ct. App. 1993).

King v. Jefferson County Bd. of Educ., 659 So. 2d 686 [103 EDUC. L. REP. 528] (Ala. Civ. App. 1995).

Kinniry v. Abington Sch. Dist., 673 A.2d 429 [108 EDUC. L. REP. 312] (Pa. Commw. Ct. 1996).

Kleinberg v. Board of Educ. of the Albuquerque Public Schools, 751 P.2d 722 (N.M. Ct. App. 1988).

Klinge v. Ithaca College, 663 N.Y.S2d 735 [121 Educ. L. Rep. 1132] (App. Div. 1997).

Korf v. Ball State Univ., 726 F.2d 1222 (7th Cir. 1984).

Krystek v. University of S. Miss., 164 F.3d 251 [131 Educ. L. Rep. 660] (5th Cir. 1999).

Kyle v. Morton High Sch., 144 F.3d 448 [126 Educ. L. Rep. 651] (7th Cir. 1998).

Landrum v. Eastern Kentucky Univ., 578 F. Supp. 241 (E.D. Ky. 1984).

Lawrence v. Curators of the Univ. of Mo., 204 F.3d 807 [142 Educ. L. Rep. 50] (8th Cir. 2000).

Lehman v. Board of Trustees of Whitman College, 576 P.2d 397 (Wash. 1978).

Linstad v. Sitka Sch. Dist., 963 P.2d 246 [129 Educ. L. Rep. 504] (Alaska 1998).

Lipka v. Brown City Community Schools, 252 N.W.2d 770 (Mich. 1977).

Lockport Area Special Education Cooperative v. Lockport Area Special Education Cooperative Association, 33 Ill. App. 3d 789, 338 N.E.2d 463 (1975).

Lovan v. Dora R. Illinois School Dist., 677 S.W.2d 956 (Mo. Ct. App. 1984).

Madison v. Houston Indep. Sch. Dist., 47 F. Supp.2d 825, 829 [135 Educ. L. Rep. 535] (S. D. Tex. 1999).

Malverne Union Free School Dist. v. Sobol, 586 N.Y.S.2d 673 (App. Div. 1992).

Manheim Central Educ. Ass'n. v. Manheim Central School Dist., 572 A.2d 31 Pa. Commw. Ct. 1990).

Martin v. Parrish, 805 F.2d 583 (5th Cir. 1986).

McComb v. Gahanna-Jefferson City Sch. Dist. Bd. of Educ., 720 N.E.2d 984 139 Educ. L. Rep. 1037] (Ohio Ct. App. 1998).

McConnel v. Howard Univ., 621 F. Supp. 327 (D.D.C. 1985).

McDaniel v. Princeton City Sch. Dist. Bd. of Educ., 72 F. Supp.2d 874 [140 Educ. L. Rep. 275] (S.D. Ohio 1999).

McGuire v. Governing Board of San Diego Comm. College Dist., 208 Cal. Rptr. 260 (Cal. Ct. App. 1984).

McKenzie v. Webster Parish Sch. Bd., 653 So. 2d 215 [99 EDUC. L. REP. 1142] (La. Ct. App. 1995).

Meckley v. Kanawha County Board of Educ., 383 S.E.2d 839 (W. Va. 1989).

Meyer v. Board of Educ. of the Charlotte Valley Central School Dist., 581 N.Y.S.2d 920 (App. Div. 1992).

Mims v. West Baton Rouge Parish School Board, 315 S.2d 349 (La. Ct. App. 1975).

Mississippi Employment Security Comm'n v. Harris, 672 So. 2d 739 [109 EDUC. L. REP. 498] (Miss. 1996).

Mongitore v. Regan, 520 N.Y.S.2d 194 (App. Div. 1987).

Moravek v. Davenport Comm. School Dist., 262 N.W.2d 797 (Iowa, 1978).

Morris v. Clarksville-Montgomery County Consol. Bd. of Educ., 867 S.W.2d 324 [88 Educ. L. Rep. 461] (Tenn. Ct. App. 1993).

Mott v. Endicott School Dist., 713 P.2d 98 (Wash. 1986).

Muggivan v. Jefferson Parish Sch. Bd., 639 So. 2d 849 [93 Educ. L. Rep. 443] (La. Ct. App. 1994).

Murphy v. Duquesne Univ. of the Holy Ghost, 745 A.2d 1228 [142 Educ. L. Rep. 383] (Pa. Super. Ct. 2002).

Nevels v. Board of Educ. of School Dist. of Maplewood-Richmond Heights, 822 S.W.2d 898 (Mo. Ct. App. 1991).

Newcomb v. Humansville R-IV Sch. Dist., 908 S.W.2d 821 [104 EDUC. L. REP. 928] (Mo. Ct. App. 1995).

Newman v. Sobo, 649 N.Y.S.2d 67 [114 Educ. L. Rep. 254] (N.Y. App. Div. 1996).

Padilla v. South Harrison R-II Sch. Dist., 181 F.3d 992 [136 Educ. L. Rep. 728] (8th Cir. 1999).

Parker-Bigback v. St. Labre Sch., 7 P.3d 361 [146 Educ. L. Rep. 1129] (Mont. 2000).

Perlin v. South Orangetown Cent. Sch. Dist., 658 N.Y.S.2d 141 [118 Educ. L. Rep. 1084] (N.Y. App. Div. 1997).

Perry v. Sinderman, 408 U.S. 593 (1972).

Petrella v. Siegel, 843 F.2d 87 (2d Cir. 1988).

Powell v. Board of Trustees, Crook County School Dist. No. 1 550 P.2d 1112 (Wyo. Sup. Ct. 1976).

Queen v. Minneapolis Public Schools, 481 N.W.2d 66 (Minn. Ct. App. 1992).

Quist v. Board of Trustees of Community College Dist. No. 525, 629 N.E.2d 807 [89 Educ. L. Rep. 916] (Ill. App. Ct. 1994).

Remus v. Bd. of Educ. for Tonawanda City Sch. Dist., 727 N.Y.S.2d 43 [155 Educ. L. Rep. 759] (N.Y. 2001).

Rivera v. Cmty. Sch. Dist. Nine, 145 F. Supp.2d 302 [155 Educ. L. Rep. 235] (S.D.N.Y. 2001).

Riverview Sch. Dist. v. Riverview Educ. Ass'n. 639 A.2d 974 [90 Educ. L. Rep. 280] Pa. Commw. Ct. 1994).

Roberts v. Santa Cruz Valley Unified School Dist. No. 35, 778 P.2d 1294 (Ariz. Ct. App. 1989).

Rogers v. Board of Educ. of the City of New Haven, 749 A.2d 1173 [143 Educ. L. Rep. 968] (Conn. 2000).

Rolando v. School Dist. No. 125, County of LaSalle and State of Illinois, 358 N.E.2d 945 (Ill. App. 1976).

Romer v. Board of Trustees of Hobart & William Smith Colleges, 842 F. Supp. 703 (W.D.N.Y. 1994).

Rossi v. Pennsylvania State Univ. 489 A.2d 828 (Pa. Sup. Ct. 1985).

Rosso v. Board of Educ. of School Directors, 388 A. 2d 1238 (Pa. Commw. Ct., 1977).

Rush v. Board of Educ. of Crete-Monee Community Unit Sch. Dist. No. 201 U, 727 N.E.2d 649 [144 Educ. L. Rep. 586] (Ill. App. Ct. 2000).

Sauter v. Mount Vernon School Dist. No. 320, Skagit County, 791 P.2d 549 (Wash. Ct. App. 1990).

School Dist. of Beverly v. Geller, 737 N.E.2d 873, 879 [148 Educ. L. Rep. 461] (Mass. Ct. App. 2000).

Sekor v. Board of Educ. of Town of Ridgefield, 689 A.2d 1112 [116 Educ. L. Rep. 1049] (Conn. 1997).

Selby v. North Callaway Board of Educ., 777 S.W.2d 275 (Mo. Ct. App. 1989).

Shaw v. Board of Trustees of Frederick Community College, 549 F. 2d 929 (4th Cir. 1976).

Sheldon Community Sch. Dist. Bd. of Directors v. Lundblad, 528 N.W.2d 593, 594 [98 EDUC. L. REP. 386] (Iowa 1995).

Snyder v. Mendon-Union Local Sch. Dist. Bd. of Educ. 661 N.E.2d 717 [107 EDUC. L. REP. 268] (Ohio 1996).

Stamper v. Board of Educ. of Elem. School Dist. 143, 491 N.E.2d 36 (1st Dist. 1986).

Stasny v. Board of Trustees of Central Washington Univ., 32 Wash. App 239, 647 P.2d 496 (1982).

Stephens v. Alabama State Tenure Comm'n 634 So. 2d 549 [90 Educ. L. Rep. 954] (Ala. Civ. App. 1994).

Stills v. Alabama State Tenure Comm;n, 718 So. 2d 1145 [130 Educ. L. Rep. 361] (Ala. Civ. App. 1998).

Strain v. Rapid City School Board for Rapid City Area School Dist., 447 N.W.2d 332 (S.D. 1989).

Strasburger v. Board of Educ., Hardin County, 143 F. 3d 351 [126 Educ. L. Rep. 677] (7th Cir. 1998).

Stratton v. Austin Indep. Sch. Dist., 8 S.W.3d 26 [140 Educ. L. Rep. 1049] (Tex. App. 1999).

Sutherby v. Gobles Bd. of Educ., 348 N.W.2d 277 (Mich. Ct. App. 1984).

Swann v. Caylor, 516 So. 2d 699, 701 (Ala. Civ. App. 1987).

Teacneck Board of Educ. v. Teacneck Teachers Ass'n., 390 A.2d 1198 (N.J. Sup. 1978).

Thomas v. Mahan, 886 S.W.2d 199 [95 EDUC. L. REP. 789] (Mo. Ct. App. 1994).

Tishey v. Board of School Trustees of North Newton School Corp., 575 N.E.2d 1018, 1021 (Ind. Ct. App. 1991).

Tomczik v. State Tenure Comm'n Center Line Public Schools, 438 N.W.2d 642 (Mich. Ct. App. 1989).

Totman v. Eastern Idaho Technical College, 931 P.2d 1232 [116 Educ. L. Rep. 429] (Idaho Ct. App. 1997).

Tweedall v. Fritz, 987 F. Supp. 1126, 1132 [124 Educ. L. Rep. 122] (S.E. Ind. 1997).

Vanasco v. National-Louis Univ., 137 F.3d 962 [124 Educ. L. Rep. 525] (7th Cir. 1998).

VanGessel v. Lakewood Pub. Schs., 558 N. W.2d 248 [115 Educ. L. Rep. 496] (Mich. Ct. App. 1997).

Walker v. Board of Educ., Unified Sch. Dist. No. 499, Cherokee County, 900 P.2d 850 [102 EDUC. L. REP. 1175] (Kan. Ct. App. 1995).

Accountable Teacher Evaluation

Walker v. Highlands County Sch. Bd., 752 So. 2d 127 [142 Educ. L. Rep. 1116] (Fla. Dist. Ct. App. 2000).

Ward v. Board of Educ. of the School Dist. of Philadelphia, 496 A.2d 1352 (Pa. Commw. Ct. 1985).

Ware v. Morgan County School Dist., 748 P.2d 1295 (Colo. 1988).

Widdoes v. Detroit Pub. Sch., 553 N.W.2d 688 [113 EDUC. L. REP. 432] (Mich. Ct. App. 1996).

Wiley v. Richland Parish School Board, 476 So.2d 439 (La. Ct. App. 1985).

Williams v. Concordia Parish Sch. Bd., 670 So. 2d 351 [108 EDUC. L. REP. 466] (La. Ct. App. 1996).

Williams v. Franklin Square Union Free Sch. Dist., 690 N.Y.S2d 682 [135 Educ. L. Rep. 1033] (N.Y. App. Div. 1999).

Wilmer-Hutchins Indep. Sch. Dist. v. Brown, 912 S.W.2d 848 [106 EDUC. L. REP. 408] (Tex. Ct. App. 1996).

Woo v. Putnam County Bd. of Educ., 504 S.E.2d 644 [129 Educ. L. Rep. 853] (W. Va. 1998).

Worzella v. Board of Regents, 93 N.W.2d 411, 414 (S.D. 1958).

Wright v. Mead Sch. Dist. No. 354, 944 P.2d 1, 4 [121 Educ. L. Rep. 312] (Wash. Ct. App. 1997).

Yackshaw v. John Carroll Univ. Bd. of Trustees, 624 N.E.2d 225 [87 Educ. L. Rep. 579] (Ohio Ct. App. 1993).

Index

A

A Nation at Risk, xii
Accountability, 3, 4, 5 51, 62, 70
Ackerman, A., 12
Adams, H. B., 35
Adjunct faculty, 320, 322
Administrative Evaluation, 35, 54, 55, 63, 69, 255
Administrative stress, 114, 116
Age Discrimination in Employment Act, 292
Aims Community College, 18
Alabama State Tenure Commission v. Birmingham Board of Education, 352
Allhouse, M. F., 292
American Arbitration Association, 225
American Association of University Professors, (AAUP), 30, 245
American Council on Education, 74, 80
American Council of Education Presidents Task Force on Teacher Education, 80
American Federation of Teachers, (AFT), 10, 29, 36, 80, 208
American Psychologist, 58, 59
Anastasia, A., 53
Andrews, H. A., 3, 5, 7, 12, 20, 22, 27, 28, 32, 54, 55, 60, 62, 65, 107, 113, 140, 157, 160, 164, 166, 173, 174, 178, 180, 184, 188, 189, 191, 196, 197, 198, 208, 209, 213, 225, 231, 233,234, 236, 239, 240, 246, 255, 258, 261, 292, 303, 323, 324, 326, 330

Andrews v. Independent School District No. 57, 298, 362
Aper, J. P., 13, 14
Arbitration, 225, 313, 317
Arreola, R. A., 5, 258
Ascher, C., 76
Aspects of hearing, 344
Aspects of notice, 274, 340
Atherton v. Board of Education of School District of St. Joseph, 361
Aulwurm v. Board, 296
Avakian, A. N., 320

B

Babbar v. M. Ebadi, 373
Bader v. Board of Education of Lansingburgh Central School District, 368
Baer, W. E., 225
Baker, G., 94, 166
Baldridge v. Board of Trustees, Rosebud School District #19, 296, 365
Barber, L. W., 139
Bay de Noc Community College, 208
Beck v. James, Superintendent Palmyra R-I School District,354
Bedell, R. C., xii, xiv
Behrendt, R. L., 329
Bennett, W., 8, 207
Benton, J., 77
Bently v. School District No. 015 of Custer County, 275, 342
Benwood Schools, 77
Berg v. Bruce, 341

K

L

X

Dr. Hans A. Andrews, Distinguished Fellow in Community College Leadership, Olney Central College, Illinois, has over 35 years of teaching and administrative experiences in secondary schools and community colleges. His background in teacher evaluation has been extensive. He is the author of *Evaluating for Excellence* (1985), *Merit in Education* (1987), *Teachers Can Be Fired!* (1995), and *The Dual-Credit Phenomenon* (2002). He has also authored over 80 articles in journals on educational topics.

Praise for *Accountable Teacher Evaluation!*

If you seek a reliable, comprehensive, step-by-step guide to the evaluation of faculty from K-12 through community college, you'll find it here. Using dozens of actual examples, Hans Andrews shows how to persuade boards, administrators and faculty to collaborate on evaluation systems that actually improve learning. The book sets a new standard for scholarly treatments of teacher evaluation.

GARY W. DAVIS, *Executive Director, Illinois Community College Trustees Association*

Excellent schools are the product of an intentional commitment to quality in every classroom, everyday. ***Accountable Teacher Evaluation!*** provides the research base upon which to build the part of the quest for excellence that often goes unaddressed in many schools. An improved knowledge base and platform for the practice of fair and rigorous teacher evaluation can be attained as author Hans Andrews demonstrates.

BOB HILL, *The Ball Foundation, Glen Ellyn, Illinois; former principal and superintendent*

Accountable Teacher Evaluation! presents a foundation for boards and administrators to **be totally supportive of good instructors** AND completely intolerant of sub-standard performance if it continues. That's the style and example that Dr. Hans Andrews has also lived as a practitioner."

WILLIAM MARZANO, *Associate Dean for Communications, Humanities and Fine Arts, Waubonsee Community College*

During my career, I have encountered far too many principals and other administrators who were unable to evaluate teaching effectiveness. Most often, they were unable to do so because of the simple fact that they were never trained to do so or they did not have the tools to properly carry it out. Hans Andrews has drawn on the research and common sense to provide them with a step-by-step guide for success in their efforts.

TED SANDERS, *President, Education Commission of the States, former acting secretary of education, chief state school officer in three states, university president and classroom teacher.*